THE END

··· OF ···

DEMOCRACY

··· AND ···

FAITH

Sean Wallace

Archway Publishing books may be ordered
through booksellers or by contacting:

Archway Publishing
1663 Liberty Drive
Bloomington, IN 47403
www.archwaypublishing.com
1 (888) 242-5904

ISBN: 978-1-4808-2821-6 (sc)
ISBN: 978-1-4808-2822-3 (e)

Library of Congress Control Number: 2016903115

Print information available on the last page.

Archway Publishing rev. date: 3/14/2016

CONTENTS

INTRODUCTION

THE JOURNEY TO ENDING DEMOCRACY

When I went into a bookstore I always had the hope of finding a book that would challenge the underlying premise or end of the state. My educational background is in economics, so, I would go to the economics section of the bookstore. I hoped to find some theory and advice on how to deal with the current state of the economy while challenging the underlying premise of the state.

Majority rule, perhaps, the biggest driver of our entire economy was never challenged or even named or mentioned. Majority rule was like the enormous elephant in the room that everyone was ignoring. Many of the authors of the books that I would pull off the shelf of the bookstore have extensive credentials, teach in universities and/or appear on television and/or manage billions of dollars in company and investor assets. Economists and even Nobel winning economists implicitly advocate monetary policies that increase the money supply and increase the national debt if we consider that their views leave the Federal Reserve and democracy intact as a viable philosophical and economic option.

After failing to find any meaningful discussion addressing democracy and democracy's effect on the economy in the economics section of a bookstore, I began to look in the philosophy section of a bookstore. There were challenges to the state in the Philosophy section. The economics and philosophy books that I could find, still failed to answer the how and why. I had to venture into biology, sociology, evolution, psychology, etc. to begin to find answers to the how and why democracy evolved in the human animal. I believe that there needs to be a bridge from philosophy and science to how these ideas could take a more specific political or economic shape. What I believe that we need is a full on assault. A comprehensive, direct challenge with specific direction on how to end democracy and faith.

The Elephant and the Rhino

While not an elephant in the room (like majority rule), our economic methodology used for US fiscal policy might be called a smaller animal such as a rhino in the room because fewer people in the "room" are aware of the rhino. Wrong economic methodology is correctly identified by a few people. The solutions of this wrong economic methodology cannot likely ever be implemented and maintained with the wrong political methodology and structure. I call economic methodology a rhino in the room because while our economic methodology has been identified by a few people, the solution needed is the end of democracy (which is quietly ignored like a rhino in the room).

The elephant and the rhino in the room largely go unaddressed publicly by professional money management. Investments can easily be affected by politics and governments. Many brokers seem to offer up a 6 month chart as a technical tool and estimate the impact from the latest words or reports from the government. From these broker offerings might be recommendations to invest. Investments should be based on the private economy. Instead, actual investment results are based in varying degree by both the private economy and government intervention in specific markets and the general economy.

I am going to start to lay the groundwork for a Voluntary State—a concept I introduce in this book. I am going to directly challenge democracy. Instinctively, people know that majority rule is simply mob rule. Majority rule is thought to be a necessary evil by some and worshipped as a god by others.

Sure, some people advocate limited government, but, not a viable functioning state that can protect people and their property and the natural resources of this country without majority rule and taxation. Sure, some people also advocate anarchy that has no majority rule and taxation, but, insufficient protection of people, property and natural resources. Minarchists might argue that there is sufficient protection with the operation of the market as protector of people, property and natural resources. I believe that a Voluntary State is a better alternative than the Minarchist model especially in the case of justice, order and defense. I believe that you can have a viable functioning Voluntary State that can protect people, property and natural resources without majority rule and taxation.

LOSING MY RELIGION

Religious faith affects democracy and investment. While both Christians and atheists can be criminals, atheists have the ability to address these issues without contradiction. How can we truly address ISIS and Islam when the Christian Bible advocates past and future murder? The government is tied to religion with our money "In God We Trust" emblazoned on coin and currency. The government is tied to religion in our schools with the Pledge of Allegiance and patriotism. Faith is a major roadblock to reason. Religious mythology has deceived people for far too many centuries. Faith deceived me for far too many decades. Far too many fictional and non-fictional lives have been lost to religious mythology. Every faith believes that their faith is the special faith. The literal fate of the world could rest on ending this mythology as we see from ISIS and governmental wars based on a mythical story.

Perhaps, in the tradition of the Christopher Hitchens book title *god is not Great*, I will try to avoid capitalizing the word "god" in this book. I want to avoid giving sanction to the existence of a special monotheistic god. We do not capitalize god when we are referring to Greek gods or other such gods. We capitalize the proper name of a Greek or other god such as Zeus, Apollo, Aphrodite, etc. Capitalizing the proper name of a monotheistic god such as Yahweh or Jehovah would be a little better for me. Capitalizing a monotheistic god as "God" is a special treatment that all other fictional gods do not have the grammatical pleasure to enjoy. Yahweh, Jehovah, god are all fictional names in the Christian Bible. While the Christian Bible and other writings may capitalize a monotheistic god in their works, I want to draw a distinction in my work. Of course, when

I start a sentence with the word "god" then it should be grammatically capitalized as "God."

Philosophy, government, the economy and investing are all linked. I wanted to write a book that showed that connection. Our technological ability has far outstripped our moral and political ability (especially in some parts of the religious world). To help calibrate twenty-first century technology and our current BCE (Before Common Era) religious morality, we must challenge the BCE beliefs and institutions (including beliefs and institutions that we might believe are twenty-first century). Some ideas of the Enlightenment and the eighteenth century are still valid, but, democracy is not one of those valid ideas. The Bible is around a 3,000 year old myth that embarrassingly still fools most of us. It is a myth that has cost much fictional and non-fictional life.

MANY TOPICS

A reader of an early manuscript of this book commented that I should break this book into separate books that cover the impact of religion on our government, the Voluntary State, investments, different government states, etc. I may write a book that cover one or two topics, but, it will not be this book. I believe that this book rightly covers multiple topics. For instance, you can, in my opinion, refute the Bible without ever having to refer to politics. The opposite is true for politics. A thorough discussion of politics may involve religion. A US government dealing with ISIS (Islamic State of Iraq and Syria) may have a much harder time denouncing murder and bad religious tenets when the majority of

US citizens follow Christianity and the Bible. A Bible that spends a majority of its pages murdering people as I will show in this book. A Bible that demonstrates atrocious acts of violence and cruelty. A US nation *under god* as the Pledge of Allegiance states. A US nation with money emblazoned with "In God We Trust." As I show later in this book, billions of Christians worship god and Christ despite the millions of people that the Bible claimed were murdered including abortions, infanticide and young children. Any government or state that we have is influenced by our own identity and how we view ourselves (this topic is explored in the History and Identity chapter of this book).

We have antiabortion violence and death based on religious beliefs as I will show in this book. Any state may have to weigh in the impact of religion when determining justice in regards to antiabortion violence. Instead of attempting to link book(s) on religion to book(s) on politics when examining ISIS, money, god, our identity as people and as a country, patriotism linked to Christianity such as the Pledge of Allegiance, antiabortion violence, etc.; I link these topics into this single book.

Protection of money is vital in any state. An understanding of what constitutes money is important. What protections exist or do not exist for the value of money. Protection or lack of protection for accounts where money is held such as banks and brokerage accounts, etc. It is important to know what governments have done regarding banks and brokerage houses and customers of these institutions. Is money protected under democracy? Is money protected under the Voluntary State? Is money protected in banks and brokerage houses under democracy? Is money protected in banks and brokerage houses in a Voluntary State? The operation of markets, theft in the markets, and justice in dealing with theft in the markets are also important topics in any Voluntary State. These questions and more are addressed in the course of this book. The topic of money is mentioned or discussed in every chapter except chapter six. The topic of banks are mentioned in chapters 1, 2, 5, 7 and 9. The topic of "brokerage" is mentioned in chapters 1, 2 and 9. I go a little beyond merely addressing the questions listed in this paragraph and try to provide some practical value for the reader regarding investments and how to possibly combat negative effects from these institutions.

Money, inflation, deflation, markets, etc. are all critical topics that any successful government or state must thoroughly understand and address if the state wants to foster free markets, if the state wants to prevent theft in the markets instead of sanction theft in the markets and if the state wants to preserve the value of money instead of stealing the value of money through monetary inflation, etc. Objects exchanged in a free market such as gold, alcohol, cash, marijuana, etc. can be confiscated under Civil or Asset Forfeiture laws. These objects such as gold, alcohol, cash, marijuana have all been illegal and/or confiscated at one point or other in our US history. Under a National State of Emergency, we have no right to a trial by jury and can be jailed for any "offense" that we or our "property" (such as gold, silver, cash, and marijuana) commits. While you can write investment books on how things *are* instead of how things *should be*, you may not be able to thoroughly write

about politics without talking about money and the economy. Leaving taxation, inflation, money supply, markets,
etc. up to the whims of a majority of people is not really
ending democracy in my view. Instead of attempting to link
book(s) on economics to book(s) on politics, I link these
topics into this single book.

I imagine that some people would prefer separate books
that they could link together. I believe that some of the
specialness that I see in this book is due to linking several
topics that all apply to ending democracy into a single book.
I believe that there is enough content to ending faith in
this book that a person could use this content to end faith
and build a better Voluntary State. I believe that there is
enough content on markets and money to help build a better Voluntary State. This book addresses the philosophical
foundation that would be needed to establish a Voluntary
State. A philosophical foundation that, I believe, rightly
covers many topics.

ACKNOWLEDGEMENTS

Many of these individuals never reviewed the book beforehand or in one person's case (Kurt Leube) even know of its existence as I write this. While I want to acknowledge and thank the following individuals below for helping to provide the tools and knowledge needed to undertake the writing of this book; it is no way indicative of any necessary agreement with the content of this book. While also providing the same preface of no necessary agreement, I also want to acknowledge the professionals who did review the book in part or in whole and provided great assistance in developing the book.

Kurt Leube is Professor Emeritus at California State University Hayward and Research Fellow at the Hoover Institution, Stanford University. He is also a Professor and Academic Director of the International Institute for Austrian Economics. Leube was a former research assistant for F.A. Hayek and co-wrote the *Essence of Hayek* among other works. I had the privilege of learning from Leube and his teaching of Austrian School of Economic thought among other topics. I appreciate the personal time you spent with me and your appointment for me to attend the Erasmus Master's Degree program. While the funding for the program fell through, the recommendation was invaluable for inspiring my effort for continuing to learn economics and philosophy.

Clarissa Wallace, my wife, who has never voted in an election and who has been supportive of the time and money needed to create this book. If you read the entirety of this book, you will understand the significance of never having voted in an election.

Steve and Debra Wallace, my parents, and authors of *The End Times Hoax and the Hijacking of Our Liberty*. Their insight through the years has been invaluable.

Scott Dreher for a time my neighbor and for another time my "trading partner." Your brokerage and pharmaceutical sales experience taught me how to make money in the biotechnology field.

John Clark for his support (Be careful what you wish for?)

Chanticleer Book Reviews for their direction and assistance in developing the early manuscript.

Archway Publishing for their editing direction and all their work in producing this book.

CHAPTER 1
RISE AND FALL OF THE INDIVIDUAL

The individual has seen many changes in freedom and identity in the last several hundred years. To have a better appreciation for these changes, we might look at the experience and nature of the individual.

OBJECTIVE REALITY

Everything is something. From the air we breathe to the ground we walk on and everything else below, above and in between. People say things like I see "nothing." I have "nothing." Uttering the word, "nothing" is something. It takes a conscious, active mind to think and then speak the word "nothing." That is something.

Everything has a specific nature. Identity is the concept that refers to the specific nature of an entity. There can only be a single identity. A dog cannot be a phone or a phone cannot be a cat or a cat cannot be a tree. The concept of identity shows that reality has a definite nature. Dogs, phones and cats are all objects of reality and can be known by their individual identity. Since each entity or object has its own identity, there are no contradictions of identity.

SUBJECTIVE VALUES

We have a metaphysical, objective reality in the objects around us. Our perception is limited by the limited sensory perceptions that we have. Our perception might change if we had different sensory perceptions. Based on our perceptions and the volition of our mind, we can begin to make choices. As we make choices, we place value on our choices and any objects of the choices. We arrange these values, subjectively, into a ranking or hierarchy.

Investing, economics, and the economy are all subjectively ranked values. Some people might think of these fields as science. Ludwig Von Mises, one of the early founders (after Carl Menger) of the Austrian School of Economics, called economics a theoretical science abstaining from any judgment of value in its task of applying means to attain the ends that people choose. The "school" of Econometrics tries to put subjective human values into mathematical equations.

Other people would contend that economics is not a science at all. Jeff Madrick stated in *Seven Bad Ideas* that, "Experimentation and empirical proof in economics rarely rise to the standards of true science." What is science? Methodology, predictability, an approach? We often try to define its scope with such terms as *natural sciences, social sciences, theoretical sciences,* etc. I would peg science with the relation of volition. Nonliving things such as a rock have no choices. The rock's behavior should lend itself to a predictable approach. This method or approach or level of predictability might be called science. A human individual has volition which gives him choices. The ability to choose is a variable which can be unpredictable. Unpredictability is not very scientific. My college, California State University Hayward, considered economics an art. I would agree.

Forming a State

Ayn Rand believed that barring physical force from social relationships under an objective code of rules is the task of a proper government. The government only has a few proper functions: (from *For the New Intellectual*)

> The only proper functions of a government are: the police, to protect you from criminals; the army, to protect you from foreign invaders; and the courts, to protect your property and contracts from breach or fraud by others, to settle disputes by rational rules according to objective law.

Friedrich A. Hayek wrote in *The Constitution of Liberty*:

> Democracy will remain effective only so long as government in its coercive action confines itself to tasks that can be carried out democratically. If democracy is a means of preserving liberty, then individual liberty is no less an essential condition for the working of democracy. Though democracy is probably the best form of limited government, it becomes an absurdity if it turns into unlimited government.

The US state was established by the founding fathers as a constitutionally limited republic that was supposed to be restricted to the protection of the "natural" individual rights of man through laws designed to protect the individual.

How have we performed over the last 200 plus years since our founding fathers formed our constitutional republic? Have we been dominated by individualism or collectivism? We will explore these questions in "Collectivism" to follow.

COLLECTIVISM

The most basic characteristic that defines a human being is the freedom to choose. In current times, "our" government violates the Law of Identity. If we are born into the United States, we are assumed to have implicitly signed a Social Contract with our government. We are left with a small handful of choices when it comes to the public realm of the government. We can choose a president, state and federal politicians, and whether to renounce our citizenship.

How did we destroy an individual's right to choose? How do we have so much coercion? In a word, collectivism. The subordination of the individual to a "higher" collective. There have been many themes of collectivism throughout time such as utilitarianism, altruism, fascism, communism and socialism. My focus will be on our current form of collectivism here in the United States which is a mix of socialism and capitalism. Voting is believed to be the only thing that keeps us from being communist or socialist or under a dictatorship. I beg to differ. Karl Marx and Friedrich Engels laid out 10 specific measures in *The Communist Manifesto*:

1. Abolition of property in land and application of all rents of land to public purposes.
2. A heavy progressive or graduated income tax.

3. Abolition of all right of inheritance.
4. Confiscation of the property of all emigrants and rebels.
5. Centralisation of credit in the hands of the State by means of a national bank with State capital and an exclusive monopoly.
6. Centralisation of the means of communication and transport in the hands of the State.
7. Extension of factories and instruments of production owned by the State; the bringing into cultivation of waste-lands, and the improvement of the soil generally in accordance with a common plan.
8. Equal liability of all labour. Establishment of industrial armies, especially for agriculture.
9. Combination of agriculture with manufacturing industries; gradual abolition of the distinction between town and country, by a more equable distribution of the population over the country.
10. Free education for all children in public schools. Abolition of children's factory labour in its present form. Combination of education with industrial production, &c., &c.

Well, Moses, allegedly had the Ten Commandments, Marx and Engels had their ten "commandments" also. How does each "commandment" first written in 1872 in German apply over 200 years later? In 1872 these were radical ideas that countered the "natural rights" and Constitutional strength of the United States in the same timeframe. Let's do a point by point comparison at modern times over 200 years later.

1.   *Abolition of property in land and application of all rents of land to public purposes.* Yes, we have a price to buy land from the "owner" (the owner apparently is the state and federal governments since they are receiving funds for the land and not distributing any funds to anyone as a result). We have to pay property taxes after we have bought the land itself. If we develop the land, we have to pay additional property taxes on those developments and any permits or license fees. Any use of the land and developments have to comply with the "owners" wishes. The "owners," state and federal governments, can take back the land through eminent domain laws if they wish.

2.   *A heavy progressive or graduated income tax.* Yes, we have heavy progressive taxation.

3.   *Abolition of all right of inheritance.* Yes and No. We have estate or "death" taxes for up to 40 percent or more? We also have 100 percent "default" and all assets go "back" to the state if there are no heirs. I say "default" and "back" because of the social contract that the state implies that we sign and "owe" the state. The state being a lienholder, of sorts, to our income and our assets. The only way that the state recognizes any right of inheritance is to have heirs, draw up a will or establish a trust. Things might still go to probate.

4.   *Confiscation of the property of all emigrants and rebels.* Yes, we tax anyone who holds American citizenship any-where in the world. We call people "enemies of the state" instead of rebels now. Enemies of the state can be US citizens or foreign citizens according to Sec. 5(b) of the Trading With the Enemy Act. We have been in a perpetual state

of "Emergency" since 1933 when the first National State of Emergency was called to close down the banks for five days. Both Democrats and Republicans have always used some pretense to continue basic Martial Law powers and declare a National State of Emergency at some point in their presidency. Under a National State of Emergency, we have no right to trial and can be jailed for any offense that we or our "property" commits. Our "property" can commit crime and be confiscated from us under Civil or Asset Forfeiture laws. Since our property has committed the crime, there is no trial for the human owners. Alcohol, Marijuana, Gold, Silver, Cash, Homes, Boats, etc. are some examples of objects that were confiscated that defied physics and philosophy and "acted" on their own. Of course, these objects did not act on their own. People "acted" regarding these objects. We can evaluate the actions of people, but, not the actions of inanimate objects. I wish the politicians would be more truthful. They could admit that they have the power under the National State of Emergency to jail us and take any or all of our assets at any time. If mainstream admissions like that were made, then the public might start to question or try to check this blatant dictatorial power.

5.   *Centralisation of credit in the hands of the State by means of a national bank with State capital and an exclusive monopoly.* Yes, we really hit this one out of the park, also. We established Central Banks of the Federal Reserve. We centralized all money into a national fiat currency that was no longer backed by commodities such as gold. Any viable competition to Central Banks and Central fiat paper or electronic currency "dollars" can be eliminated through the National

State of Emergency powers described above and other laws. That certainly seems to constitute an exclusive monopoly to me.

6.   *Centralisation of the means of communication and transport in the hands of the State.* Yes, communication and transport is centralized and controlled. We have the FCC and NSA among others. We have some free speech as long as it doesn't pose any danger to national security (or more accurately, national interests). The FAA, IRS, police, etc. and a whole host of others regulate transport in some fashion or other. Transport can cover almost anything? Whether we are transporting ourselves or property in trains, planes, autos, trucks, sending money overseas or domestically; we are subject to a myriad of state and federal oversight to our actions.

7.   *Extension of factories and instruments of production owned by the State; the bringing into cultivation of wastelands, and the improvement of the soil generally in accordance with a common plan.* No, we have private production that is heavily regulated. The state does not own all the businesses and farming across the land.

8.   *Equal liability of all labour. Establishment of industrial armies, especially for agriculture.* Yes. Labor has some "centralized protections." These protections may not be all bad or all coercive.

9.   *Combination of agriculture with manufacturing industries; gradual abolition of the distinction between town and country, by a more equable distribution of the population over*

the country. No, there was no centralized effort at population distributions that I am aware of.

10.   *Free education for all children in public schools. Abolition of children's factory labour in its present form. Combination of education with industrial production, &c., &c.* Yes, obviously everyone is aware of public schools for children. These schools are "free." The cost of these schools comes from property and other involuntary taxes. The state has the monopoly of power in regards to "free" education. Despite the "public" paying taxes and paying for "free" education, the public is coerced into one "free" choice, public schools. There is no "voucher" program that allows this coerced, taxed money to be used for private schools of the individual choice of the students and parents. So, any parents that choose to put their children in private school must pay BOTH the cost of public school and the cost of the private school of their choice. Of course, individuals who have grown kids or never had children must fund the public schools for everyone else's children.

The term Capitalism was popularized from Marx in *Das Kapital* (1867). Marx was not the first to use the term, though. While we still have private ownership of capital. That ownership and use is becoming increasingly socialistic or communistic over time as you can see from my point by point comparison of the *Communist Manifesto.*

The Fatal Flaw of our Founders

Currently, our premise for the state is life, liberty and the pursuit of happiness. Life and liberty imply the freedom to live and the condition of liberty. The pursuit of happiness implies freedom to "pursue." Happiness is a relative concept. It is a comparison. Happiness actually works against us here. Happiness is an end state or end condition or end. It is a fatal flaw in the Founders creation of our republic. The Founders left the ends of the state to a majority. A majority of voters and a majority of politicians to decide what ends they want. The ends are limited by a few laws in the Constitution.

Allowing a majority to determine ends or outcomes has had dire consequences. The state is allowed to use other people's money through coercion to achieve its ends or outcomes. Voting minorities pay for voting majorities ends despite possible direct opposition to the ends or outcomes. Everyone pays for everyone else's government programs, ends and outcomes.

In addition to majority rule, ends and outcomes; we have allowed for the concept of a *national debt*. We have allowed the state to have a *national currency*, the US dollar, which is allowed to be inflated and increased to pay for the ends and outcomes of majority rule.

The last section "Collectivism" has shown some of the damage that this fatal flaw has done. Later, we will show the sheer size and scope of the government's growth as we show how large our national debt and state and federal departments, agencies, administrations, entitlements, etc. have become and continue to grow.

THE FATAL FLAW CORRECTED

The Voluntary State should have the following premise: It is illegitimate to initiate or promote aggression against non-aggressors.

There are no ends or outcomes. The state should not determine the end or outcome. Each individual determines his or her own end or outcome as long as each individual does not initiate or promote aggression against non-aggressors.

Put another way: The only end or outcome of the state is to help provide a means for the individual to freely choose his or her own ends and outcomes without coercion or aggression from other individuals, majorities, entities, or the state itself as long as coercion and aggression of others people or property is not part of the ends and outcomes chosen.

SUMMARY

The individual has an objective identity as an object in reality. An identity that has a fundamental right to life, a fundamental right to retain the efforts of his labor (production, capital, property, etc.), a fundamental right to not have aggression used against him. The US government has eroded the influence that the individual was able to exercise within its borders. The individual had the ability to keep his own income. Now, the majority decides how the individual should use his income. The individual no longer makes those choices. We can see that the "wishlist" that Karl Marx wished for around 200 years ago has almost come to full fruition. Many people even celebrate democracy as if it is the greatest thing since sliced bread. Perhaps, they compare it to communism or totalitarian regimes and pride themselves with their "voice" and "influence" they believe they have through democracy. This majority thinking is so prevalent that even groups that consider themselves bastions of freedom such as the Libertarian Party still run candidates for president and other public seats.

Investments can affect you at the most fundamental level. We are surrounded by the basic theft and thievery of monetary inflation and high frequency trading. Various investments can be manipulated at the margin or more or even much more. Often, we can go for a while and not have a bubble or crash. How many people knew of CDO (collateralized debt obligations), CDS (credit default swaps), MBS (mortgage backed securities), total return swaps, interest rate swaps, forward rate agreements, forward contracts and other derivatives and securitization before the 2008 "great recession?" How many people were aware of the OTC (over the counter markets) where investment banks make markets in the above derivatives and do transactions with hedge funds, commercial banks and other investment banks?

The assault against the individual will continue in varying degree. The 2008 "great recession" was aided by money being given (loaned at almost zero percent) to banks by the government. The banks funneled much of this money and risk into derivatives. The government stepped in again and "insured" the money that they had just given to the banks. Through a bailout of AIG, derivatives use by Fannie Mae and Freddie Mac, FDIC accepting derivatives debt from bank issued bonds and setting consumer deposit insurance of at least 100,000 dollars for each consumer account that the banks can use as insurance against their speculation in stock or other markets; the government assaulted the individual through collectivism. Fueled by this almost free money and the security of the insurance that the government provided to use it, banks had the license and leverage to make more loans on lower standards of creditworthiness. This government money and insurance increased the size and damage of the housing crisis. The free money and insurance given by the government is a product of majority rule and democracy. The individual left to himself would not loan money to the bank for free. That would be all risk and no reward. When groups take other people's money politically through majority rule, the individual connection of risk may not be felt. It is not their own money. As I said before, investments can affect you at the most fundamental level. The majority or collective helped cause the last "great recession" of 2008.

The answer to the problem of free money and insurance that helped cause the "great recession" is not more free money and insurance. That is exactly what has occurred. The government still hands out free money and insurance. Derivatives have grown from a notional value of 95.2 trillion dollars in 2000 to 672.6 trillion dollars in June, 2008 according to the Financial Crisis Inquiry Report which cited the Bank for International Settlements data on semiannual OTC derivatives statistics. The gross market value of these derivatives grew from 3.2 trillion dollars to 20.3 trillion dollars in the same timeframe. From June, 2008 derivatives have grown from 672.6 trillion dollars to an estimated 1.2 quadrillion or 1,200 trillion dollars now in 2014. The world's GDP is around 85 trillion dollars by comparison. Of course, some might be quick to point out that only interest payments may actually change hands in many swaps. Or that the notional value is a leveraged multiple of the actual money put up for collateral or that will actually change hands in an exchange. So, they might argue that comparing world GDP to the notional value of world derivatives is misleading. They might argue that derivatives are notional. That is mostly true. In the case of a CDS (credit default swap) the notional value could become the actual value. The purchaser of a CDS makes payments for a certain period of time. The seller of the CDS accepts payments from the purchaser in return for an agreement to pay off the debt of a third party loan that is owed to the purchaser of the CDS if that third party defaults on the loan to the purchaser. The global CDS market alone equals a large majority of the value of our annual US GDP. You can make a comparison between world GDP and world derivatives as long as you make distinctions in the nature of derivatives.

However you want or are able to measure it, the fundamental assault against the individual is growing with each "cure" usually being more collectivism to "solve" the last dose of failed or damaging collectivism. All the while, we embrace majority rule and collectivism hoping this time will be different. This is the same sentiment that a gambler has when he or she pulls the lever of the slot machine hoping that this time will be different. This is part of the danger of the fall of the individual. Most individuals don't understand the damage to their freedom and finances. They don't understand the individual at the most basic levels. This lack of understanding helps to affect the individual's own demise and fall.

CHAPTER 2
MARKETS

The state should exist to protect the means not the ends. The one and only end of the state is to protect the means. We examined this theme for the individual, at large, in the last chapter. We will focus a little more on markets. The means in this case is the market exchange. The means to make an exchange could be broken down into some key components: type, participants, access, items exchanged, units and prices of the items exchanged. We have different types of markets such as a stock market, bond market, black market, etc.

Who represents a market? Ayn Rand in *Philosophy: Who Needs It* stated that

> Only producers constitute a market—only men who trade products and services for products and services. In the role of producers they represent a market's "supply"; in the role of consumers, they represent a market's "demand."

The source of a market participant's exchange is supposed to be freedom, not coercion. It is supposed to be based on voluntary exchange. In the case of many black market exchanges and even stock, bond and other exchanges there is an involuntary third party. A third party who might have been a victim of theft. It is the producer to producer exchange that can be voluntary without any third party damage.

Many people get confused or otherwise when the term "labor market" is used. Most exchanges occur in seconds or minutes. Labor exchanges are an ongoing exchange. Many people confuse a labor market with market failures or market externalities. By proper definition, the terms "market failure" and "market externality" do not exist. Perhaps, this confusion arises because of the longer duration of the labor exchange or the high expectation of the labor exchange. Whatever the reason, a labor market refers to the available supply of labor (individual workers) and the available demand (jobs). If the labor market exchange does not provide the wages, benefits, health care or retirement package(s) that you want then that is not a failure of the market. Supply was met with demand, voluntarily. Otherwise, the exchange would be kidnapping, slavery or such.

You can have discussions about wages, benefits, retirement, health care, air pollution, noise pollution, odor pollution, good working conditions, fair practices, etc. You can say that you don't have enough of one or more of these things. What you cannot do is call these things market failures or market externalities. Call them what they are specifically without a larger generalization that can be bundled with some collectivist plan. Call it what it is without it making it sound larger with the word "market" beside it.

Money

Our current government chooses ends. One of the biggest drivers of markets is money itself. Money should be under the sphere of control of the individual. Instead, we have collectivized money under collective control. The government has ends as we see when Congress amended the Federal Reserve Act in 1977 under a new "dual mandate" to "promote" the "goals of maximum employment, stable prices and moderate long-term interest rates." On January 25, 2012 the FOMC (Federal Open Market Committee) released specific targets of a 2 percent inflation target and a 5.2 percent to 6 percent unemployment target.

Money is supposed to be a medium of exchange that replaces exchanges such as bartering. Under bartered exchange, you exchange one thing of value for another thing of value. Money can be more convenient and divisible. It also can be much easier to store and transport. Often, money does not provide a medium of exchange. Instead, money has been collectivized for government ends. Our US dollar has no value. Our dollar is debt. Our dollar is *fiat* or *fiat currency*. It has no backing by any commodity or good or service. Our dollar has no value in and of itself. Each dollar issued is more debt or more promises of production that the government coerces from all of its "citizens." Each dollar issued is not an issue of value, but, an issue of debt. The Federal Reserve has been a sort of "dictatorship" for the market. The Federal Reserve is an unelected entity.

Allowing the state the power to "print" money or increase the money supply has led to an "oversupply" of money or "national debt" and entitlement obligations. If money was controlled by the individual then there would not likely be any national or collective debt because each individual would not likely spend more than he was able.

There is a belief likely held by a vast majority of people that money needs to be controlled collectively by a government that will seek certain "beneficial" ends with money itself. It is believed that the government is a lender of last resort. The government has even labelled itself a lender of last resort when the Financial Crisis Inquiry Commission released a report which was published in January 2011 by PublicAffairs. The report stated that "To stabilize financial markets, Congress created the Federal Reserve System in 1913, which acted as the lender of last resort to banks."

Among general market observers there is a belief that an ever increasing money supply or velocity of money is needed or the economy might contract and head into a recession and might cause bank withdrawals from panicked depositors. A much more discerning observer, Frederick Hayek, in *The Essence of Hayek* (Chiaki Nishiyama and Kurt R. Leube) stated that "The first necessity now is to stop the increase in the quantity of money – or at least reduce it to the rate of the real growth of production."

What would happen if the government was no longer a lender of last resort? The government currently runs a budget deficit for each year's budget. The budget could not be met without printing more money itself. The government would actually need to spend less and/or tax more. If an individual spent more than he made, he should spend less and/or make more. Why should the government be any different?

Interest rates would likely go higher as there is less

money in circulation and there is no more "free money" being "lent" to banks on a continual basis. While mortgage payments might be higher because of higher interest rates, prices for most every other good or service would likely deflate and lower as each dollar is worth more. This deflation should more than offset the higher mortgage prices. Since each dollar is worth more, interest and fixed income investments will be higher which helps retirement income and growth.

A few less homes might be built without the collective money of the government "lender of last resort" outflow of money to the housing market. Though the "great recession" or "housing crisis" of 2008 helped many people lose their homes. Personally, my wife and I had upgraded from a townhome to a large home in the "housing boom" that preceded the "housing crisis." We lost this home around two years after the housing crisis. Our pre-crisis townhome mortgage payment was cheaper than the rent we had to pay to live in an apartment after we lost our home post-crisis. Were we better served by the government "lender of last resort" for homes?

Contraction is inevitable. Contraction is one of the great fears of not having an ever increasing supply or velocity of money. Stocks, commodities, assets, etc. cannot keep going up forever. They must fall or contract at some point if even for a short period of time. Trying to prevent this contraction will make this contraction much more severe when it finally arrives. We will return to contraction in the next section.

TECHNOLOGY, TIME AND MONEY

The excuse for much of the destruction of our wealth, our money and the economy comes from the most unlikely of sources, bank runs. In the late 1800s and early 1900s we needed actual cash and coin to conduct business transactions. If it was believed that this cash might not be available then banks might have panicked depositors demanding cash. The government created the Federal Reserve System and FDIC and many acts and regulations to try to instill depositor's confidence in banks.

This is the point where the use of money really began to become collectivized. There was no longer a direct exchange between banks and depositors. There was now a third party, the government. This third party uses taxpayer money, collectively, to backstop depositors and banks. By backstopping banks, it gave banks the leverage to pursue a "fractional banking system." Only a small portion of actual cash and other reserves need to be physically on hand or deposited elsewhere. The rest can be loaned out because the government, the third party taxpayers, have the bank's back.

If depositors and banks had to work things out without government (taxpayer backing) then things would have been different. Banks would likely to have been fully funded and backstopped themselves. Interest paid out would be meager as banks would need to slowly and carefully build their own capital base. Once banks built their own capital base then they could slowly start loaning out money to the most creditworthy borrowers. If this borrowing was successful then a larger capital base could be built to extend credit to less creditworthy borrowers.

If fully funded banking that built its own capital from the ground up had been the way things happened then money might have avoided collectivist usage for a while longer? Instead, we borrowed money from ourselves. The government merely stole our present and future money from taxes and used it to promise our own present and future bank deposits. They extended us credit from ourselves. They extended us time. Deposits held in the future will be protected, the government claims, but, Cyprus may foretell a different story for our future deposits (as we shall examine in the chapter Going All In).

For any society, group of people or state to survive effectively requires the ability to manage time well. Time is surplus production or savings. It requires more time to develop more complex technology and tools. This development time requires surplus production or savings. Sometimes, this surplus production or savings comes from a third party in the form of credit. If this surplus production or savings or credit is used well then additional production or profit is generated.

We gave the banking a massive amount of credit or time. The banking industry funneled this money into a notional value of hundreds of trillions of dollars. Instead of a few bank runs, we had an "economy run" as the entire economy contracted into recession. Contraction is inevitable. Instead of dealing with bank runs in the short run, we are dealing with massive debt and a global recession in the long run.

We kicked the can way down the road on this one. Our massive ability to produce and create surplus production created a lot of time before our surplus production started to dwindle. We might blame derivatives, Subprime lending, government and banking practices, etc. The big offender is collectivism. The government chose an end. It chose the short run end of preventing bank runs.

Instead of addressing the collectivist roots of the banking problem, we want to find the "right" collectivist tool that can kick the can down the road. Many look to the Federal Reserve with the hope of finding the "right" tool that can fix the problem.

Another reason that we were able to kick the can way down the road was technology. We didn't need actual physical cash to perform almost every financial transaction available. Technology allowed us to use "electronic markers" to represent physical cash. We have electronic transfer, credit and debit cards, etc. We began to forget that cash represents money. Money is a medium of exchange. An exchange of a product of production for another product of production. An exchange of value for value. Technology helped us lose sight of this representation. We began to exchange production for non-production, value for non-value. We gave banks production or money. Overall, this money was not used to generate more production or money. It was used to generate derivatives and create instant millionaires for successful derivatives traders. This lack of production ultimately helped create the "great recession" of 2008.

The good news is that technology can help us create production and a Voluntary State where freedom can reign as we will see through the progression of this book.

INFLATION

As we mentioned earlier, The Federal Reserve openly advocates inflation with a 2 percent target. Nobel Laureates such as Milton Friedman and F.A. Hayek wanted to target the money supply to 3-5 percent annually (Friedman) or tied to the real rate of production (Hayek).

The government doesn't need any help increasing the money supply, they have been increasing the money supply by double digit figures annually. Every year we increase the money supply with the federal budget deficit, growing national debt and growing entitlements and other government spending. The money supply is growing. However you might like to characterize our additional annual debt, it is additional money. It may not be directed as we would like. It should not be ignored as if it is not money or not a part of the money supply. It is additional created money supply whether we call it debt or interest or otherwise.

What would happen if we stopped inflating the money supply through government spending? Does the private market need physical money to conduct business transactions? No, we have been using technology for decades. The same technology that helped mask the banking and housing crisis can actually help us in this case. Electronic markers that represent money. Real businesses producing real production use electronic markers every day. Actual cash rarely exchanges hands. In fact, we could likely exist in a cashless society. Would we run out of electronic markers to represent money? Of course not. It is only when there is a perception or a possibility that our money may no longer represent production. The gold standard was abandoned long ago.

There is no longer any redemption to money anymore. There is no commodity to exchange our US dollars for. It is all perception. If there was an actual commodity that backed our US dollar then you would need to increase the quantity of the commodity backing to correspond to the increased production of the economy.

When asset prices start falling, the government jumps in with trillions of dollars of Quantitative Easing to "boost employment." The hidden agenda is to keep inflation going. Modest inflation such as the 2 percent target is the optimal condition for the Fed. Too much inflation or hyperinflation might threaten the dollar's very existence. Too little inflation threatens to make debt and deficit spending too expensive as fewer dollars are coming into the tax coffers. The government takes in less dollars in sales tax, income tax and all other taxes. Past debt and future debt the Fed wants to support is now more expensive.

Money in a Voluntary State would operate differently. To increase the money supply, you would need to increase the commodity backing used to represent money, which should be gold. The last gold audit was in 1953. We have had a *fiat* currency for a very long time. We have lived on promises and perceptions. The past has shown that increasing the money supply has meant promising many non-producing entities such as many government agencies and banks more money to spend on derivatives and other non-producing endeavors.

These promises of money to non-production inflate the supply of money. This inflation decreases the value of money as there is only so much actual production to redeem for the money. The government needs to stop giving away our future production. Increasing the money supply is like the banking example we discussed earlier. You can deal with the bank runs in the short run and work to solve the problem directly as a direct exchange or you can indirectly kick the can down the road and have everyone else collectively produce for you until there is a severe contraction like the "great recession" of 2008. If we increase the money supply, and that increase in the money supply gets used for non-production then the stakes of kicking the can down the road will be much higher than the "great recession" of 2008. There will be less capital or surplus production left to recover from an increased supply of money or promises of production.

So, will decreasing or stopping governmental money supply cause bank runs or a recession. It is possible. It is also possible that if someone is no longer able to reach into my pocket and take money out then that might cause income problems to the thief who steals my money. Do we cater to the thief and allow him to keep stealing? The thief may have some short term pains by no longer being able to reach into my pocket for money. Do we allow the thief's coercion and aggression?

Ayn Rand in *Philosophy: Who Needs It* stated that,

> Inflation is a man-made scourge, made possible by the fact that most men do not understand it. It is a crime committed on so large a scale that its size is its protection: the integrating capacity of the victims' minds break down before the magnitude—and

> the seeming complexity—of the crime,
> which permits it to be committed openly,
> in public. For centuries, inflation has been
> wrecking one country after another, yet
> men learn nothing, offer no resistance, and
> perish—not like animals driven to slaugh-
> ter, but worse: like animals stampeding in
> search of a butcher.

Inflation is a crime. It is committed openly. It helps feed asset bubbles. Inflation makes the bubbles bigger. The "cure" to inflation is deflation. The government wants you to believe that deflation is "evil." They want to keep heaping larger and larger doses of new inflation to "fix" the current or last deflation. These new doses of inflation such as QE (Quantitative Easing Bond Buying) programs or setting low interest rates fuel the next deflationary cycle. These doses of inflation are not evenly spread. They will create bubbles that will eventually burst to cause the next deflationary cycle. This keeps on going in a vicious cycle until we get a hyper-inflationary destruction of the dollar or the US dollar gets replaced as a reserve currency, whichever comes first.

When a company increases shares of a publically traded company there is a news release. There is some kind of ratio-nale as to how the sale of more shares will add value to the company and share price in the future. The company might be developing a drug or expanding manufacturing or some other endeavor that is supposed to add value to the company and share price in the future. When the government adds to the money supply there is usually no press release and no honest rationale for how the additional money supply will create value for our "share price" the US dollar. There might be some vague mention of new jobs or spending cuts years down the road. By the time the "years down the road" pass then someone else is likely in office drawing up some new plan with spending cuts years down the road. There is almost never any cuts, let alone, any cuts that offset the growing spending of the present government. The plain proof is our rising national debt and other entitlements.

If a company suddenly started selling more shares than the total number of shares that are supposed to be outstanding then the company is engaging in an illegal practice known as naked shorting or fail to deliver. The government can merely increase the number of outstanding "shares" (money supply or national debt) and it is never considered naked shorting since the government does the devaluing instead of an individual company.

Asset bubbles are not always so easy to see coming. Inflation over so many years or even decades might make you believe it will continue forever. You might buy into the belief of a Federal Reserve "target" and "dual mandate." Inflation is not natural. It runs counter to survival. It runs against the production needed to survive. It siphons off production. It usually transfers production to non-productive sources. Many people may have never imagined that housing prices could collapse or that banks could fail. We came up with many reasons and excuses to skip steps in our due diligence and research. Failure to understand and appreciate the starting point that the government and Federal Reserve start from. Inflation can go unseen, for the most part, in our economy. We hide the inflation in seasonally adjusted, auto and energy excluded, randomly small sampled manners. We hide it in the technology and performance of our markets that in normal circumstances would be deflationary and raise our standard of living. Instead of natural deflation, we have unnatural inflation that robs us of a higher standard of living. We hide a lot of debt and inflation in our reserve (still barely a reserve) currency the US dollar or our future and present production. There is no natural rate of inflation despite what the Federal Reserve might say. In fact, there is a natural rate of deflation as technology and economies of scale kick in.

SUBJECTIVE VALUES IN COERCIVE MARKETS

A large part of the markets are coercive acts of aggression. You buy ownership in shares of stock, commodity contracts, shares of funds, etc. You are also "buying" access. Access to the market where you placed ownership. Access is supposed to be the same for all. Michael Lewis in his book, *Flash Boys*, showed that HFT (High Frequency Traders or High Frequency Trading—depending on the usage) perform trades in less than a second. High Frequency Traders can front-run your trade and sell it back to you at a higher price and pocket the difference in less than a second. High Frequency Trading has additional order types (dozens or tens of dozens). High Frequency Trading firms have their own software and hardware and their own actual computers often sitting in the actual market exchanges to help give them that extra speed due to the close proximity to market exchange servers. The days where people are walking around the market floors in an "open outcry" are long gone. Now, we have rows of computers that automatically buy and sell in fractions of a second. They have the full blessing, to date, of federal regulators.

There is no subjective value hierarchy or choice for High Frequency Traders. They do not prefer one share or company or commodity over another. It is coercive theft plain and simple. They have bought special access from the markets in their placement inside the market exchanges themselves. They may have bought special access from federal regulators through some means or other. High Frequency Trading continues to be considered to be a legal practice with High Frequency Trading computers still residing in the market exchanges. High Frequency Trading is pure coercion and theft. I don't understand how High Frequency Trading is still legal and allowed to continue unabated in the market exchanges?

If you buy shares from a brokerage house as a retail investor or trader then you pay a commission and other market fees. These fees are automatically generated with the trade or investment. High Frequency Trading is really no different than an automatic generated fee. All of these fees occur in a split second automatically as the trade or investment is made. The brokerage house is buying or selling shares for you. The High Frequency Trader is doing nothing for you except stealing your money by acting as an unwelcome, unwanted middleman who collects a stolen fee in the form of making you pay for a higher stock price.

The next example of coercion and theft is, at least, rightly considered illegal. This next example is called *naked shorting* or *fail to deliver*. It is where registered or unregistered shares are sold without finding a buyer that you actually sold the shares to. The CUSIP numbers might be real or fake (registered or unregistered). Regardless, you may never locate a buyer for these sold shares. You are supposed to find a buyer as you are selling them or at least by the end of the business day that you sold them. While, by no means inclusive, I, at least, wanted to provide a few examples of legal action regarding naked shorting.

In February, 2007 Overstock.com CEO Patrick Byrne filed a 3.5 billion dollar lawsuit naming Morgan Stanley, Goldman Sachs, Bank of America, Merrill Lynch among others of basically "naked shorting" Overstock shares to more than the number of available outstanding shares of the company. The case was dismissed on the grounds of "venue" (California). The plaintiffs argued that none of the alleged actions occurred in the state of California.

In June, 2013 the SEC ordered Optionsexpress former chief financial officer and a customer to pay 4.8 million dollars in fines and return 4.2 million dollars for illegally selling shares they did not own (Reuters June 10, 2013).

In October, 2005 CMKM stock was deregistered after the SEC allegedly set up a covert sting operation to catch naked shorters. Besides, the alleged naked shorters, the SEC "caught" legitimate registered shareholders who allegedly had no knowledge of the SEC covert sting operation. The SEC never compensated the registered shareholders and a 3.87 trillion dollar lawsuit was filed.

It is unknown how large naked shorting is or how many companies are affected and to what degree. Derivatives got to a "notional value" of around 600 trillion dollars before derivatives helped cause a recession. Derivatives mostly flew completely under the radar before the recession of 2008.

While High Frequency Trading and *naked shorting* are clear acts of coercion and aggression, there are other market participants that may be on the "cusp." "Automated Algorithmic" trading systems which use high speed computerized trading systems to read keywords of newswires and volatility in the markets to instantly buy or sell stock often without prompting from traders. Their high speed allows them access to instant news and moves in market price faster than retail investors and traders. This enhanced access might be on the "cusp" of coercion and aggression. The extra profits from enhanced access might be a coercive act of aggression? *Market makers* are also on the "cusp." Market makers are a broker-dealer firm that is supposed to provide extra "liquidity" for a security by offering to buy or sell the security from their own inventory or buy or sell later in the trading day. There are hundreds of market makers across the market exchanges.

Market makers get special access. They get "Level 3" platform access. They can see any orders that are placed in a security. If a retail investor placed a "stop-loss" order, the market maker can see that. They can see the exact price and quantity of the order. If a market maker can see a certain number of limit orders to buy and certain amount of limit orders or stop loss orders to sell then the market maker may be able to initiate a "bear raid" and "domino effect." The market maker may start selling from their own inventory to put downward pressure on the price of the stock. Once the market maker starts triggering stop-loss sell orders that the market maker sees on the Level 3 platform then the market maker can start replenishing their sold inventory used to start the bear raid. The market maker can start buying these stop-loss sell orders. The market maker can then sell the cheap shares later. I have seen bear raids such as this occur in mere seconds and return to their previous highs. The special access allows the market maker to manipulate some nice profits at the expense of the retail investor.

To avoid this type of bear raid victimization and profit from a bear raid, you might consider these strategies. Be very careful about placing standing orders. Market makers and others can see these orders. They are likely trying to think of ways to use your order to their advantage. Try to avoid stop loss orders. If it is time to sell, then place a market order and sell. Stop-loss orders can become a self-fulfilling prophesy. The fear of loss used to place a stop loss order can create the feared loss by the market makers that are able to exploit these orders. If you still think that a stop-loss order is worth the risk then place the stop-loss order.

To profit from bear raids, you can keep available cash on hand. If you believe that this is an artificial bear raid with no fundamentals behind it, you might decide to buy some shares at these low prices the market makers have created for you. You could pre-plan with a buy limit order at a price where you think a bear raid could degrade price to. This is risky as these pre-planned buy limit orders are vulnerable to fundamental changes that might occur after you place the buy limit order. News or other events might suddenly change the fundamental value that might be placed on the stock price. If you are lucky and skillful enough to profit from a market maker induced bear raid, it can be a very profitable return of up to 30 percent or more in less than a minute or a day.

THE FOUNDING FATHERS AND MONEY

The starting point of the state or congressional republic or government was, at the founding, a pursuit. A pursuit of life, liberty and happiness. A pursuit of ensuring the natural rights of man. Rights that the founders believed were conferred by god. If the founders had said, "natural freedom," instead of natural rights they would have been much closer. Any claim to a right automatically imposes or corresponds to an obligation to everyone you claim a right against. If you claim a right to white oak trees then you impose an obligation on others to recognize or provide white oak trees. If others have agreed to provide you with white oak trees then you have a valid right that does not coerce or impose on people who have agreed to provide you with white oak trees. If you coerce or impose your right to white oak trees then you have an invalid right. You have an invalid right because your right imposed an obligation. An obligation that was not voluntary.

If 51 percent of all people agree to give you white oak trees and 49 percent of all people do not agree to give you white oak trees is any right you claim to white oak trees valid? Under majority rule, you could tax the 49 percent to get your white oak trees. Under natural rights there are no income taxes. For around 130 years from 1776 – 1913 there was no income tax. Founders believed there was a natural right to your own income. Using your own income should be a voluntary choice. The founders likely believed that sales or excise taxes had some voluntary components to it in the sense that you choose how much or how little to buy.

Ironically, much of their basis for founding the United States of America was to escape the type of taxation that infringed on a person's natural right to their own income. Today, probably, any definition of taxation or explanation of taxation has to do with how progressive or regressive the tax is. Once you remove natural rights and add majority rights, discussions on taxation get increasingly unclear. An upper class person's social security taxes are capped at around the first 110 thousand dollars of their income. This equates to around 16 thousand dollars or so factoring in all employer/self-employed/employer combined contributions. Many upper class taxpayers would be paying over 150 million dollars versus 16 thousand dollars. Additionally, they would be "means tested" out of any social security when they reach retirement age. Upper class taxpayers are said to regressively pay a lower percentage of their income as taxes. Wealthier people are more likely to use "already taxed and lower taxable" capital gains as income. Instead of questioning whether a wealthy individual has a right to his or her income as a natural right or freedom, we turn to the realm of social politics and majority rule. Nowadays, we skip over the individual's right to his own income.

To the lower class's interest, the wealthy individual is an offender as the wealthy individual is not paying the same percentage of income to the social program, Social Security. The cap might represent less than a tenth of one percent to the wealthy individual. To the upper class, they are victims because they are paying for something, Social Security, which they will not be able to use because they make too much income. Even if these wealthy individuals were allowed into the program, the cost could be greater than the benefit they could collect in many lifetimes. As it exists now, the income cap might make it possible to recoup the cost of their contributions if they were allowed into the program.

The farther we get away from the starting point of the supremacy of the individual, the cloudier and corrupt we are to the individual. The envy of the "social" starting place of a collective societal whole can be infinite. We can envy everything. You could flip it around, of course, and say that an individual's greed is insatiable. There are benefits to individual selfishness. There are no benefits to envy. Individual selfishness has to involve productivity at some point. The men who made great fortunes employed thousands, tens of thousands. They produced. Envy never produced anything. Envy is about wanting to steal outright or steal through, majority rule, the productivity of others. The best that envy can do is to try to deceive people into believing about what is the best "resource allocation."

There is a market version of "resource allocation." The government tries this "resource allocation" or redistribution through taxing the people and then providing government stimulus. This stimulus could be in the form of a check directly to taxpayers. It can come through the purchase of mortgage backed securities and long and short term bonds. Mortgage backed securities and bonds do nothing for the unemployed or people who can't take advantage of a rising stock market or low interest rates to purchase homes or autos, etc. There are around 320 million US citizens. The 2008 QE (Quantitative Easing, Mortgage Backed Securities and Operation Twist Bond Buying) increased the Federal Balance Sheet to about 4.5 trillion dollars. If we paid each citizen a stimulus that would be 16,425 dollars per person. Everyone besides savvy, leveraged Wall Street investors would likely prefer to take a direct stimulus per person over a general QE that favors the upper class. The QE raised Wall Street, but, not Main Street. The increase in jobs would have happened whether we had a QE or not. Would a 16,425 dollar stimulus have been better than QE at generating short-term demand and raising employment by a more broad based demand of a wider target group (Main Street)? Either way you believe is better is based on an out-come based approach. Taxation and majority rule stole the 4.5 trillion dollars used here. This fact is often and almost always overlooked.

Yes, I know, the Federal Balance Sheet where the 4.5 trillion dollars supposedly resides is not "lost" or spent money as the government still has control of it. What will become of the 4.5 trillion dollars? The important detail is the direction of the events. The outcome may not always be clear to forecast or follow. It doesn't matter if you have a Republican or Democratic president or majority, the biases are the same. They have past debt and obligations. They use majority rule (they need votes). Any policy will probably involve future debt where plans are years or a decade into the future with the spending reductions later versus now. We only see reductions to the increase of the next spending year(s). There are almost never true cuts where less money is actually being spent. The past debt means that they need to keep inflation going. They need to continue growing the debt and increasing the money supply which all means inflation. They need votes so they have to promise to do something in the future, but, never really do anything in the present. Doing something might offend a voting group. A cut of any social program, defense spending, infrastructure, health care, etc. could offend a group of voters. You need to please more voters than you alienate while beating out the political competition.

SUMMARY

For any group or society to survive, there has to be production. The only real source of production comes from conditions of freedom. Use of coercion, deception, inheritance or charity can transfer or steal production. So many policies and principles depend on stealing or transferring production from the ones who actually produce. This theft or transfer is often packaged as majority rule or democracy. There is nothing democratic about it. At best, you can call it a representative democracy where around one congress person represents one million citizens. I don't imagine there was a single feudal king who ruled over that many people. The majority never sees, let alone votes, on laws that the "congressional king" decrees. True democracy would at least have over half of the people voting in favor of each law. In our computer age, this should be relatively easy. How good is true democracy? Majority rule is simply mob rule. Sometimes a mob is right, sometimes, the mob is wrong. Our government is supposed to be a constitutional republic bound by the Constitution and laws. The Constitution is ignored more than it is followed.

So, what is the right starting point? The right starting point is the freedom to produce and the freedom to use your production of your own choice in a manner that does not infringe on the equal right of others to produce and freely choose how to use their production.

So, what does this have to do with markets? The market is considered to have failed if the market doesn't have the "right outcome." Freedom to produce and choose is replaced by a myriad of social values. Many of these social values are theft and transfers of wealth. Some of these social values falsely try to portray themselves as freedom and rights.

These social values violate the freedom of producers of wealth. Wealth is stolen and redistributed to non-producers and people who derive unearned wealth. These thefts and transfers hurt the overall production of the market as less production is attained.

The greatest threat to production may be money itself. Without sound money, a single keystroke can devalue all producers and income classes at the same time. New money and debt can be created instantly and instantly devalues all other money by the additional supply. With all this influx of money, false principles and policies are believed and accepted. People actually believe in a natural rate of inflation. The Federal Reserve even includes a 2 percent inflation "target" along with an employment target as part of its "dual mandate." There is actually a more natural rate of deflation. As economies of scale and production efficiency and technologies improve, prices deflate or fall. This is the last thing that the government wants to see. It takes more dollars to service the debt and deficits that the government has incurred and is incurring. With less dollars, it is also harder to siphon off money to line their own pockets and own personal causes as "congressional kings."

The Federal Reserve's starting point is to kick the can down the road. One well known case in point, Alan Greenspan. He was an advocate of sound money and sound thinking. He wrote an essay, *Gold and Economic Freedom*, which was originally published in Ayn Rand's "Objectivist" newsletter in July 1966, and reprinted in her book *Capitalism: The Unknown Ideal*. Greenspan had to renounce his mind and past to work for the Fed. Sound money and sound thinking is the polar opposite of kicking the can down the road. Sound money and sound thinking would pick up the can and fix the problem despite any short-term pain. Most "congressional kings" know some of the right things to do. If it were simply a matter of informing or convincing them then it would be much simpler. Instead, the "congressional kings" try to sell ideas that have some pretense of helping, but, in actuality, kick the can down the road. When 10 year plans are written up, the plans are written to do almost nothing in the first couple years. Then the "real work" begins at the tail end of the 10 year plan. By the time the tail end of the plan comes around, the plan has been mostly forgotten and a new 10 year plan is now written and on the forefront of the attention of the press. This cycle repeats itself over and over again.

CHAPTER 3
BREAKDOWN

A broken clock is right twice a day. Different movements might be right once in a while or some of the time, but, their flaws manifest themselves. The same could be said for majority rule. Many movements have no philosophy or premise behind them. These movements consist of principles or beliefs that may contradict themselves and can break down. Other movements or schools of thought have a premise, but, the premise is entirely incorrect.

LABOR THEORY OF VALUE

Communism or Marxism is based on the premise of the Labor Theory of Value. The Labor Theory of Value holds that all labor has value. The total amount of labor required to produce a good or service determines the economic value of the good or service. Goods and services are created all the time that may have value for some people and no value or a "negative value" for others. Prostitution has value for the prostitute who receives money for their services. Prostitution has value for the people who pay for the services. Prostitution may have a "negative value" for the people who don't like to see that type of activity occurring in their neighborhoods. These people have a "negative value" for prostitution and would pay to see prostitution removed from their neighborhoods.

If you accept the Labor Theory of Value that total labor determines total value then your arch-enemy or nemesis becomes capital. Capital can reduce the total amount of labor involved in a good or service. This reduction of labor is a reduction of value under the Labor Theory of Value. This is probably the reason that Karl Marx wrote several manuscripts that became *Das Kapital*. Minimum wages may be a modern variant of the Labor Theory of Value.

CONSERVATISM

To my knowledge, conservatism has no directly stated premise. Conservatism sees the state as an end not a means. Liberalism, as a generic term to distinguish from conservatism, considers the state as a means. Liberalism considers the state as a means to the ends of individuals. According to liberalism, as a means to an end, the state can be contained in a body of rights, obligations, laws or a constitution. Conservatism might point to the civil society of language, customs, traditions, institutions and common law that preceded the creation of the "liberal body of means." Conservatism might believe that there should be no separation between civil society and state. To conservatism, the state is not exclusively an intellectual exercise defined by explicit laws, but, an organic unity that is formed by bonds of family, community and institutions.

Edmund Burke was a forerunner of conservatism. Modern conservatism removed some parts and kept the rest. Modern American conservatism certainly did not follow Burke's advocating the British constitution. Modern conservatism does not have "rules of prudence" or higher or lower order prudence. Modern conservatism does not strive for a "true natural aristocracy" as Burke prescribed. Prudence to Burke was sovereign over all theoretical rights or metaphysical first principles. In the *History of Political Philosophy* edited by Leo Strauss and Joseph Cropsey

> Prudence is "first of all the virtues, as well as the supreme director of them all." This means, in particular, that "practical wisdom" justly supersedes "theoretic science" whenever the two come into contention.

Self-restraint was valued over choice for Burke. He believed that morality must be understood as in a contract which cannot be broken without the consent of all parties versus a founding or a revolution where choice can come into play. Government, to Burke, was a process of change, balance and adjustment with room for growth. Burke thought of the state as a social contract between the living, dead and the unborn. In a contract, each generation is equal; past, present and future. Burke believed that the means to the end of the state cannot have universal rules. Burke stated that means are determined by circumstances which are infinite and determined by chance.

A huge percentage of Burke's ideas come through in one way or the other into modern conservatism. Among some of Burke's influences include supremacy of institutions over individuals, avoidance of theory and the state serving as an end not a means. Roger Scruton in *The Meaning of Conservatism* stated that

There are two principles so basic as to constitute axioms of conservative thinking. First, the principle that there is no general politics of conservatism. The forms of conservatism will be as varied as the forms of social order. Second, the principle that conservatism engages with the surface of things, with the motives, reasons, traditions and values of the society from which it draws its life.

Property, to conservatism, is an institution that requires allegiance and membership to the state. To conservatism, ownership is only possible through the state. To liberalism, the state is only possible through the individual. In liberalism, many individuals choose to create a state to own property among other things. The individual should not be lost in the shuffle or have his value diluted by the number of individuals in a state. To conservatism, the state takes primacy over the individual and from that primacy it is the state that controls property. To conservatism—taxation, forfeiture and other forms of property theft arise from that supremacy. Under conservatism, you might say that there is an implicit underlying debt of obligation to the institution of the state that is *greater* than the sum of rights, obligations or contracts that you may consent to as an individual. Under conservatism, you are eternally bound by obligations to each other and the state.

When you have obligations and place value for others that *exceed* the value or rights that you hold for yourself then you can sacrifice yourself to the state. Under conservatism, you obligate yourself as a sense of duty to acknowledge the bond that you share with others and the obligation that you have to the institution of the state. Under liberalism, you might say that the state should acknowledge that the individual is the standard of value that makes property, the state and even survival possible. As I hope that we will learn through the course of this book, when the state is the standard of value then we can have catastrophic consequences as seen by the Nazi State of Germany. We have a standard of value for ownership of property or income which is the state instead of the individual (I say *have* because we *have* already met most of the financial conditions that Marx envisioned).

If you think that I have gone too far in drawing parallels between conservatism and fascism and Marxism then consider the following passage again from Roger Scruton *The Meaning of Conservatism* (p. 179)

> In this book I have argued for a view of
> legitimacy that places public before private,
> society before individual, duty before right.

Scruton goes on to argue in later pages to finish the book with the thought that politics is a matter of choosing which myth to pursue. Which myth to promote while concealing the true meanings of the myths from the voters.

In the course of this book I will demonstrate how ideas of conservatism, namely subordination of the individual, can be leveraged by fascism and Marxism to extreme ends and results. When the state is your end as conservatism, fascism and Marxism share in common then the consequences can be catastrophic.

When I began this book, I didn't know how great a threat that conservatism poses. I believed that conservatism was only a movement without a premise, consistency and some wrong ideas. I now understand the danger that conservatism poses. There may be people within conservatism who place a higher value on the individual or do not consider conservatism a myth. Scruton has the philosophical knowledge and understanding to state precisely the assertions and values that he is making and following. A conservative like Rush Limbaugh will contradict himself all day and have no clue of philosophy or logic. Limbaugh will see no contradiction in voting, democracy and the placement of the individual or the state as an end. This can be done by Limbaugh all day long. He claims he has "rugged individualism" or something to that effect, but, at the same time subordinates the individual to the state. This is the evidence I have seen, at least, from the books in the Further Reading section that I list under Limbaugh (and when I listened to his radio show around the same time frame as these books). Scruton also has books in the Further Reading section. I can respect Scruton's books on philosophy. I highly appreciate these books. Though, I am cautious when his work touches ever so briefly on institutions in these books. I think I have stated well enough the reasons why above.

Under conservatism, you are not a self-owner. You do not own your own body or reproductive rights. You do not own your own income. A majority decides what you do with your income and reproduction. The fact that a majority chooses what you can and cannot do demonstrates that your ownership rights depend on the whims, desires and ends of the majority. If you are not a self-owner, you are a slave.

ANARCHO-CAPITALIST AND STATIST

The basic belief of the Anarcho-capitalist is that if the state exists, it will grow. The obvious implication is that the government growth will be a negative and unavoidable once initiated or in existence. The state does grow if left to its own devices. The state does grow when we allow mere one in a million representation of our congressional kings to write law and control our right to our own money.

The Voluntary State contends that if individuals retain their right to their own income and we can craft law to reflect individualism then we can limit the basic tools that the state uses to grow. If the state grows without money or law then we can clearly see that the state is a dictatorship that should be put down.

The basic premise of the anarcho-capitalism is that every problem that the government currently handles can be worked out to a root decision of voluntary choice with a profit motive. The failure that I see with the anarcho-capitalism view is that not every government problem is voluntary or can be worked out to be a problem that can be solved with a profit motive. I see certain areas of justice, national defense and natural resources as areas that are not voluntary or lead themselves to a profit motive. I expand on these areas in the Voluntary State chapter. I wanted to help define and state the positions in this chapter that I will expand upon in later chapters.

THE SEARCH FOR REALITY

How a person examines many fields, disciplines, studies, etc. might be determined by a single theme of reality. For me, the best way to understand reality comes from John R. Searle and Ayn Rand. Rand shows there is an objective reality. Searle is a modern day successor to Rand in terms of the topic of reality. Searle builds upon our understanding of reality. Searle has several great books that touch on reality in part or in whole that I list in the Further Reading Section of this book. I wish I could spend a hundred pages or so discussing reality. It is of critical importance. Reality is a critical threshold that helps determine the state, institutions and the nature and direction of politics and wealth. Our view of reality can even influence how we view our self and our identity.

I can only scratch the surface here. I really hope that people understand the independent nature of reality. Otherwise, we have surrendered our philosophical foundation to collectivism, pragmatism, fascism, etc. If we give up our self as an individual and we give up an independent reality then we have a small philosophical base to mount against collectivism and subjectivity and the pragmatism, fascism and all kinds of other ideas and movements that have proceeded and could precede from it.

While reality is independent of our consciousness, what triggers our consciousness of reality? How does our perception of reality affect the scope of reality? If we perceived objects at the molecular level or had the sensation of color determined by sound waves or smell instead of light waves then does the scope of reality change in relationship or time and space? Can reality for humans be deterministic? Is reality a causal chain? Searle writes in *The Mystery of Consciousness*, "How is it possible for physical, objective, quantitatively describable neuron firings to cause qualitative, private, subjective experiences?"

Jean-Paul Sarte in *Existentialism and Human Emotions* stated, "existence precedes essence, or, if you prefer, that subjectivity must be the starting point." Subjectivism is where consciousness determines reality. Whatever you think reality is, that's what reality becomes according to Subjectivism. F.A. Hayek posited in *The Counter-Revolution of Science*, "things are what the acting people think they are." Subjectivism holds that objects might exist outside of our mind, but, we can only subjectively perceive or conceptualize the objects. A subjectivist might posit that it is the purpose or design which determines what objects are. We could replace design and purpose for feelings and whims.

Hayek appears to want to entirely close the door on objective or external reality or metaphysics. Hayek appears to want to conclude that human purpose determines what an object is. Hayek states in the same book "An ordinary hammer and a steamhammer, or an aneroid barometer and a mercury barometer, have nothing in common except the purpose for which men think they can be used." Hayek argues that human attitudes trump physical characteristics. According to Hayek, objects have to be defined by human attitudes toward them.

Purpose can be influenced by the objective reality that Hayek excludes. The reality of an object can influence the purpose that we find for the object. Time itself can be a reality. Gravity can be a reality. There is the old question that if a tree falls in the woods and there is no one there to hear it, does it make a sound? Do we need to exist in a specific area to "hear" the tree fall? Or, does the tree fall and make a sound independent of our existence (essence—tree fall—precedes existence)?

Again in the same book, Hayek states,

> And it is probably no exaggeration to say that every important advance in economic theory during the last hundred years was a further step in the consistent application of subjectivism.

I would state that, and it is probably no exaggeration to say that every important *decline* in *political* theory during the last hundred years was a further step in the consistent application of subjectivism.

I agree with Hayek that mathematics has been used incorrectly in many instances. Many schools of economics have used mathematics incorrectly. Equilibrium is only one point in time. Supply and demand can change rapidly and dynamically. Objects of reality may not lend themselves to quantifiable relationships expressed in many mathematical economic models. Advancements in economic theory have come from an understanding of dynamic human action. I would not characterize these advancements as having subjectivism as their source. I would characterize these advancements as a placement of dynamic human action in economic theory. For that placement of dynamic human action in economics, I credit Hayek among others...

I fail to see how subjectivism advances economic theory. Perhaps, Hayek equated dynamic human action with subjective choice? Perhaps, human choice and purpose were thought by Hayek to correlate to subjectivism? In any case, first, let me discuss a few paragraphs about subjectivism and then show how subjectivism erodes political theory. Hayek was concerned with calling the facts of reality "objective" or "true." Hayek did not want facts of reality quantified in a mathematical form where their weighting or qualitative nature could be mistakenly identified. We get to or can make mistakes in how we interpret the facts of reality. The facts of reality about the earth may have led us to believe that the earth was flat at one point. Reality is objective whether the earth is flat or round or otherwise. There is an objective reality regardless of how we interpret it.

The trap that we fall into by believing that reality is dependent on our purpose is the belief that we can make reality become anything that we wish. We can easily fall into pragmatism, hedonism, relativism, utilitarianism, totalitarianism, fascism, communism, etc. A dictator, Fuhrer or small group can decide the purpose that we will have for an entire population or country. If reality is independent of any dictator, Fuhrer or small group then their purpose is subordinate to reality. The shape of the earth is not dependent on the accuracy of our interpretation of the earth.

Put other ways, you could say that subjectivism states that essence is dependent on existence or object is dependent on subject. I believe objectively that the object is independent of the subject. We, as subjects, can subjectively give an object a use or purpose to us. While we can designate a use or purpose for an object, it is presumptuous for us to assume that we have absolutely defined or characterized the essence of an object. We may or may not have defined or characterized the essence of the object. Our knowledge or use surrounding the object may change. Imagine if we had different sensory perceptions. If we had different sensory perceptions, it would not change the essence of the object. The object has an essence regardless or independent of our perception. This independent essence is objective.

A subjectivist doesn't believe that truth can be found. With no truth all objects are the same. They are all part of the same subjective reality. There are no distinctions between the objects of reality. There is no separate or distinct identity for each object. The distinct metaphysical essence of an object is replaced by random consciousness and whatever purpose, design, whim or feeling that any random person might conjure up for the object. If there is no truth then you are implicitly saying that there is no reality. If the purpose of *The Counter-Revolution of Science* is a Frisbee for me, but, a book to others then the purpose alone may not determine the truth. For a subjectivist, there can be no "facts" or reality. Since we cannot prove the absolute essential characteristics of an object then there can be no truth the subjectivist might reason.

There can be truth or falsehood. You are either pregnant or not pregnant, A or not A, it is The Law of Identity. There is identity and truth. To deny truth would be to deny The Law of Identity and reality. Sometimes, you misidentify the truth with false facts of reality. At an earlier time, we believed that the earth was flat. Truth does not have to be universal of all time and space. We are not omniscient. The truth is true until it is not. You are pregnant until you have given birth, had a complication that killed the pregnancy or had an abortion. Your pregnancy is not dependent on my consciousness. Truth is not dependent on consciousness. Truth and reality exist independent of consciousness. The earth may metaphysically be round in an absolute sense. Roundness may be an essential characteristic of its identity.

What is subjective and what is objective? Objects, metaphysically, are neither true or false. We can take facts of reality (existence) and use reason (consciousness) to form concepts than can be formed into propositions. The propositions might relate to characteristics of an object or objects and any relationships between them. Those characteristics may define or describe an essential characteristic of the object. The truth or falsehood is not in the objects themselves, but, the characteristics or facts of reality that we ascribe to them. So, objects or reality is objective. Truth is objective because it deals with facts of reality or existence. Rights, as we shall see in the next section, are objective also.

Value is subjective. There is no intrinsic value. You have an objective reality and have subjective value. Reality is what it is objectively. How you value that reality is your subjective choice. While there is no intrinsic value, there is a standard of value as we explore more in the next section.

Now, let's finally discuss how subjectivism can affect political theory as noted in my discussion about Hayek. If objects of reality are dependent on purpose, as Hayek claimed, then objects (reality) can vary from person to person. Purpose, reality and truth can be variable according to his view. Hayek reinforced the idea that reality is dependent and variable. Pragmatism holds that reality is dependent and variable. Instead of reality being dependent on purpose, pragmatists hold that reality is dependent on consequences. Reality is shaped by what is deemed a good or bad consequence. Hitler and Mother Theresa had different ideas about what are good and bad consequences. Under variable, dependent reality; anything is possible. Since pragmatists base things on consequences then there is definite bias to the short-run and what consequences can give us the quickest "fix" immediately.

Individualism takes a long-term commitment in terms of planning, producing, saving, investing, etc. Pragmatists use any political configuration that might attain the instant gratification of a beneficial short-term consequence at the expense of individualism or whomever may stand in their way to a quick fix. As we shall explore in the History and Identity chapter, the political landscape is filled with pragmatists ranging from judges, scholars, politicians, etc.

There is a primacy of existence. Reality is not flexible or dynamic to changes in consciousness, sensory perceptions, etc. Reality is independent of consciousness. Reality would not change if we were to have a different set of sensory perceptions or were able to arrange a different sensory order. Reality is not subjective and left up to what we think. Life is a process of self-sustaining and self-generating action. Your life is a result of past production. Other people had to produce and give you the nutrition and other vital elements to give you life. Your past, present and future life depends and depended on production. Someone had to produce something to sustain and generate your life. We wrongly surrender the individual to the majority. Let's not take away truth from the individual. Let's not take away the concept that an individual has an ability to reason that is not limited or dependent on the consciousness of others.

REASON, NATURALISM, NIHILISM, EXISTENTIALISM, OBJECTIVISM

It took a very long time for reason to dominate philosophy or the world of ideas. The Age of Enlightenment or Age of Reason was eroded by Romanticism. You might say that the Age of Reason suffered some missteps and oversimplification. The Age of Reason, at least, put us in the right ballpark. Romanticism and many movements that followed had us walking off the field. Romanticism was a return to faith, myth, and a lack of reason. Romanticism placed a high value on heroic individuals or achievements.

Naturalism emerged around the same time frame as the Enlightenment. Naturalism holds that there is no purpose in nature. James W. Sire in *The Universe Next Door* categorizes naturalism as

> matter exists eternally and is all there is. God does not exist. The cosmos exists as a uniformity of cause and effect in a closed system.

Naturalism is a materialistic approach where matter is the primary characteristic. Matter might be considered the only characteristic. Matter is the only value for naturalism. God, ghosts, the human soul or any supernatural entity does not exist as they are simply matter acting upon matter.

Nihilism is set up by naturalism. Naturalism has no value hierarchy. Naturalism has one value which is matter. There are no other values of comparison. You cannot compare good or bad, happiness or sadness or find truth, justice or other values. It is a short step from one value (that is not an idea or concept, but, a simple physical characteristic or component) to no value.

Any nihilism that has been exercised has been a limited nihilism. An absolute or total nihilism would mean no values at all. If you tried to walk down a street, get dressed, drive a car, plan a meal, look or gaze a certain direction, hold a job, play a sport or any non-random action then you would be placing one value over another. How many actions are totally random or have no value attached? Even if we could think of a random action; would it really be random? Actions our conscious minds tell us are random might not be random as we might have a non-random cause which originated in our subconscious mind.

Fascism, for instance, was a blend of limited nihilism and naturalism. The standard of value for fascism was the Fuhrer or the state. Any hierarchy of values were to serve the state or German nation. Objects or ideas only had a limited value as a means to serve the state. These objects had no value by themselves. Where naturalism has matter as its only value, fascism had the state or Fuhrer as its only value. Nihilism had wiped out almost all value from any idea, concept, right, sense of justice, object, etc. that wasn't from the state.

Existentialism transcended nihilism. For existentialism, the individual gives meaning and value to life and reality.

Existentialism holds that the starting point is the subject (individual) or subjectivity. The problems with existentialism are solipsism, relativism and reality. Solipsism is where values are determined by the subject or individual which means there are as many centers of value as there are people. If every single individual subject or person is his own standard of value then anything or everything or nothing (of course, nothing is something) can be "the good." "The good" could vary from person to person and there might never be any universal "good." Morality, justice, etc. and all value set by the subject become relative.

To believe that subjectivity is the starting point, as preeminent existentialist Jean-Paul Sarte had stated, takes a certain view of reality. It takes a naturalistic or materialistic view of reality. It takes an internal or dependent view of reality. Reality is dependent on the subject with existentialism.

As we know from objectivism, reality is independent of the subject. Reality exists regardless of how we value it. Existentialists may try to separate what they believe is a physical world (of the natural sciences, objectivity or other such dividing lines) from what they believe is a non-physical world (of the social sciences, subjectivity or other such dividing lines). Existentialists might allow for rules, theories and laws in nature or natural science. They might allow for universal standards of value for the physical world. The non-physical world for existentialists is subjective with no universal standard of value. Value is determined by the subject. The subject is the standard of value for the existentialist. There is no universal standard of value for the existentialist in the non-physical world. To the existentialist, each individual or subject is free to choose his own standard of value.

There are universal laws of nature. We may get the facts of reality wrong at times, but, objects in reality have an essence. The essence of an object is independent of the subject. The essence of an object exists regardless of any value that a subject may or may not place on the object. The essence of the object is universal to any subject. A problem with existentialism in regards to reality is that the existentialist believes there is no essence of an object that should be universally applied to the subject. The existentialist believes that reality (essence of an object) is totally dependent on the valuation of the subject.

We place value on objects all the time. The basis of the stock market is placing different values (prices) on objects. There are standards of value in the stock market. Any stock, fund or other instrument that is traded on the stock market uses money. If you tried to open a brokerage account or buy stock with Monopoly money, I am sure that you would have a difficult or impossible time trying to find someone who would accept your standard of value (Monopoly money). How about if there was a crime Friday, where any crime or action is acceptable on Fridays. If an existentialist tried to assert his standard of value such as crime Friday then how well would that go over? There are standards of justice. As I explained in the chapter Markets, money is a concept. Justice is a concept. There are standards of value for money and justice. Concepts can have a standard of value.

Rights

What is the origin of rights? Many people claim to have a right to this or that. Do rights come from god, an individual or a collective or some other place or juxtaposition of places? The Founders believed that rights came from god as "natural rights." Rights were believed to exist as a part of the biological nature of being human. Rights were believed to be an inherent part of being human. If being human gives us rights, then how can we take the life and rights of others even if they are trying to take our life and rights? If we all have equal human rights then how can I deny a person's natural rights or make a person's natural rights unequal without contradiction?

Rights are not natural and cannot be considered "natural rights." An object such as a cat, dog or rock are natural objects. These objects exist in nature whether man recognizes their existence or not. While objects exist in nature, rights do not exist in nature apart from man's consciousness and reason. A right is a mental integration of observed facts of reality or nature. A man may need entities in nature, mental integration or perception, consciousness, existence, experience and the mind to form a concept that exists and is valid. A theory is not "natural." It is an objective mental integration of many observed facts of existence or reality. It is objective mental integration because basic consciousness is objective as a biological process of neuron firings. Reality and the objects of reality are objective. Our observations are subjective and any "facts" or "concepts" are subjective also. Principles refer to facts of nature. The facts themselves, however, are not laws or principles. The laws or principles are mental integrations of facts. For facts to become a law or principle, someone has to conceptually integrate them (subjectively).

Even the "founder" of "Objectivist" thinking seems to implicitly conclude that concepts are subjective. Ayn Rand in *Introduction To Objectivist Epistemology* states:

> The primary purpose of concepts and of language is to provide man with a system of cognitive classification and organization, which enables him to acquire knowledge on an unlimited scale; this means: to keep order in man's mind and enable him to think.

These perceptions, classifications, organizations, hierarchy rankings, higher or lower order rankings, observations and the mental integration used to form a theory may be proven to be correct or incorrect. The theory may be correct or incorrect. It may be contradicted by degree or in full or not at all.

Rights are derived from man's nature as a rational being, but, never inherent in man's nature. Rights must be acknowledged. Rights are a conscious choice and an implicit or explicit assertion. To walk down a street or walk into a building or any number of conscious activities may assert an implicit right to do so. To steal, vandalize or commit murder may or may not be asserting an implicit right to do so. You may or may not believe that you have a right to commit these acts, but, you did them anyways.

The origin of rights is choice. To make a choice you have to have the freedom to make that choice. Otherwise, that decision is coercion not choice. We choose the obligations that we want. If the thief, vandal or murderer wants to steal, vandalize or murder; we are under no obligation to accept any rights that he might assert. There is no contradiction with the freedom of choice. Without freedom of choice, any other concept of rights contradicts itself.

Reality is objective and does not allow contradictions (see Chapter 1, Objective Reality). Rights that are derived from reality have no contradictions. You could call these "objective rights." The thief, vandal or murderer could not "qualify" for objective rights. They never had consent or voluntary choice from the people that they robbed, vandalized or murdered. Otherwise, with consent, the theft would be charity, the vandalism would be art, and the murder would be suicide. Consent and voluntary choice can completely change the nature of the actions. The thief, vandal or murderer never had any consent to commit those actions, so, they have no objective rights. So, punishment, consequences, restitution or some form of justice does not violate their objective rights as long as it is commensurate with the degree of violation of rights that they inflicted.

Any other form of rights beside objective rights can have contradictions. Majority rule can generate "collective rights." Collective rights are rights that may have voluntary consent and obligation for some of the people and may have involuntary consent or coercion and aggression for other people. An obligation has been made that only some of the people may have had the freedom to voluntarily choose. This is part of the reason that collectivism destroys the individual in so many ways. Collectivism may use coercion, aggression and contradiction to create obligations for the individual that were not of his choice.

JUSTICE

How do we define justice? Roger Scruton in *Modern Philosophy* states that:

> Questions of justice arise in two contexts— first, when there is some good to be distributed among those with a claim to it; secondly, where a person deserves something through his actions, whether a reward or punishment, and where justice is the measure of what he has earned.

First, let's look at when there is allegedly some "good" to be distributed. There are several different ways to "distribute" goods through what you could call "distributive justice." Here are a few different ways as offered up by *Wikipedia* (as of 12/15/14 as internet sites can change from day to day).

> *Equity:* Members' outcomes should be based upon their inputs. Therefore, an individual who has invested a large amount of input (e.g. time, money, energy) should receive more from the group than someone who has contributed very little. Members of large groups prefer to base allocations of rewards and costs on equity.

Equality: Regardless of their inputs, all group members should be given an equal share of the rewards/costs. Equality supports that someone who contributes 20% of the group's resources should receive as much as someone who contributes 60%.

Power: Those with more authority, status, or control over the group should receive more than those in lower level positions.

Need: Those in greatest needs should be provided with resources needed to meet those needs. These individuals should be given more resources than those who already possess them, regardless of their input.

Responsibility: Group members who have the most should share their resources with those who have less.

Robert Nozick in *Anarchy, State, and Utopia* discusses the theme of distributive justice when he explains that some good is only "*just*" and not theft if that acquisition or transfer is a gift, sale or other agreement. Currently, we have a need approach to justice in the context of goods. We are tearing out a page from Marxism when he popularized a well-known thought in his day, "From each according to his ability, to each according to his need." People with less income have more need according to this form of justice. Consequently, our progressive taxation has a lower tax rate for those with more need and a higher tax rate for those with less need according to this form of justice. Income is collectivist according to this approach. In both Marxism and our US socialism, we do not own our own income. We do not own our labor, our time and our mind in any exchange of those inputs for income. The state tells us what our need is and what our income will be. We have no choice in what the state decides that our need and income will be. We have no ownership. If we do not own our income then how can we own the inputs used to produce the income?

Our approach to justice in the context of goods affects justice in the context of actions. The second context of justice "deserved" through action could be called "retributive justice." Some retributive "themes" might include retribution, deterrence, rehabilitation, incapacitation, reparation and denunciation. Our form of distributive justice affects our form of retributive justice. We have no retribution for distributive justice. We have no retribution for the theft of our income through income taxes, sales taxes, licensing, permitting, fees, fines, etc. We have no retribution for the theft we experience through the inflation of the US dollar. We have no retribution for the national debt that we did not create. We have no retribution for the entitlements that are promised to some at the expense of others. We have retribution in punishment. We have no retribution for rewards. We are self-owners only in punishment. We own the whole crime and own the whole punishment. According to our justice system, we are individuals when it comes to the crimes we commit, but, a collective whole when it comes to our income and the labor, time and brilliance that might have went into earning that income.

There is a certain amount of force that is unavoidable whether you are in a state of nature, anarcho-capitalism, democratic state, a Voluntary State or any state. There is likely to "always" be crime, competition for money, food and land within and from without any area or group of people or nation. For instance, when crimes such as sex crimes and murder occur there can be force involved regardless of how it is handled. If we use market justice and demand financial restitution and set the criminal free, there is force involved. First, detaining the suspect for court, imposing any financial sentence and finally the force that is implicitly unleashed by allowing such an offender to roam the streets endangering the general public and his or her next victims. State justice involves the same force of detaining suspect for court. State justice has the force of imprisoning a criminal instead of the force imposed on the criminal's next victims. The force should be leveled against the criminal instead of the future victims.

Justice is one "unavoidable" use of force. Internal or external security or defense is another use of force. Defending borders and national resources may take force. There is already force built into any social contract. Emigrating from an area or nation can exert force upon an individual. There is implied or actual force in any state of nature to defend your life or property. We should allow a person to choose if he wants to consent to a social contract.

A proper understanding of rights and the state changes how justice unfolds to some degree. Currently, most people don't believe that an individual has a right to his own income. A collective majority decides what an individual does with his own income. If you fail to pay taxes you can have your house, vehicles, bank accounts and even your cattle (Bundy Standoff), etc. have liens or be seized. You can even be jailed. How we judge taxation would be different if taxation was illegal. Non-aggression actions that are, currently, considered crimes such as drug use and prostitution would be judged differently. The judgment would shift from issues of legality to issues of access and damages. Drug or prostitution access to children under age 18, drug or prostitution use on public property and other access and damage issues would be judged instead of the overall legality of drugs and prostitution. We discussed distributive and retributive justice. In the Voluntary State chapter we will discuss market justice and state justice.

NATURE

Biology is not an area of expertise for me. Still, I felt obligated to understand Charles Darwin before I made any conclusions on Social Darwinism and any impact biology and nature might play in politics and the state. An interesting development in my inquiry is the limits that are placed on any thoughts on nature.

There are so many characterizations of nature that to isolate the Social Darwinist's (namely Herbert Spencer's popularized phrase) "survival of the fittest" as the defining characteristic of nature seems simply incorrect and wrong to me. There are instances of cannibalism, killing, cooperation and freedom to name a few. To me, you could never pick out one single characteristic and define the totality of nature in a single ideal. The Founding Fathers did this with natural rights. Social Darwinists generally used the biological concept of natural selection to make characterizations of how nature, at times, supports the strong and punishes the weak. Cannibalism, incest, killing and a kill or be killed attitude does exist in nature. Still, nature does not have to be a model for human society.

SOCIAL DEBT

Our standard of value and the values that follow (even if those values are a lack of values) can be influenced by how we define our self as man. Whether we believe in a monotheistic god, evolution or are undecided or some combination in between can affect the level of responsibility that we may believe that we have towards our actions and values. Whether we believe that we originated from design or chance can affect our standard of value and any hierarchy of values that follow. Whether we are following god's choices or our own individual choices by reason. The amount of responsibility that we believe we have is relative to the amount of choices that we believe that we have.

We might consider the quest for the answer of the origin of life as a desire. Nobel Prize recipient Jean-Paul Sarte in *Existentialism and Human Emotions* in The Desire To Be God (cont.) chapter of the book writes

> If man possesses a pre-ontological comprehension of the being of God, it is not the great wonders of nature nor the power of

society which have conferred it upon him. God, value and supreme end of transcendence, represents the permanent limit in terms of which man makes known to himself what he is. To be man means to reach toward being God. Or if you prefer, man fundamentally is the desire to be God.

The level of responsibility we may believe that we have can be affected by the "social debt" we may feel that we have. This social debt may come in the form of any debt we may feel that we owe the Creator (unmoved mover or prime mover) who we may believe created us. This debt can affect our values, responsibility and how we live. Many people may also feel that we owe our state a social debt. Some philosophers have described this as a social contract that we have with the state. This unsigned, unwritten social contract is a social debt that obligates us at birth to accept or repay a debt that preceded our birth. This social debt may be some of the reasoning that many people may use to accept the obligations that the state places upon them. The obligations or loss of our right to our own income. Submission to the rule of congressional kings appointed by numerical majorities or mobs or democracy as we like to call it.

Naming our interaction with the state as a social contract is an utter exercise of irony and deceit. A contract is supposed to be a voluntary agreement. As a single individual, I have no input to the terms and conditions of a social contract. The social contract is not a voluntary agreement. If you want to live within the 3-4 million square miles that bound the United States of America then you are forced to live by the terms and conditions of the US social contract.

The state never "resets" to a new starting point. We may feel that we owe institutions or past generations of people. This debt is expressed as a fundamental belief in conservatism. The state is not customizable to the individual consumer. Many people likely consider themselves citizens with attached social debt and obligations. They do not consider themselves a consumer of the state. A consumer does not walk into a store and owe the store money before he or she even walks into the store. A consumer does not have to buy goods and services for other patrons or consumers in the store.

I consider myself a consumer of state goods and services. While I may feel that I owe a debt of gratitude to past generations, I will not sacrifice my individualism. I will not sacrifice my right to my own income and my right to self-rule. I may be coerced into sacrificing my income and some individualism. This sacrifice on my part is due to coercion not agreement.

MAJORITY

Once the individual is subordinate to a tribe, group, class, collective or majority, etc.; the individual no longer lives for himself, but, lives for the collective. The consequences for accepting this subordination can be staggering. The way that incentives form in the state and the directions that the state takes is just a small part of the narrative.

A scientist builds upon the science that precedes him. If a scientist says that the Law of Gravity is not working on the earth anymore, but, there is no recordable evidence of this gravity failure happening anywhere on earth then the scientist is likely discredited and unemployed. A judge builds on the case law and general law that precede him. It is even called precedent. An economist should reference past price behavior, cycles, effects and other data, phenomenon and behavior. Politicians are not ignorant. Many politicians graduated from Ivy League schools and had at the least some general courses in a wide range of subjects as core requirements in addition to whatever major, minor, post-graduate, Masters or Doctoral disciplines or degrees that they choose. They should be well aware of the differences in historical, economic and political approaches. They should be well aware of the formation and development of socialism, capitalism and other movements and schools of thought.

Politicians deliberately choose to follow socialism, Keynesian economics and failed policies of history. They know that they are growing the debt and expanding the size of government and expanding socialism. They can grasp basic math and accounting and can measure the loss of freedom through socialism. Politicians instead of protecting the individual have grouped individuals into groups and classes. From this collective grouping, they have built a vast, growing bureaucracy to service not individual rights, but, social ends of collective groups. Their work more closely mirrors the work of collectivists Karl Marx and Adolph Hitler than Thomas Paine, John Locke or Alexis de Tocqueville. Karl Marx believed in the subordination of economic classes. Adolph Hitler believed in the subordination of races. An individualist does not subordinate rights, freedom or life based solely on the grouping of race and economic class. Majority rule is a form of collectivism that is no different than fascism. Both fascism and majority rule subordinate the individual to the collective. It is only a matter of the degree and direction of the subordination.

Politicians have incentives to do the wrong thing. There is an incentive to create a culture of dependence on the government. Politicians can try to provide national (socialized) healthcare to all. In a zero sum game, people with jobs and health insurance subsidize people who don't have or cannot afford healthcare. Our retirement is already socialized with Social Security where many people will never get what they paid in and many people will get more than they paid into Social Security. If the government can make our health and retirement depend on the government then they have created a huge dependence. The more things that people are dependent on the government to provide, the more indispensable the government is and less likely they will be downsized or replaced. Not only is dependence wanted, but, putting down any possible resistance is wanted also. The government has kept a standing National State of Emergency since 1913. Martial Law and all resistance can be squelched. To make things easier and less risky, gun bans been attempted many times with varied success. The goal is to start banning the most controversial or high powered weapon which may start opening doors to all weapons being banned. The more control and influence that politicians can wield, the more they can siphon off for their own personal compensation, influence and power.

This cycle of dependence even takes on more elements

when it is applied to the economy. There is an incentive to create or sustain two economic classes – rich and poor. Giving amnesty and work permits to immigrants creates votes and dependence. The votes will come from the poor. The rich are needed to give politicians campaign contributions, board positions on companies, high dollar speaking engagements at events and promotions, etc. Politicians can provide the rich with cheap immigrant labor, inflation and Quantitative Easing stimulus spending to prop up investments in the markets and low interest rates to spur spending in companies that the rich own. Politicians have an incentive to use the middle class as a host to suck out the life-blood of the middle class to feed the poor and help the rich.

The first president, George Washington, had no Party affiliation. We have had other early presidents with different Party affiliations such as the Federalist, Democratic-Republican, Whig and Union parties. We then moved to the predominate influence of the Republican and Democratic Parties. We have had 18 Republican and 14 Democratic presidents. There are many estimations or remarks that you could make about the order of presidents. Let me start with a hypothetical situation that might illuminate some of the reasons for our order of presidents.

Imagine, if the US government gave you a choice. You could receive an immediate payment to you of one thousand dollars or immediately reduce the national debt by ten thousand dollars. Would you choose an immediate payment to you or a larger reduction in the national debt? Would it make a difference if the choice was a one hundred thousand dollar immediate payment to you or a one million dollar reduction of the national debt? What about a one million dollar immediate payment to you or a ten million dollar reduction of the national debt. Imagine if you could get exactly what you put into government in a financial sense. Imagine you could simply vote to have more than you put in. Imagine if you chose the one million dollar immediate payment. Initially, you might be happy, but, perhaps down the road you start to feel the effects of massive national debt that you created by choosing the immediate payment. Imagine if you chose the ten million dollar reduction in the national debt and now feel like you missed out on what others are enjoying.

After 4 or 8 years, voters usually have some picture of what they would like to see change. The "other" party (that has no president in office) will probably always offer this change to them. Any candidates from the same party (as the current president) will likely be "tainted" and not be trusted to deliver these changes during this election cycle. This may explain some of the reasons why we toggle back and forth between parties and have had 18 Republican and 14 Democratic presidents. A relatively even toggle back and forth.

There are other themes that could be at play here. Alexis De Tocqueville believed that people want to be led, but, want to be free at the same time. People may want expansionary spending during one term and restraint on the next term to counteract the excess spending. People may want money spent one way as one party should do and spent another way 4 years later as the other party should do. This cycle of alternation may repeat itself as the likely failed promises and failures of one party are countered with the alleged promises and success that the other party now offers.

Roosevelt created a vast safety net and was elected 4 times to be president to "guide us through the war" and "create jobs?" We had the same expansion of government in the Reagan "Cold War" years as Reagan increased the percentage of the national debt likely as much or more than any president before or after. The bigger the fear, the bigger we spend. It is an incentive for the politician to create fear and then "solve" it with more government spending.

Any move to a voluntary government will be met with politician's attempt to cause fear and victims. This fear and victims might be used to bring back taxation. Taxation and majority rule run hand in hand to create coercion and big government. Once the government has the power of the purse through taxation then the sky is the limit.

There is a point where an ordinary person would have to stop. Stop spending. Cut back on spending categories. The government never wants to admit that there is a time to stop spending. There is always some real or imaginary government "dependent." The government finds or creates victims and hides behind the victim's plight (a plight that often has some measure of government origins) to try to avoid spending cuts. The government fails to stop at their own marginal utility. Marginal utility holds that there is an optimum point of consumption or production.

There is what they call a moral hazard here. Politicians can take risks or alter their behavior because the negative costs or consequences that could result will not be felt by the politician taking the risk and will be felt everyone else collectively.

The majority, as a whole, usually does not reference science, history, mathematics, law or economics in any meaningful way. We repeat the same historical mistakes again and again. If a scientist, lawyer or economist repeated failures of the past or ignored past case law and past theory and effects then, in most cases, they would be unemployed or disbarred. Socialism and Keynesianism were disproved decades ago, yet we use them as if they are still valid approaches for the economy. Parts of the Bill of Rights are ignored. Early case law about taxation are ignored such as our right to our own income. Law is mostly ignored or unused by the people. Laws such as the Affordable Health Care Act or "Obamacare" is over 1,000 pages long and most people have never seen or read the Affordable Health Care Act. No voters got to directly vote on it. The "representational democracy" of one in a million congressional representation voted for us.

MORAL HAZARD

When you remove the chains of collectivism and free the individual, the individual can rise to the occasion or falter with the free choice. The choice between individualism and collectivism is an all or nothing proposition. You are either free or not free. Freedom or coercion.

Once you allow coercion and taxation, for one thing, you open the door to coercion and taxation for all things. You violate the individual right to income. You violate a right, as voluntary exchange, between the individual and the employer. If we replace individualism with altruism then what do we get? There are adults and children starving and dying every day. Is our altruism limited to geography? Is it limited to certain boundaries or certain results? Is it limited to a certain percentage of your income? At what point, if any, do you stop your altruism? Can you stop your altruism? If the implicit end of altruism is equality then can altruism be stopped? No two people are equal. There will always be inequality. If there is always inequality then altruism has a perpetual ongoing task to bring about equality. How do we bring about that equality? Is it just a financial thing? Do we try to "balance" our inequality on a daily basis? How about on a weekly or bi-weekly basis? Do we take our paychecks each week or every other week if bi-weekly and balance the United States financially making every US citizen financially "equal" in weekly income for a moment. Do we confiscate past inequality and take land, assets and property? If we could get a momentary US altruistic equality then do we stop there? There is a whole world to "save" with altruism and equality.

The majority does not want absolute altruism and equality. The majority wants to somehow mix altruism and freedom. The majority wants to control freedom. Nowhere is this perhaps more clear than a "social safety net" of collectivism. One implicit premise is that we can save more lives through coercion than through freedom. It is a false premise as I will show in this section. What if people use free choice and don't voluntarily help starving people in the US if that should occur? The solution for the altruist is to coerce them to do it through taxation and the loss of the right to income and the loss of individualism.

Once the individual is subordinated to the collective then there are so many forces at play that it is very difficult to limit the power of the collective. Once you can tax for one thing, you can tax for all things. Once your money is no longer yours to control then the collective has taken control of your money. When the collective controls the money then inflation can start to arise. Once inflation starts, it is a pretty unstoppable force that keeps growing. The collective can promise your past, present and future money and production to the collective. You can promise more production or money than you can make or produce. These promises can create debt. This debt usually leads to more flawed policies to correct the past debt. The inflation, debt and growing non-productive efforts of politicians and the growing number of dependent people they help create eventually leads to starvation, war and death. It can take a while to see it. A little bit of freedom can go a long way, but, can erode over time as I showed in the first chapter. The erosion is subtle enough that it likely goes unnoticed by the majority. The majority continues to pursue the collectivism that will eventually lead to their own demise.

R.J. Rummel in *Death By Government* shows that 169,198,000 people were murdered by government in what he calls "democide" which he defines as "the murder of any person or people by a government, including genocide, politicide, and mass murder." This may be what we have to look forward to. The majority believes that *this* cannot happen to them. The morals, principles, rights and laws are already set in place. The economic consequences of these laws are set in motion. Time gives us the illusion that we are doing the "right" thing. We may not "feel" the consequences right away or for a very long time. Lessons from one generation are rarely passed onto the next generation. So, we keep repeating the same errors and keep getting the same, growing, result.

Besides collectivist government murder or democide, we have millions die to starvation due to collectivist policies. The source of the following statistics come from the internet. Sources on the internet often get "revised" or "edited" and then reposted. You usually don't know the exact changes that were made. So, these are the statistics as of 12/7/2014. From *faminegenocide.com* and *wikipedia.org* we get the following:

> An estimated 14 million people died of starvation in the Ukraine Famine of 1933. Stalin's forced farm collectivization program was a man-made famine in one of the world's most fertile regions.

> An estimated 6 million people died of starvation in the Russian Famine of 1921 due, in part, to political collectivist Communism.

> An estimated 15-45 million people died in the Great Chinese Famine of 1959-61. These deaths were due, in part, to the policies of the Communist Party of China.

Those deaths were historical clusters or groupings of deaths. Thousands of people die of democide and starvation every year. While the United States has separation of church and state, much of the middle east has no such separation for all practical purposes and thousands die each year to conflict that stem from religious beliefs. These religious conflicts involve conflicts between collectivist governments and collectivist rebels.

The majority might think they are "safe" under democracy. Much of the collectivist thinking and policies that generated the millions of deaths above exists in our democratic collectivism. Inflation and debt are eroding our wealth. We are undermining our future to combat growing inflation and debt. If inflation is under the Federal Reserve "target" of 2 percent a year then we are "fine" according to the Federal Reserve and most economists and advisors. How many hundreds of trillions of "notional" dollars can be absorbed into derivatives? How many trillions can be absorbed into our national debt and entitlement programs? How many trillions can be absorbed into bonds? What are we overtly or covertly exchanging to other countries for our bonds and treasuries? What foreign policies are being conducted to protect "national" interests? The most central of those national interests most likely being the protection of the US dollar as a reserve currency to keep growing debt and inflation that is necessary to the politician? Domestic skirmishes such as Waco and Ruby Ridge and other suspected incidents involved attempts to control guns and other objects that might present some threat to collectivism and democracy?

So far, I am not aware of any starvation that has occurred in the US to date. We survived the "great recession of 2008" without any starvation deaths. How about the next recession that might occur in bonds and/or derivatives? How about the eventual inflation and hyperinflationary collapse of the dollar? Will we be able to continue to evade starvation in the United States? Will a European country under democracy have starvation deaths first?

Even if there are starvation deaths under democracy, it will likely be blamed on the "free market" or "capitalism" as a "market failure." It will unlikely be blamed on democracy or collectivism. How many things do we call "market failures" now that are actually collectivism that have nothing to do with voluntary choices of the individual? We should be calling many events *collective failures* or *collective externalities*. These events had nothing to do with markets and everything to do with collectivism. As long as we consider the source of the problem to be the market then the source of the solution will be collectivism. Once we consider the source of the problem to be collectivism then the source of the solution can be individualism.

There can be political moral hazard by politicians. Under democracy there will always be the temptation to try promise some goodies (money) from one group to another larger group. If the politician gains more votes and can get into office by some gerrymandering of manipulation then the politician wins at the expense, often, of individualism. Imagine, if the politician had to list the names and dollar amounts of the people that would subsidize this gerrymander. Imagine, if the politician also had to list the names and dollar amounts of the people receiving the subsidy. Imagine, if this was all public information accessible on the internet. If this was done by individuals it would be called theft. If it is done by the government it is called democracy.

If we are ever able to try to have a voluntary state then moral hazard would be one of the Voluntary State's greatest obstacles to overcome. Despite millions of deaths through collectivism, just one alleged starvation death through individualism might be used to destroy individualism. If collectivism were reintroduced to "prevent starvation" then we would just reset the time table for millions of starvation deaths that may be inevitable under collectivism.

According to *wikipedia.org* (I want to remind the reader of the potential problems of internet sources I cited earlier in this section—I pulled this data on 12/7/2014) "there has been a total of 3,551,332 motor vehicle deaths in the United States from 1899 to 2012." We have not tried to replace motor vehicles with horses. A single alleged death due to individualism would likely lead to an effort to replace individualism with collectivism. Despite millions of deaths due to collectivism and cars, we do not seem to question collectivism and cars. A single death due to the freedom to make our own choices and live by our own consequences would likely lead to collectivism.

CHAPTER 4
BREAKDOWN AND MORALS

TRUTH

Does truth exist? Yes, truth does exist. Where can we find truth? We can seek truth and morality from the universality of reality and the Law of Identity. The facts of reality can be true or false. Reality is universal. There can be universal facts of reality. Objects of reality have essential characteristics that are independent of existential subjectivity, Hayekian subjectivity or any individual subjectivity. The essential characteristics of objects have a Law of Identity. The identity or essential characteristics of an object are universal.

Let's use the example of man with the Law of Identity. Man's life, existence and consciousness are all part of his identity or nature. To have an identity of man, man must exist as man. To exist as man assumes a right to exist as man. A right that does not need to be natural or conferred by some god or some nation. A man cannot exist as a fish. A man cannot act in contradiction to the nature of a man. He cannot act in the nature of a fish. He can act like a fish, but, not in the nature of a fish. Change presupposes the concept of what changes. If you change from man to a fish or from a fish to a man; in both cases you have an identity of what changed from what to what.

To try to act in contradiction to the identity of man could be to deny the nature or identity of man. To deny your own reality, your own consciousness your own life can be an attempt to act against your own identity. This denial is still the actions of a man even if you are attempting to deny that you exist. There are many who try to deny or act against the identity of man. Despite any actions or denials, you are still human—woman or man.

There is at least one nearly universal boundary. A boundary that I am calling nearly universal. This boundary is not a source of truth or morality. While I am describing it as a nearly universal boundary, Robert Nozick called it the Libertarian moral side constraint. A moral side constraint can only constrain or restrain morality or truth. The Libertarian moral side constraint goes as follows (though the exact wording has changed at times): it is illegitimate to aggress against non-aggressors. Affirmation by signing a written form of this Libertarian premise or oath has been used for years as a prerequisite to joining the Libertarian Party. Regardless of my disagreement with joining any political party aside, this moral side constraint is something that I find useful and nearly universal.

How is this moral side constraint nearly universal? This moral side constraint is like a public good. A public good is a good that can be consumed by everyone without exclusion while not diminishing the use of the good to others. Air is a good that would fall under the category of public good. Current "political goods" consumption cannot be consumed by everyone without diminishing the use of others. Taxation diminishes the use of income while often excluding the "political goods" to narrow social goals.

Non-aggression is like a public good in the sense that

it can be used without exclusion and without diminishing the use of others. Concepts such as charity or money might provide kindness, but, are limited. Money is a limited commodity. The use of charitable money directed at one or more charities can eventually diminish or eliminate the money directed at all other charities. You can only make so many charitable contributions until you are broke. For the most part, non-aggression can be used without exclusion and without diminishing the use of non-aggression. Terrorists, murderers, rapists, etc. might initiate criminal aggression. The non-aggression or pacifism of some people to avoid stopping this criminal aggression can diminish the ability of other people to use non-aggression. Someone will have to counter the initiation of aggression by these criminal aggressors. Asking or forcing the use of non-aggression is an act of aggression. Still, forced non-aggression is the least possible amount of aggression in most cases.

A theist might argue that god exists. An atheist might argue whether god exists. From god's existence can come existence of truth the theist might argue. There is a difference between defining truth by reality and defining truth from god. Reality as a set of objects do not define truth. Humans define truth from characteristics or relationships from objects. The truth comes from any correct definition of characteristics or relationships between objects. Having god define truth is like a human being defining truth except that god is supposed to have more knowledge and power.

Using god as a standard of truth backs you into a corner pretty quickly. There is the temptation to define *what* the truth is from a supposed succession or progression. This can lead to a belief of a succession of inspired people and inspired religious texts. In a court of law, any conversation that any "inspired" man allegedly had with god should be barred from any court proceeding. We have no way to cross-examine god or to examine any evidence of god. The Bible's authors cannot be cross-examined either. Not that cross-examination is necessary for truth, but, some clear evidence to support truth should be necessary.

Who can we accept this evidence of truth from? God killed or conspired to kill millions of people according to the fictional Bible. Jesus was born of a virgin, performed miracles and was resurrected from death according to the same fictional Bible. Where is the credibility, proof or evidence for any of these events happening? Deriving truth from god, Jesus or the Bible is impossible.

Can the observation of reality lead to a standard of morality? There is no inherent standard of morality in the objects of reality. The theist might argue that there is an inherent standard of morality in god. Do we need an inherent standard? Does theism have an inherent standard? What would the theist need to have in order to have an inherent standard? First, the existence of god. Next, god's omniscience and omnipotence has always seemed to have been assumed to be "the good" or omnibenevolent. You could be a psychopathic, amoral, omniscient, omnipotent being who chooses to do what we consider evil. If god exists and is "the good" then what can we do with that? The Bible is an insult to any concept of "the good" as we will see in the moral section. These biblical morals, if consistently applied, would lead you to prison. I cannot imagine an omniscient being "inspiring" or participating in the Bible. An omniscient being that I could imagine that "correctly" exercises their omniscience for "the good" would likely be insulted and angry by their portrayal in the Bible. I cannot imagine any inherent standard of morality from the Bible or other religious texts. Do we need an inherent standard of morality? No, we can follow "the good" if we choose to. We don't need an inherent standard to choose "the good." There is no inherent standard of morality anyway.

Reality and the Law of Identity are universal. The universality of their potential application takes us away from relativism and nihilism. We can seek truth and morality from the universality of reality and the Law of Identity. The facts of reality can be true or false. There can be universal facts of reality.

MORALITY

What is the origin of morality? There is something that might come before we sense or reason that we have a right to exist or we should constrain our aggression. In the most basic sense of being human we share a language and self-awareness or self-consciousness that separates us from the animals. We can imagine how things *ought* to be. If we *ought* to exist or use aggression. We can decide if we ought to be a part of a community or be an isolated individual. If we don't feel bound by the duties and obligations of a community or state then we may be able to exist outside of societal obligations, but, may not be able to rely on any protection that society might offer. We can keep or revoke our pre-birth implied social contract or citizenship to the country of our birth. The distinction between science and morality is how we treat the object that is the human being. Science treats humans as objects that have properties and behaviors. Morality treats the object that is a human being as a subject. A subject that is sacred. To remove all sacredness or value from the subject that is a human being we have to remove all morality from the subject until he is a mere object. An object that can be used or disposed of at will.

While this may seem like a simple or low threshold for a person who has moral values, it is threshold that many leaders of governments breached. Fascist and other dictators killed people in the millions because of their race or other factors. People were objects in a collective to be used or destroyed. We will look at things that morality can and cannot properly assert. Morality starts from the most basic concept of identity and can proceed rightly or wrongly into a complex set of codes or values.

Let's look at some moral assertions. Man *must* produce. Man *must* exist for his own sake. *Must* is an imperative. An imperative is an ultimate commandment of reason from which all duties and obligations derive. An imperative is a necessary action to attain certain ends. A categorical imperative denotes an absolute, unconditional requirement that must be obeyed in all circumstances and is justified as an end in itself. There are no categorical imperatives. Self-proclaimed amoralist L.A. Rollins states in The *Myth of Natural Rights* that

> If there are no unconditional "musts" or "oughts," then there are no "duties" or "moral obligations." Which means there is

> no "morality," no "system of the principles
> and duties of right and wrong conduct."

The absence of categorical imperatives does not negate morality. We cannot logically deny our existence or ability to reason. There is truth and right and wrong conduct. Truth is the product of identification of facts of reality by means of concepts. The concepts can be organized into propositions which truth and falsehood rest in the definitions of the concepts and whether these designations could be essential objective characteristics from objective reality. Elsewhere in the same book, Rollins claims that morality is arbitrary. Morality may or may not be arbitrary. Your individual standard of morality can be arbitrarily based on anything. Morality can also have objective, absolute qualities if man's reason correctly perceives, learns and integrates any objective, absolute qualities that exist in our objective, absolute reality. Reality objectively has different identities. These different identities have different effects and consequences to our mind and senses.

Arbitrary decisions require complete discretion without restrictions or exclusions. Arbitrary decisions require the ability, but not the necessity, to be random. If every amoralist murdered every moralist and every other person and then every amoralist committed suicide then you would have extinction of the human species. What if every "moralist" committed suicide at the same time that every amoralist and all others committed suicide causing an extinction of the human species? Are the examples the same? No, a consistent moralist could not use aggression against himself and destroy the standard from which morals are derived. That standard being life itself. Any consistent morality has life itself as its standard, otherwise, that morality is arbitrary. Initiating voluntary aggression against your own life violates the standard from which consistent morality follows. The only way to avoid extinction without contradiction in the previous examples is if one or more people exercise non-aggression.

Amoralism is not a self-sustaining value. If everyone exercised aggression against themselves and others and they use that aggression to exterminate the human species then extinction is possible. The possibility of extinction was made logically possible by the use of aggression. Under amoralism, everyone could exercise aggression and make extinction possible. The only way to make extinction logically impossible is through non-aggression. Only random, arbitrary use of non-aggression by the amoralist or deliberate, purposeful, moral use of non-aggression by the moralist prevents the logical possibility of human extinction. Since an amoralist has no preset standard or code or ranking of morals, it is an arbitrary action as to which moral or lack or moral he might choose to exercise.

It is ultimately choice that determines our moral code. The individual chooses the morals and any ranking or hierarchy he wants to arrange the morals in. You should make individual choices on morality on the merits of reason.

The "naturalistic fallacy" in philosophy is that you cannot derive *ought* from *is*. If everything falls under the "naturalistic fallacy" then ethics or morality cannot be possible. Daniel C. Dennett explores ethics among many other topics in *Darwin's Dangerous Idea*.

From what can "ought" be derived? The most compelling answer is this: ethics must be *somehow* based on the appreciation of human nature—on a sense of what a human being is or might be, and on what a human being might want to have or want to be. If *that* is naturalism, then naturalism is no fallacy. No one could seriously deny that ethics is responsive to such facts about human nature. We may just disagree about where to look for the most telling facts about human nature—in novels, in religious texts, in psychological experiments, in biological or anthropological investigations. The fallacy is not naturalism but, rather, any simple-minded attempt to rush from facts to values. In other words, the fallacy is *greedy* reductionism of values to facts, rather than reductionism considered more circumspectly, as the attempt to unify our world-view so that our ethical principles don't clash irrationally with the way the world is.

Peter Singer in *Practical Ethics* wrote about purpose and goals that, for some people, might give meaning to our life.

If our life has no meaning other than our own happiness, we are likely to find that when we have obtained what we think we need to be happy, happiness itself still eludes us.

> Our own happiness, therefore, is a by-product of aiming at something else and it is not to be obtained by setting our sights on happiness alone.

No doubt that morals are influenced by cultural evolution. Steve Pinker in *The Better Angels Of Our Nature* shows how norms and taboos shape moral behavior. You can track human suffering and law and see how norms and taboos have shifted through time and shape what we define as a crime. These laws, norms and taboos affect our moral feelings and values. Peter Singer in *The Expanding Circle* shows an expanding circle of morality that naturally evolved. Providing a reason or defense of a decision grew larger than only an obligation to family, kin or tribe.

I want to return to the moral assertions from earlier. Man *must* produce. Man *must* exist for his own sake. With our understanding of morals now, we can change those imperatives to proper assertions. Man must produce if he wants to survive. Man should exist for his own sake.

Production is a self-sustaining value. You cannot survive without production. Someone has produced is producing and will produce something for your past, present and future survival. You cannot live long without food and water and other essentials to your survival. These essentials have to be hunted, gathered or produced. If there are more non-producing people than producing people then, at some point, you can start losing quality of life and may find yourself facing starvation. If there are no more producing people then your saved money may become worthless. Money is a redemption or exchange of your saved production for other people's production. They say that money is the root of all evil; money is the root of all that is good, namely production.

Man should exist for his own sake. He should not exist for the sake of others. If he is enslaved then he cannot act on his own judgment which makes him unable to live as a rational being able to use his reason. It is hard to imagine that coercion and aggression could be a self-sustaining value. Eventually, you would think that the captives would overthrow the captors. Freedom is a self-sustaining value. Having the freedom to live for yourself is another strong moral value. Freedom works well with the moral value of production.

Freedom is a condition. Absolute freedom may not be possible. You can take away some freedom in order to agree or cooperate with others which limits or invalidates an absolute set of free choice. Cooperation or agreement can limit the absolute amount of choices that you could have. An agreement is usually a constraint to avoid acting in a certain way or a call to act in a certain way. Freedom, in a general sense, is the absence of coercion. Absolute freedom includes coercion or the freedom to act with coercion. This, of course, entails the contradiction of freedom and not freedom or freedom and coercion.

You can create limited freedom from absolute freedom with the "Libertarian" side constraint of not aggressing against non-aggressors. This side constraint adds an obligation, but, removes coercion and aggression. An individual may want to further limit his freedom in exchange for a right to something else from someone else. This obligation or rights exchange could be for a myriad of reasons or ends that the individual may want to pursue for his survival, security, pleasure, etc. Limiting freedom with a Libertarian moral side constraint and voluntary rights exchange can be an optimal or best set of freedom and morality. Absolute collectivism would be where the collective makes every choice for the individual. Any freedom of choice derived from the collective is a whim of the collective.

Under a proper Voluntary State or individualism an individual is his own end with the state being a means. There is reciprocity of means and ends. An individual may be his own end while serving as means to others. Likewise, others may provide a means to the individual's ends. Under a collective state, the individual is a means to the ends of the state. Those state ends have varied from fascism (race), communism/socialism (class and labor), utilitarianism (utility), consequentialism (consequences), environmentalism, etc. and many points in between. The ends of individuals can vary also. The individual can be blessed or cursed with the choice of his own ends.

No state can survive long term with the wrong morals. If you have altruism instead of selfishness, theft instead of production, coercion instead of freedom then these moral values will eventually catch up with the state and implode it from within.

Morals are optional (that doesn't mean there won't be consequences). There are many things we *ought* to do. Any *must* is implicitly followed by an *if*. If we choose to avoid moral action then there can be consequences. These consequences, rightly or wrongly, may come in the form of the justice system. The justice system is legitimized (legal) sanction for retributive and/or preventative aggression. Retributive aggression for a past crime and preventative aggression for crime that you are likely to commit. Another aggression is self-defense or returning aggression that was initiated towards you. If aggression is initiated against you (falsely implying a right to use aggression against you) then a right to respond with aggressive self-defense is rightly implied. Justice supports self-defense as we have a basic right to our own person and property.

The state, as we know, goes much farther than justifiable self-defense. The state initiates aggression in several forms and manners. The state determines or imposes outcomes on non-aggressors for non-aggressive voluntary acts. The choice isn't as much between the Involuntary State and the Voluntary State, but, between coercion and non-coercion or aggression and non-aggression.

Basically, I have attempted to justify aggression in the sphere of self-defense. The state attempts to justify all manner of aggression as it enacts law and asks for your vote as an endorsement of the state's aggression. The state still uses aggression by taxing your own income (regardless of whether you vote or not). The coercion of the right to your own income can be compounded by actions the state can make with your stolen income. When anything can be argued, by the state, "for the greater good" then any measure of coercion might be possible

If we want a Voluntary State then we need to understand and act on morality in a different, non-coercive manner. Until we understand the coercion that we inflict or sanction on others through democracy, we will not move past democracy.

FAITH AND MURDER

The belief in faith has almost no bounds as to the aversion of reason, logic and science and inclusion of the imagination. So, I am starting from a place where no amount of aversion or imagination can deny. Murder is detailed throughout the Old and New Testaments of the Bible.

Steve Wells in the book *Drunk With Blood* shows that the Bible details 2,821,364 murders. Wells shows there were 24,994,828 estimated murders in the Bible. Steve Wells details how the mountains, rivers and lands will be consumed with the blood and carcasses of the murdered dead (Isaiah 34:3-7, Jeremiah 25:33, Ezekiel 35:8, Amos 8:3, Amos 9:1-4, Nahum 3:3, Zephaniah 1, Revelation 2:23, Revelation 8:8, Revelation 11:9). It is implied that everyone will go to hell except the 144,000 Jewish male virgins according to Revelations 14:3-4. Revelations 14 discusses murdering 24 trillion people as Steve Wells shows if you calculate the blood spilled based on 5 liters of blood per person and the dimensions described in this chapter of Revelations. Wells also goes on to show how Revelations shows that more than 4.7 billion people will be murdered by Death, Hell and four angels. Ironically, Wells states how Satan has no recorded plans to murder people in the future.

I cannot begin to cover the totality and immorality of millions of murders for the myriad of reasons that god chose to conspire or directly murder people. I will give a few of the statuses or groups of people that god chose to murder for their inclusion into that group. God chose to murder infants and children (1 Samuel 15:2-3 RSV, Psalms 135:8 RSV, Psalms 136:10 RSV, Psalms 137:9, 2 Kings 6:28-29 RSV, Isaiah 13:15-18 RSV, Ezekiel 9:5-7 RSV, Leviticus 26:21-22 RSV, Jeremiah 19:7-9 RSV). God wants a monopoly on supernatural worship as any man or woman claiming supernatural powers or speaking ill of god is to be murdered (Exodus 22:18 RSV, Leviticus 20:27 RSV, Zechariah 13:3 RSV, Deuteronomy 13:6-10 RSV, Deuteronomy 17:2-5 RSV, Leviticus 24:10-16 RSV). Adultery, fornication and being a victim of rape are capital offenses (Leviticus 20:10 RSV, Leviticus 21:9 RSV, Deuteronomy 22:20-21 RSV). I imagine that most everyone is familiar with the Bible's homophobic mandate of death to homosexuality (Romans 1:26-32 RSV). These examples are a few of the non-aggressive victims of aggressive murder. These victims were not murdered for being aggressive. Being an infant, small child, practicing non-aggressive supernatural activities, a victim of rape, consenting sex such as adultery, fornication or homosexuality are all non-aggressive acts that god murdered people for.

FAITH AND MORAL HYPOCRISY

The moral hierarchy of the Bible is horrendous. For example, is adultery the worst sin? Adultery is the only acceptable reason for divorce as Matthew 5:32 (RSV) states "But I say to you that every one who divorces his wife, except on the ground of unchastity, makes her an adulteress; and whoever marries a divorced woman commits adultery." To me, there are many things worse than adultery such as murder, rape, incest, assault, terrorism, etc. Divorce is not offered up as an option in these cases.

In a severe case of the most distorted moral hierarchy from John W. Loftus in *Why I Became An Atheist* we have

> A female captive in war was forced to be
> an Israelite man's wife (Deut. 21:10-14). If
> a virgin who was pledged to be married was
> raped, she was to be stoned along with her
> rapist (Deut 22:23-24), while if a virgin
> who was not pledged to be married was
> raped, she was supposed to marry her rapist
> (Deut. 22:28-29).

A father could even sell his daughters into slavery (Exodus. 21:7 RSV). Or cannibalize their children (Jeremiah 19:9 RSV) or wipe out present and future generations (Exodus 20:3-5 RSV).

In the story of Sodom and Gomorrah, homosexuality seemed to be the chief reason whole cities were destroyed. Homosexuality is a sin to keep violators out of heaven? Religious teachings like "the meek shall inherit the earth" and "the first shall be last and the last shall be first" teach humility and unworthiness. In the crucifixion of Christ, Christ sacrificed himself as a perfect, sinless person to cleanse the sins of the sinners. Are we supposed to live for others with everyone living for everyone else? God asked Abraham to offer up his first-born son, Isaac, as a sacrifice to god as a testament of Abraham's faith and loyalty? This is the type of loyalty that street gangs, despots, tyrants and dictators try to command. Is there still church authority in men with direct lineage or authority going back for over 2,000 years? Are these men any different than you are or I? Do they talk to god, walk on water, turn water into wine and perform miracles? Are we supposed to treat church leadership as ambassadors of god? Does the Bible foretell a future apocalypse or was the apocalypse the end of the Judaic age?

Ayn Rand wrote in *For The New Intellectual*

> What is the nature of the guilt that your teachers call his Original Sin? What are the evils man acquired when he fell from a state they consider perfection? Their myth declares that he ate the fruit of the tree of knowledge—he acquired a mind and became a rational being. It was the knowledge of good and evil—he became a moral being. He was sentenced to earn his bread by his labor—he became a productive being. He was sentenced to experience desire—he acquired the capacity of sexual enjoyment. The evils for which they damn him are reason, morality, creativeness, joy—all the cardinal values of his existence. It is not his vices that their myth of man's fall is designed to explain and condemn, it is not his errors that they hold as his guilt, but the essence of his nature as man. Whatever he was—that robot in the Garden of Eden, who existed without mind, without values, without labor, without love—he was not man.

More hypocrisy would include Guy P. Harrison *50 popular beliefs that people think are true* when he stated

> Yes, when it comes to religion, every believer is a skeptic—almost. The only difference is that they stop analyzing, doubting and asking questions when their thoughts arrive at the doorstep of their own religion. That's where critical thinking ends and faith begins.

FAITH AND MORAL RANKING

Organized religion is a different variation of the same theme as Marxism and fascism. They all seek to subordinate the individual. Marxism subordinates on the basis of economic classes, fascism subordinates on the basis of race and organized religion subordinates on the basis of faith. Organized religion gives imperatives and commandments that must be followed. Organized religion gives you a moral hierarchy that you cannot question or dispute. Organized religion gives you a collective church and helps program you for the collective rule of the majority or majority rule. Organized religion subordinates the individual's reason to the alleged omniscience of an alleged omnipotent god. I have an easier time believing that there could be an omniscient, omnipotent being than believing that the Bible is an inspired authentic work of an omniscient being. I might give the possibility of an omniscient, omnipotent, omnibenevolent being a one in a billion odds of actually existing. I would give the Bible no odds of being an inspired work of an omniscient, omnipotent, omnibenevolent being. The Bible is a total work of fiction that may have had, at best, actual people (people who went by those names) or event(s) like a local flood (Noah's Ark). To say it is more fiction than fact would be an understatement. I would have to estimate that the Bible is 99 percent fiction.

It seems difficult to imagine cobbling together a moral or ethical hierarchy with faith as the base. Anything that you might put together will be mixed with inconsistencies and contradictions. There are a million different excuses such as that was the Old Testament, Judaic Law, Mosaic Law, Joseph Smith or Old Testament people could have multiple wives, that was god's will that this or that happened, it is not for you to question god, you will have to take it on faith. The faithful are often willing to settle for inconsistencies, contradictions and any poor ethical hierarchies. This complacency in ethics can increase the acceptance level of state power and authority.

There are at least two main categories or reasons that people might use god as a standard of value. The first category or reason is the assumption of "the good." God's supposed omniscience and omnipotence has always seemed to have been assumed to be "the good." Any assumption of "the good" would be cherry picking (picking only moral or biblical or historical reference that you want while ignoring the morals or biblical or historical reference that you don't want) or guessing the moral hierarchy that god would want you to have. If we could know an absolute set of moral values "the good" and were forced to follow them to avoid hell then how deterministic and coercive would that be? Even non-aggressive action and behavior seem poised to send you to hell. Examples of non-aggressive action and behavior might include homosexuality, pre-marital sex, prostitution, masturbation, adultery, divorce, lack of baptism, lack of asking for forgiveness, lack of confessing sins.

The second category or reason that could be used to affirm god as a standard of value is the Bible or other religious texts that are believed to have a standard of value that we are supposed to follow. We have no idea if an omniscient being such as a god has established or practiced some absolute standard and/or hierarchy of moral values. The Bible does not provide any clear standard or hierarchy of moral values. The Bible surely didn't exercise any such moral value hierarchy in Bible times (it oscillated between psychopathic murderer to forgiving saint and many places in-between).

Following god from a heaven/hell or reward/punishment equation is basing morality on aggression. "The meek shall inherit the earth," according to Matthew in the New Testament. So, if you do non-aggressive sin with meekness then maybe you can still inherit the earth. Makes about as much sense as many other things regarding the Bible.

There are a few conclusions or questions that you can draw from using god as a standard of morality or "the good." God is the "the good" because god is omniscient, so, the Bible's account of god's behavior must be explainable? God never ordered the genocide, infanticide, slavery, child sacrifice of the Old Testament and the Bible is not true and is a fictional story? We cherry pick and ignore any negative aspects of the Old Testament? We focus on positive parts of the New Testament such as parts of Jesus's life and not god's conspiracy to commit murder that lead up to Jesus's crucifixion and murder? We ignore genocide of the Old Testament for the possible salvation of all mankind? We perform the largest utilitarian exercises ever performed and sacrifice the "few" actual living breathing lives for the eternal ethereal soul of the many that followed and follow?

Some people see some of the problems with faith and believe that there is still room for god. There is no room for god in morality. Either the Bible is true in whole or part or it is not. If the Bible is true then even if we ignore the entire Old Testament, we still have to contend with New Testament murder and moral hierarchy that defy reason and logic (contradiction).

ORIGIN OF THE BIBLE

Michael Shermer in *The Believing Brain* states that

> Around five thousand to seven thousand years ago, as bands and tribes began to coalesce into chiefdoms and states, government and religion co-evolved as social institutions to codify moral behaviors into ethical principles and legal rules, and God became the ultimate enforcer of the rules.

Shermer, in the same book, states

> God is the ultimate pattern that explains everything that happens, from the beginning of the universe to the end of time and everything in between, including and especially the fates of human lives. God is the

ultimate intentional agent who gives the universe meaning and our lives purpose.

Michael Onfray in *Atheist Manifesto* shows how the Bible could have took up to 2,700 years to complete.

> Conclusion: if we go upstream and take the most ancient Old Testament dating (twelfth century BCE) and then voyage downstream to the final establishment of the New Testament corpus at the Council of Trent (sixteenth century), the construction sites of the monotheisms were constantly at work for twenty centuries of action-filled history. For books directly dictated by God to his people, the opportunities for human intervention are numberless. At the very least, they call for and deserve serious archaeological spadework.

Where did the Bible come from? It is at least very clear to me that the Bible was inspired by the Epic of Gilgamesh that was written around 2,000 BCE (I will use BCE—Before Common Era instead of BC—Before Christ because I don't want to give credence to the son of an alleged omniscient being roaming the earth over 2,000 years ago). Loftus stated that the Genesis Flood Myth could not have taken place before 1250 BCE because of the events that need to occur first in the Bible myth such as the death of Jacob in Egypt and the Exodus. Loftus's timeline supports Onfray's twelfth century BCE timeline. The Epic of Gilgamesh predates the

Bible and the correlations are very staggering. The Bible books Ecclesiastes and Daniel have some influences from the Epic of Gilgamesh. The Flood Myth in the Epic and the Bible are pretty much point for point. The Garden of Eden myth might even be a little closer point for point. In any case, the Garden of Eden myth is shorter than the Flood Myth, so, I have detailed it the next paragraph.

In the Epic, Anu creates Enkidu. In the Bible, god creates Adam. In the Epic, Enkidu is a wild man of the forest. In the Bible, god places Adam in the Garden of Eden. In the Epic, Enkidu is naked in the forest. Enki an Epic character (though this myth was not directly in the Epic of Gilgamesh) had a rib removed to create Ninti, the Sumerian goddess of life, who healed him after he had eaten forbidden flowers. In the Bible, Eve is created from Adam's rib. In the Bible, Adam and now Eve are both naked in the Garden of Eden. In the Epic, Enkidu is tempted by the harlot Shamhat. In the Bible, Adam and Eve are tempted by a serpent (many assume that to be the devil—we will look at this later in the book) to eat the forbidden fruit. In the Epic, Enkidu falls to Shamhat's charms. In the Bible, Adam and Eve eat the forbidden fruit. In the Epic, Enkidu loses his strength but gains knowledge. In the Bible, Adam and Eve gain knowledge.

The Bible took around 2,700 years to complete. As we see in Steven Pinker *The Better Angels of our Nature* the evolution of violence has culturally evolved from torture and human sacrifice to equal rights (in most of the non-Muslim world). Animal sacrifice, slavery, stoning, crucifixions, heretical or apostate murder, murder for people in "your land" that was allegedly promised from god; these are all what you might expect from people of the timeframe when the Old Testament myth was written. Thousands of years of cultural evolution finally lead to Jesus's admonishment of Old Testament torture, punishment and death. The New Testament Bible myth in the book of John chapter 8 speaks of a woman who had been caught in adultery. This woman was brought to Jesus to be stoned under Old Testament Mosaic law. Jesus then told them that "Let him who is without sin among you be the first to throw a stone at her."

By the time the New Testament was written, in most parts of the world, adultery was not a crime punishable by stoning. As with most things, the Muslim Middle East is morally centuries behind the rest of the world. With a static book of the Koran, the Middle Eastern moral compass may stay locked in the middle ages. Stoning is still legal in several Middle Eastern countries. There have been dozens of reported stoning deaths in the last decade in the Middle East primarily for consensual adultery or homosexuality.

It might be similar to creating a new myth where the Old Testament is described in terms of Middle Eastern morality and culture of today. Then the New Testament comes along describing the morality and culture of the rest of the world. If this myth was given to people 3,000 years in the future and they were somehow unaware of the differences in morality then the contrast of cultures would seem so extreme and miraculous. A character such as Jesus would be an enlightened man of morality that must be due to faith and his proximity to an omnibenevolent god. The character Jesus, for the most part, is morally like you and I.

Unfortunately, in a Koran style version of this myth, there is no evolution of morality. It is a static moral entity for the entire 2,700 years. Imagine, if some of the people 3,000 years in the future, were somehow unaware of the history and morality of this time, then believed the morality of the Koran style myth. They might be locked in the moral compass of morality of 5,700 years ago and continue for another 5,700 years into the future with this static moral compass if the human race didn't kill each other off because of their ignorance.

Determining the New Testament was a long process as Loftus in the same book stated

> The process of determining the present collection of twenty-seven books that Christians now call the New Testament took roughly four hundred years, leading up to the Third Council of Carthage (397 CE), which declared them to be scripture. That being said, James Barr reminds us that when it comes to the question of the canon, "it was impossible to provide scriptural proof for this most central of questions, namely, which precisely were the books which had been divinely inspired. No passage in either the Old or New Testament gave a list." There was "no scriptural evidence to decide what were the exact limits of the canon. Books do not necessarily say whether they are divinely inspired or not, and many books that do in some fashion

claim divine inspiration were nevertheless not accepted as canonical."

THE EVOLUTION OF THE DEVIL

I was taught as a child that the devil, in the form of a serpent, tempted Adam and Eve. The devil is never mentioned here. The creators of the Bible myth wanted man to bear the full responsibility of his actions or sin at this point. The Bible myth creators didn't want such an evil scapegoat such as the devil. In the Old Testament, Satan is mentioned chronologically after the Genesis myth. In Job 1:6 (RSV) Satan is a son of god. In the first two chapters of Job, god and Satan have a conversation where god said that Job is a special servant of god unlike any on the earth. Satan argues that Job's special faith is a result of the blessings that god has bestowed on him. God gives Satan the task to challenge Job. There is no hostility or condemnation or nothing to suggest any evilness on Satan's part. Satan is seen as an obedient servant acting upon god's wishes to test Job. 2 Samuel 24:1 (RSV) said that god cited David against Israel and Judah. In 1 Chronicles 21:1 (RSV) it is Satan who cites David against Israel (these two connecting scriptures came by way of John W. Loftus *Why I Became An Athiest*). Reading the whole chapter from these two connecting scriptures shows that Satan was acting as a proxy for god as 1 Chronicles 21:7 (RSV) states that god smote Israel himself and in 2 Samuel 24:15 (RSV) god murdered 70,000 men.

Satan was never mentioned directly among the sons of god who were on the earth in the days of Genesis 6:4 (RSV).

If Satan was a fallen angel in direct defiance of god who was procreating offspring (Nephilim) from human women in the time of Genesis then shouldn't the leader of the supposed fallen angels, Satan, be mentioned here? The passages from 1 Chronicles and Job show to me that Satan was following the direction of god as a loyal servant of god. Another Old Testament passage Zechariah 3:1 (RSV) shows Satan as a servant of god that has accused Joshua. God passes judgement in verse 7 and says that if Joshua walks in the way of god and keeps god's charge then Joshua shall rule god's house (as high priest) and have charge of god's courts. Satan had the job of an "adversary" (Hebrew) as part of god's kingdom or court.

As if a switch is turned on or something, Satan goes from loyal servant of god in the Old Testament to an evil arch nemesis or something in the New Testament. Whether New Testament writers wanted to shift the blame from god and man to Satan is not known for sure? In the fictional Old Testament Bible, god and man murdered millions in the name of the Lord. Maybe the New Testament writers wanted to change the mood or shift the focus from an angry murdering god to a loving god? Sin was derived from an inability to serve god correctly in the Old Testament. In the New Testament, sin appears to be shared by man and Satan. God is now the reformed murderer. Ironically, Satan never murdered anyone in the Bible myth.

THE LOGICAL PROBLEMS OF GOD

God cannot logically be omniscient, omnipotent and omnibenevolent simultaneously if evil and suffering exist.

Let us imagine that we could forget the past murder and suffering that was committed and conspired by god in the fictional Bible. Could god be omniscient, omnipotent and omnibenevolent in the present and future? Being temporal is being in one point in time. An omniscient and omnipotent being in the present could know all the thoughts of all mankind, the animal kingdom and know all environmental events across the universe or multiverse as they occur. Even if you could travel backward or forward in time, you can only exist in one point in time. If you exist in the future then you cannot temporally exist in the present. A temporal being cannot exist in two places at once.

If you travel back in time from the future to the present then the future that you left is unwinding without your temporal presence. Of course, any single point of time in the future is just one moment in time. If you are a year in the future then how about two years in the future? What about a year and a half or three or four years in the future? What about sixteen years or seven years in the future? There are 31,536,000 seconds in a year (60 minutes in an hour * 60 seconds in a minute = 3,600 seconds in an hour * 24 hours in a day = 86,400 seconds in a day * 365 days in a year = 31,536,000). There are 31,536,000,000 milliseconds in a year. There are around 7 billion people in the world. If my math is correct that would be 220,752,000,000,000,000,000 milliseconds in a year just to keep up with the human animal.

I don't even want to begin the numbers for all the animals and natural events that would need to be tracked to prevent murder and human evil and suffering. To be omniscient even within the limited parameters of the present and future would require a possibly limitless number of points in time. The surface of the earth is around 200 million square miles. The average depth of the ocean is 3 miles deep. We have satellites in space and events overhead. There is a massive amount of "3D Space" (or should I say eleven dimensional space as some have shown?) for a god to monitor. Just the time and space of this earth would be a pretty tremendous thing to have total knowledge of. If you had total knowledge of all time and space of the earth then you would only have an infinitesimally small sliver of the knowledge of the multiverse to qualify for your omniscience merit badge.

Let's say that god can be atemporal or outside of time. Let's say that god can exist in all places at all times. Let's say that god can have knowledge and power over a possibly limitless number of different combinations of outcomes as an omniscient and omnipotent being. Can omniscience and omnipotence create an omnibenevolent outcome? To be omnibenevolent implies the omniscience and omnipotence to be benevolent at all times. This benevolent ability would require foreknowledge of all people and events and the ability to act on that knowledge.

What is an omnibenevolent outcome? Stopping evil and suffering before it starts by stopping life before it starts at the sperm and egg selection level? Allowing life, but, controlling events deterministically to avoid evil and suffering? Allowing any freewill to the point just before any evil or suffering? Any way that I can imagine removing evil and allowing any possible freewill involves coercion on some level. Is any coercion compatible with an omnibenevolent being? As we should know, god is not even close. God has never tried to reduce evil or suffering except in the fictional Bible or the deluded patterns or events that people might falsely attribute to god as a miracle or blessing.

I am not sure that god reduced any evil or suffering in the Bible. I am sure god increased murder in the Bible. Things god did to reduce evil and suffering seem to be caused by god's indifference or direction in the first place. God told Abraham to murder his first-born son Isaac as an offering to god. When god saw that Abraham was capable of being a murderously loyal evil servant then god told Abraham to offer up a ram instead. God only "saved" the murder he was going to conspire to commit. I would not call this a reduction of evil and suffering.

First, I would say that being omnibenevolent is not likely possible under any definition of avoiding aggression and coercion. Second, I would not even call god benevolent, let alone, omnibenevolent. I would classify god's fictional character in the Bible as evil as I would classify any similar mega murderer.

If god is omnibenevolent, omniscient and omnipotent then god would foresee that man would sin (omniscience). God could have made a sin-free version of man (omnipotence). With omniscience and omnipotence, god could not be omnibenevolent after the creation of man. Man was known in advance to not always be good. Many men are downright bad. While you could argue that any alleged introduction of mankind is, on balance, benevolent—I do not believe that you could effectively argue that this introduction of mankind is omnibenevolent. Any alleged creator is either introducing evil and suffering through the creation of mankind or using aggression to stop perceived future evil and suffering through death of their life, freedom and free will. God had foreknowledge of the murder and suffering these evil men would inflict. God allows the murder and suffering. This alleged omniscience and omnipotence make god's foreknowledge and subsequent inaction or indifference a lack of "the good" or omnibenevolent.

For omniscience of the past, present and future, we would need god to be atemporal or outside of time. God would need to be able to exist in the past present and future and be able to travel backwards or forwards in time. Somehow, god would need to be atemporal or exist everywhere at every time at all times at once to truly be omniscient. To be atemporally omnipotent might involve the ability to act on everything at the same time. God is said to be in the form of man. A single entity such as a human form only takes up a very limited point in time and space. As impressive as creating any planet or universe in 6 days might be, it is not an omnipotent exercise of power. Omnipotence would be acting on time and space (the multiverse) simultaneously in any creation scenario. It would not be 6 days. It would not even take 6 seconds for an omnipotent being. Taking a whole 6 seconds could show some lack of power and not omnipotence.

If we took that same level of precision and applied it to omnibenevolent action then god would not have a single murder, sacrifice or act of suffering in the entire Bible. Instead, the Bible is littered with millions of people murdered in the past and trillions prophesied to be murdered in the future. There is no proof of any omniscience, omnipotence or omnibenevolence from any alleged god. A Christian apologist may say that god has unlimited knowledge, power and goodness, but, has not used them, yet. I could say the same thing of myself. Both god and I have not proved our unlimited abilities so far. I would give myself better odds of success since I actually exist. Both god and I both are supposed to exist in human likeness and physically speak to men. I exist in human likeness and can actually speak to women directly. Find some instances in the Bible where god spoke directly to a woman without some angel or intermediary? I don't think you will find god having a direct conversation with a woman? You may have just as difficult a time finding where a woman performed a miracle in the Bible? You may try to call birth or a so-called virgin birth a miracle, but, the "miracle of birth" is more of a saying than a fact. Birth is not a supernatural event such as a miracle. If we took the Bible as literal truth then it would seem that omnibenevolence is referring to some specific faith, race, gender, sexual preference and other qualities that do not seem to have any "omni" characteristics that I can see. Omnibenevolence would include all faiths, races, genders and sexual preferences that could act in a non-aggressive moral fashion. A non-aggressive attempt at omnibenevolence is much better than the morally depraved racist, sexist, misogynistic narrow minded approach that oozes off the pages of the Bible.

To get around some of these logical impossibilities a Christian apologist could claim that god has innate knowledge of future events and is therefore omniscient. While no human has innate knowledge, a Christian apologist might claim that an omniscient god has innate knowledge of the future. Without the existence or access to such an alleged omniscient being, it is impossible to prove or disprove this innate knowledge just based on logic alone.

Another way the Christian apologist might engage god's allowance of evil and suffering is what they call Theodicy. Theodicy attempts to answer why an alleged good god would allow evil and suffering. Theodicy might even try to rise to the level of implying that evil is a victory or triumph of god. The Christian apologist might argue that by allowing evil, god allows freewill and the opportunity to choose right from wrong. This freedom of choice can provide a means for god to decide who is going to heaven or hell. Of course, an omniscient and omnipotent being could circumnavigate our experience and just place us in heaven or hell and avoid evil and suffering altogether.

THE CHRISTIAN RESPONSE

What is the Christian response? Ravi Zacharius wrote an entire book *The End of Reason* to one of the most effective atheist books *The End of Faith* by Sam Harris. Sam Harris's *The End of Faith* is full of chapter and verse examples of god's orders for the murder of men, women and children and other atrocious acts in Old Testament scripture. Harris, on pages 118-123, has a non-stop list of dozens and dozens of similar orders and acts in the Koran. Many Christians acknowledge these scriptures. It is impossible to deny them unless you affirm that the Bible is partly or wholly a work of fiction. It is interesting how some Christians circumnavigate the scriptures.

Zacharius seems to be attempting to show a superiority

of Christianity over atheism. The biggest thing, to me, for the Christian to defend is the standard of morality. If god is your standard of morality and there is clear undeniable proof (if you believe the Bible) that god commanded the murder of men, women and children in the Old Testament then that should be something that you defend against. Instead, Zacharius states,

> Harris is clearly assuming that God kills innocent people, and thus he is violating his own laws. Let's grant this for a moment. Why is killing innocents wrong? Is it wrong because God says so? Is it wrong because Harris believes that an innocent ought not be killed? If we assume the first, namely, it is wrong because God says it is wrong, then God contradicts himself through his actions—saying it is wrong but killing innocents anyway. Harris, however, is not relieved of the responsibility of proving his argument that innocents ought not be killed. To genuinely believe this he must assume a moral framework that supports the intrinsic value of innocent life. But based on his atheistic starting point, he has no grounds for such a moral framework.

I can hardly imagine a bigger circumnavigation. God is let off the hook and gets a free pass from his biblical murder because Harris has allegedly not proven an argument that innocents ought not be killed from an atheistic starting point? Talk about misdirection and avoidance by Zacharius. Zacharius states that intrinsic value is needed to support any argument of saving innocent life. Why does this value have to be an intrinsic value? Zacharius should prove why this value *must* be an intrinsic value? Zacharius should also prove why it is okay for god to murder as long as Harris allegedly has not proven why innocents ought not be killed from an atheistic starting point?

Is intrinsic value inherent from god's alleged omnibenevolence? If god is the standard of value then intrinsic value is mired in Old Testament murder and anger? I fail to see how any intrinsic value *must* be necessary for any moral framework. I really fail to see how a Christian based intrinsic value *must* be necessary for any moral framework. *But based on his atheistic starting point, he has no grounds for such a moral framework.* Thank goodness.

Zacharius goes on to say on the same page on the same topic that this "distorts the Bible's finer points while denying its big picture." Also, same page, same topic, he states that the atheist picks and chooses particular values to applaud while refusing to allow the other side the same benefit.

Exactly, the atheist can be free to pick and choose values without contradiction. The atheist can use reason. You could pick any number of arguments to show why innocents should not be killed. Utility, consequences, fair play, rights, justice, reduction of suffering, non-aggression, etc. could all be used as arguments why innocents ought not be killed. Zacharius is correct in saying that the atheist could not use intrinsic value from god in his arguments. *A priori* (before experience) arguments such as intrinsic value and natural rights give the appearance of giving an argument a "natural edge," but, you end up having to use *A posterior* (after experience) definition and arguments or an unprovable appeal to faith to attempt to define abstract concepts such as intrinsic value and natural rights. The theist using god as his standard of value must use faith *before* reason. To escape contradiction, the theist must accept the murder that god commits or conspires to commit. Otherwise, the theist's standard of value is not wholly god and faith. It is some hybrid of reason and faith. Instead of addressing, perhaps, the biggest flaw in faith (god committing, conspiring or allowing murder and suffering), Zacharius circumnavigates this flaw and chalks it up to atheistic relativists not playing "fairly."

Zacharius charges atheism with abortion and the deaths from Hitler and Stalin. Hitler's theism has been a matter of debate. He was a Catholic. The Catholic Church never excommunicated a single fascist Nazi. The Catholic Church has excommunicated women who have had abortions. What Hitler believed in terms of faith when he tried to take over the world might have changed. Hitler may have wanted to keep churches on his side as much as possible instead of opposing them directly?

I will assume for Zacharius's sake that Hitler was an atheist and argue from that perspective. The Old Testament had great numbers of abortion and infanticide with the great flood of Noah alone. So, the Bible cannot claim high ground on that count. Atheism does not have Hitler and Stalin as a standard of morality. Sam Harris in *Letter to a Christian Nation* explains that 'atheism' is a term that should not even exist. There is no specific view or philosophy. I would not call myself a non-female as a male. I would not call myself a non-Greek mythology believer. We have made up a term for a non-Bible or non-god believer—atheism. Christians have attributed many values or assumptions, as Zacharius has, of what an atheist might be defined as. Christians worship the abortion, infanticide and millions more that were murdered in the Bible when they sing songs of praise and thankfulness to the god who committed these acts. There are not atheist houses of worship for Hitler. Billions of Christians attend houses of worship. Billions of Christians worship god and Christ despite the millions of people that the Bible claimed were murdered including abortions, infanticide and young children.

At this point, a Christian might try to argue a connection between nihilism and atheism. The problem with this argument is the standard of value. Christians, by nature of being a Christian, have Christ as their standard of value. Christians may choose individualism or a Voluntary State in their political sphere of life while submitting to a collective or hierarchal morality of Christ in their spiritual life. That is a contradiction. A Christian is obligated to worship god and Christ and follow the moral hierarchy of the Bible even when it goes completely against reason. If this spiritual obligation of following god is not fulfilled then you can go to hell. Whether following god is voluntary or a coerced practice, it is an obligation.

Hitler, Stalin and others did not use reason or observation of true facts of reality or scientific method to base their decisions for war or genocide. On one hand, you could argue that Social Darwinism and nihilism were contributing factors to the war or genocide. On the other hand, you could argue that selflessness and putting a god, Hitler, Stalin or other dictator as a standard of morality or value were contributing factors to the war or genocide. Nihilism and selflessness are both dangerous ideas. When you subordinate and devalue yourself the primacy of value is open to allow an empty set of values, or worse, an evil set of values. The atheist can use reason and individual freedom to choose whether to make nihilism his standard of value or not. The atheist is under no inherent obligation to make nihilism his standard of value. The atheist can use reason to avoid contradiction and increase individualism at the same time.

CHRISTIANS AND MUSLIMS

If faith is your standard of value and the Bible or the Koran is believed to be true then a moderate position could marginalize or devalue your standard of value. If apostasy is believed to be a capital offense by both the Bible and the Koran then do we ever know if and when capital punishment will occur for the apostate? Daniel Dennett in *Breaking The Spell* wrote

> It is equally unknown how many Muslims truly believe that all infidels and especially Kafirs (apostates from Islam) deserve death which is what the Koran (4:89) undeniably say. Johannes Jansen (1997, p.23) points out that in earlier times Judaism (see Deuteronomy 18:20) and Christianity (see Acts 3:23) also regard apostasy as a capital offense.

Even Muslims "on the inside" really don't know what Muslims think about apostasy—they mostly aren't prepared to bet their lives on it. ISIS (Islamic State of Iraq and al-Sham) is merely a militarized form of enforcing apostasy for the Islamic faith? Any Muslim at any time may enforce the Koran's apostasy and enact capital punishment. It is a matter of enforcement of existing law and commandment instead of taking a step towards a new direction in faith.

Can there truly be a moderate Muslim position on apostasy? I think the Koran is quite clear with a resounding "no."

> The Koran (9:11) says to "make war on the leaders of unbelief."

> Koran (9:14) states "MAKE WAR on them: God will chastise them at your hands and humble them. He will grant you victory over them."

> Koran (9:73) "PROPHET, MAKE war on the unbelievers and the hypocrites and deal rigorously with them. Hell shall be their home."

> Koran (9:5) "Slay the idolaters wherever you find them."

> Koran (2:89) "God's curse be upon the infidels!"

Koran (2:191) "SLAY THEM wherever you find them."

Koran (3:149) "We will put terror into the hearts of the unbelievers."

The Hadith also has apostate murder—"Whoever changed his Islamic religion, then kill him" (Bukhari's Hadith Volume 9, Book 84 Number 57). While some might define apostates as past-Muslims, should there be that much distinction for killing people who are non-Muslim? Whether a non-Muslim used to be Muslim or not should make no difference in the capital punishment of taking someone's life. Koran (9:73) appears to make no distinction a past-Muslim or a non-Muslim—it appears that all are "unbelievers" that shall have Hell as their home. Koran (3:87) and Koran (3:91) speak of a curse and punishment for those who lapse into unbelief after embracing the Islamic faith. Koran (2:171) "The unbelievers are like beasts which, call out to them as one may, can hear nothing but a shout and a cry. Deaf, dumb and blind, they understand nothing."

Can there truly be a moderate Christian position that is safe? Moderate Christianity is a danger to others. I am not aware of the Bible proscribing capital punishment for having abortions. In fact, scriptures dealing with the death of children are where god has commanded the death of infants. Generally, modern Christianity has engaged a pro-life stance where abortions are considered murder. Modern Christianity is about saving souls. A baby has a soul that should belong to god according to Christians. With a Christian view—despite the mother being almost the sole owner of the fetus minus male sperm—the mother no longer has a choice or any ownership rights while the fetus grows within her belly. The fetus growing inside her belly is god's property a devout Christian might believe. Under Christian thinking, the mother has no choice as to whether or not she wants to make an obligation (creating a right for the life of the future baby) to the baby. The modern Christian sees the pregnant woman as a baby murderer.

God's alleged ownership of alleged souls and an Old Testament view of an eye for an eye or some similar view can set the groundwork for radical violence. Since 1977 in the United States and Canada, there have been 11 murders, 17 attempted murders, 383 death threats, 153 incidents of assault or battery, 13 wounded, 100 butyric acid attacks, 373 physical invasions, 41 bombings, 655 anthrax threats, and 3 kidnappings committed against abortion providers (Anti-abortion violence, *Wikipedia.org*, December 2015). I would venture to guess that all these antiabortion crimes were committed by Christians. Moderate Christians can provide the foundation for antiabortion violence.

Moderate Christianity can provide the foundation for branching off into cults. David Koresh and the Branch Davidian cult participated in having David Koresh commit statutory rape of the young daughters of adult cult members. Some cults may be terrorist cults that are hostile to others such as the Army of God, Christian Identity, Christian Patriot Movement, Lambs of Christ, Concerned Christians, The Covenant, The Sword, The Arm of the Lord, Defensive Action, The Montana Freeman, Hutaree Movement, etc. Some of these listed cults have individual group members that have used violence against abortion clinics, a gay night-club, anti-Semitic robberies and bombings, etc.

The Christian and Muslim faith demonstrate piety and apostasy. A Christian might be "designed" to feel "special" in his own mind. If it is believed that god chose man to share his likeness, carry an eternal soul and have the opportunity for eternal happiness in heaven then man must be special. We can add to the "specialness" by following some special interpretation of the Bible among the thousands of churches that exist. It might be believed that our proper selection of church ensures our opportunity to be saved. This proper selection and wisdom on our part, gives us piety and extra-specialness. How can I be so sure? I carried that piety around when I was a Christian. Christians may believe that god will judge and that some other people from some other churches may be saved, but, it may be very selective or it may not happen at all as Matthew 7:13-14 (RSV) says "Enter by the narrow gate; for the gate is wide and the way is easy, that leads to destruction, and those who enter by it are many. For the gate is narrow and the way is hard, that leads to life, and those who find it are few." For the Christian, passages likes this create piety and a feeling of specialness and can create a lack of concern and distance for the damned who will not be joining you in heaven.

Christians can take a step and add a religious text like the Book of Mormon to the testimony of the Bible. They can add a prophet like Joseph Smith. As a special "inspired" prophet, Joseph Smith can add a second wife. Smith's successor, Brigham Young, was a polygamist. Modern Day Mormons appear to have gotten a "feeling" or "communication" from god at the Mormon Temple or while wearing special underwear or something or somewhere that polygamy should not be followed anymore. Other Latter Day Saints did not get that "feeling or communication" from god and continue to practice polygamy. Mormons got this special "feeling" or revelation again about the "Lamanites" of dark pigment around the time of the Civil Rights Act of 1965. If you can have modern day revelations supporting women and people of color then why not throw in some holocaust victims in the mix also. The Mormon Church got Nazi war records and started baptizing murdered Jews of the holocaust.

Imagine, for instance, if one Christian religion in the United States went on an apostate rampage. Let's say the Baptists (I am picking at random; no special offense to Baptists) went on this rampage. There would likely be moderate Baptists, Mormons (LDS), Catholics, Church of Christ, Church of God, Lutheran, Episcopal Church, Anglicans, Orthodox, Evangelical Church, Pentecostal Church, United Church and tens of thousands of other churches that would stand up against the extremist Baptists. These Christian religions should all be using the Bible, I believe. The apostate Baptists would likely be put down quickly biblically and perhaps physically.

We do not see this outcome in the Muslim world. There are only so many possibilities. Fear of ISIS, fear of fighting with ISIS, strong sympathy with ISIS, mild sympathy with ISIS, no sympathy with ISIS... Of course, ISIS is not the only threat in the Middle East. There are many groups and countries fighting apostasy in varying forms of punishment and severity. If reason is a tool for reaching your standard of value then you can have a moderate position on issues by using the tool of reason. Faith, on the other hand, may have a more difficult time reaching moderate positions? There is apostasy in the Bible. The moderate Christian has to show how "non-apostasy" is "more Christian" than apostasy despite apostasy in the Bible. A moderate Muslim must carve through a large volume of apostasy in the Koran, Hadith and Shariah Law. It would be a difficult task of persuasion and hypocrisy for a moderate Muslim to argue for "non-apostasy." It could even be a dangerous task that might label you as a near-Kafir or Kafir supporter despite a moderate position. Of course, the best choice would be to emigrate and leave the Muslim faith altogether. While a moderate Christian can safely voice their opinion in this country, it would be better for the Christian to become an atheist.

A possible short term answer for moderate Muslims might be to try to be fanatical and extreme about the moral wrongness for capital or other punishment for apostasy. Maybe there is an Islamic answer to counter the plethora of verses supporting capital punishment for apostasy? It is for the Muslim to find and decide what prophets or texts might serve as an example or inspiration to other Muslims. Whatever an apostate or Kafir says may be of no value to a fanatical, extreme Muslim. Long term, moderate Muslims validate the Muslim faith and provide validation to terroristic Muslims that may consider themselves more "faithful" to the cause. The children of moderate Muslim may be more "faithful" to the murderous brutality of the religious texts. The children of moderate Muslims may want to be "better" and more "faithful" than their parents.

Until the Muslim faith sees the value of this life on earth as important and sacred and not subordinated to any perceived afterlife then we may continue to see fanatical and extreme movements like ISIS. This lack of value for this life is a kind of religious nihilism. It should be the opposite of religious nihilism. If we believe in the afterlife and we believe our memories and knowledge are fully transferred to this afterlife then who wants to be remembered as the suicide bomber that wiped out scores of innocent lives?

There is no likely revision that will "solve" the Muslim faith. Only abandonment of this faith is probably the only true solution. As Sam Harris in *The End Of Faith* writes

> The world, from the point of view of Islam, is divided into the "House of Islam" and the "House of War," and this latter designation should indicate how many Muslims believe their differences with those who do not share their faith will be ultimately resolved. While there are undoubtedly some "moderate" Muslims who have decided to overlook the irrescindable militancy of their religion, Islam is undeniably a religion of conquest. The only future devout Muslims can envisage—as Muslims—is one in which all infidels have been converted to Islam, subjugated, or killed. The tenets of Islam simply do not admit of anything but a temporary sharing of power with the "enemies of God."

While the Old Testament Bible is as violent and as murderous (perhaps more violent and murderous) as perhaps anything in the Koran, the Old Testament is followed by the New Testament. The New Testament while having some violence and wrongful deaths is not a handbook for apostate murder. The Koran, Hadith and Shariah Law are generally, with few exceptions, a handbook for apostate murder. Moderate Muslims may ignore or view the directives for apostate murder in a non-violent way. Islamic nations are certainly not civil societies as Harris details in the same book

> What constitutes a civil society? At minimum, it is a place where ideas, of all kinds, can be criticized without the risk of physical violence. If you live in a land where certain things cannot be said about the king, or about an imaginary being, or about certain books, because such utterances carry the penalty of death, torture, or imprisonment, you do not live in a civil society.

I would also add that you do not live in a civil society if members of your society are treated differently just based on their gender. Female genital mutilation, death for being raped, only male jurors or witnesses, permanent house arrest for adultery, limited interactions with others, permanent access to husbands for sexual gratification (there is no marital rape). Women are property of men in Muslim countries. A male shall inherit twice as much as a female Koran (4:11).

The Koran, unlike the Bible and the New Testament, has no stopping point to advocating murder. Murder is throughout the Koran. It extends into the laws of Muslim countries or Sharia Law. Government and Religion are codified as one into law. The laws of the land are based on the laws of religious faith. It is like going back in time to the time of the Old Testament or tribalism. There are dozens upon dozens upon dozens of examples where the apostate or unbeliever is vilified in the Koran or other religious text. Harris, again, in the same book (p.118-122), provides a long compilation showing a vast array of passages from the Koran demonstrating moral atrocity. Like finding murder in the Old Testament Bible, finding murder for the apostate or subjugation of women is so numerous in the Koran.

While religious freedom and tolerance kept the peace hundreds of years ago when the United States was founded on freedom of religion; today, religious tolerance will destroy the peace as the Muslim faith grows in numbers and violence.

Unfortunately, millions will likely die as faith and government converge in the Middle East. It is like people who believe in the flat earth having machine guns and nuclear weapons or as Harris puts it in the same book

> Paleolithic genes now have chemical, biological, and nuclear weapons at their disposal is, from the point of view of our evolution, little different from our having delivered this technology into the hands of chimps.

Yet, in the Middle East, science, evolution and reason will be ignored and the killing will continue for who knows how long?

FAITH AND SCIENCE

Over time, faith is running out of places to hide its myth and tradition while science continues to reduce the odds of a creation by design. The majority of people believed at one time that the earth was flat. This belief persisted for hundreds of years. The human authors of the Bible believed in the flat earth when they wrote the Bible. In Revelation 7:1 (RSV) it says "After this I saw four angels standing at the four corners of the earth..." Foundations for homes are typically relatively flat and square. Foundations would not be thought of being round or spherical. They would be a flat level surface that can be built upon—a foundation. In Psalms 102:25 (RSV) we read of the *foundation of the earth.* In Psalms 104:5 (RSV) we have "set the earth on its foundations, so that it should never be shaken." A round ball would roll very easily. A flat, four-cornered square set on a foundation to never be shaken is no round ball. It is very clear to me what the authors of the Bible believed about the shape and nature of our earth. A fact that was never corrected by the alleged omniscient creator of an inspired Bible. The majority of people today believe in the Bible myth as they believed in the myth of the flat earth. Like the flat earth myth, the Bible myth will eventually be understood as a myth in history.

Scientifically, theology was safe when the earth was thought to be the center of the universe. Theology was relatively safe in the nineteenth century when thermodynamics provided an argument for a finite, created universe. As we march into the twenty first century, theology cannot effectively hide behind thermodynamics.

The Second Law of Thermodynamics states that an isolated system will tend towards disorder or that order does not arise from chaos or disorder. When I was young, I wrongly believed that god created order from disorder. I believed that design was the only way that order could arise from disorder. The key here is the whole system. The whole system is the multiverse. The source of matter and lower entropy can come from inflation and expansion of our universe and the multiverse that likely surrounds our universe. Parts of a system can increase in order while other parts decrease in order. For instance, a mother might give birth to an offspring. The offspring is an increase in order while the aging process of the mother is a decrease in order. The same cycle occurs for plants and animals. Life is an increase in order from the disorder of the water and other resources we take from the earth. The earth in turn takes light and heat from the sun and creates photosynthesis. The sun is certainly affected by the Second Law of Thermodynamics and the heat and energy from the sun will eventually end over a very long period of time. As you can see, human life is not an isolated system.

The Christian apologist might simply try to write off the Revelations flat-earth passage as human error or nonliteral description. The apologist can try to avoid any unwanted conclusions. The same avoidance can be attributed to when the earth was thought to be the center of the universe. Human error is no game changer for the apologist.

There are enough suggestions, theoretical evidence and probabilities for a multiverse that any good physicist could not ignore it without making excuses or being improbable.

Christian apologists were still toting around thermodynamics over a century after it had been clearly disproved as a means to support intelligent design. If science proves the multiverse as it seems likely and probable to do then it may take a century or two after the proof of the multiverse for the apologist to begin to capitulate. The apologist might try to somehow infuse a multiverse into religious mythology. The multiverse would clearly refute a biblical beginning (creation) and an end (judgement, second coming of Christ or Fall of Jerusalem). Time might be proven to be infinite with no beginning and no end? Time might be seen as a relationship between objects and their positions in the multiverse?

There would be no need for a creator. The multiverse and infinite time have always existed? Time for us is a relationship between our universe and the multiverse? The energy transferences between our universe and our lives will eventually run out. We will have to change the relationship or go to a different point in time or space (universe or planet) for the survival of our species?

An omniscient god could have explained how in the future we could be able to see and travel to distant planets in the multiverse through time and space. A specific physical description in detail of various planets in our universe could have been provided that we could later verify with satellite imaging. The speed of light, expansion of the universe, and a myriad of other cosmological equations and truths from the future could have been given. Instead, we are given a flat earth with four corners that serves as a foundation to never be shaken. Our sun will destroy life on earth if a life-ending cosmological event doesn't occur first. If there were an omniscient, omnibenevolent, omnipotent god then we could surely use some knowledge, benevolence or power to help the earth before all record of the earth's life and knowledge is destroyed from the multiverse forever.

It is a marvel to me that as I type these words, I am hurdling through space at around 66,000 miles per hour with a side rotation of around 1,000 miles per hour. How much would the earth need to slow down abruptly to throw me from my keyboard into the wall? Why would an alleged omniscient, omnipotent and omnibenevolent creator need to design such a dangerous planet and universe?

The human authors of the Bible were unaware of the dinosaurs. They had not unearthed them yet. If the earth is only about 6,000 years old as the Bible myth states then dinosaurs would have coexisted with biblical man. I would have imagined that it would have "came up." With primitive weapons and scant numbers, man would not be at the top of the food chain. If the dinosaurs were wiped out, how did man survive? There are dozens of references to horses, assess, birds, snakes and lions to name a few. No dinosaurs? Dinosaurs could have affected outcomes of wars, affected livestock and shepherding. David was said to have slew Goliath. How about a pack of raptors at full speed? Not worth mentioning?

Reason, science and morality are not on the side of anyone who uses the Bible as a standard of value. The only thing that the Bible has on its side is hope. Heaven is the obvious reward the Christian can hope for. What people do not discuss is the hope in hell. Hell itself has hope. If you are alive in hell, you exist. It is hard to imagine extinction on a personal level or on the species level. The science is that 98 percent of the species that have existed are now extinct (Christopher Hitchens *god is not Great*). Even in hell, we are not extinct as an individual or a species. Even in hell we could have hope. Hope that we will continue to exist and maybe hell may not be eternal as promised or that hell's severity of punishment might diminish for us personally.

Science tells us that there is no hope of the afterlife. Some have argued that god has to exist and even if the Bible isn't true, god does exist. They point to the things of the earth as proof. According to the Bible, the earth is either about 6,000 or 12,000 years old. 6,000 years old if it took 6 literal days to create the earth. It took 6 days to create the earth, genealogy shows about 4,000 years from Adam to Jesus and over 2,000 years from Jesus to present day. We add in another 6,000 years if you believe that each day of creation is a thousand years as 2 Peter 3:8 states.

In that alleged short span of time 98 percent of the species went extinct (including the dinosaurs), continents drifted apart and the light from millions of stars from millions of light years away are somehow impossibly visible after a few thousand years. How well "designed" is a 98 percent extinction in a supposed few thousand years? The Christian circumnavigates this bit of science and may tell us to look at the complexity of the human eye as proof of god (a Christian coworker used the human eye as proof of god to me once).

Christopher Hitchens in *god is not Great* quoted

> Initially a simple eyespot with a handful of light-sensitive cells that provided information to the organism about an important

source of the light; it developed into a recessed eyespot, where a small surface in-
dentation filled with light-sensitive cells
provided additional data on the direction
of light; then into a deep recession eyespot,
where additional cells at greater depth provide more accurate information about the
environment; then into a pinhole camera
eye that is able to focus an image on the
back of a deeply recessed layer of light-sensitive cells; then into a pinhole lens eye that
is able to focus the image; then into a complex eye found in such modern mammals
as humans.

Hitchens explains that all intermediate stages of this
process exist and have been shown to work. The creationist's
supposed "designed" eye still carries design flaws to this
day. For example, as Hitchens pointed out in another quote
"For optimal vision, why would an intelligent designer have
built an eye upside down and backwards?" The retina is
backwards, installed back to front.

The human eye is so complex that even Charles Darwin
doubted that natural selection could explain it. We have
come a long way in over 150 years. In addition to an understanding of the evolution of the human eye, we understand
how the human brain compensates for the defects in the eye.
We have a blind spot in the visual field that corresponds to
the lack of light-detecting photoreceptor cells on the optic
disc of the retina where the optic nerve passes through the
optic disc. Although all vertebrates have this blind spot,

cephalopod eyes, which are only superficially similar, do not. In cephalopods, the optic nerve approaches the receptors from behind, so it does not create a break in the retina.

High extinction rates and "design flaws" are to be expected if understood from evolution. Most mutations are negative. These negative mutations are usually weeded out through natural selection over consequent generations over time unless the environment prevents it such as living in a cave, deep sea, etc. Still, there can be "unfiltered or uncleansed" mutations that were never culled and evolution found a "work-around" such as the human eye.

The human eye has evolved to detect light in the 380-780 nm (nanometer) wavelength range. Light travels as waves of energy. Electromagnetic waves are capable of transporting energy through the vacuum of outer space. Electromagnetic waves are produced by a vibrating electric charge and as such, they consist of both an electric and a magnetic component. There are different lengths of waves. In order of longer to shorter waves we have these types of waves: Radio, Micro, Infrared, (Visible), Ultraviolet, (Xrays) and Gamma. I put (Visible) in parenthesis to show where waves that are perceptible to human vision show up in the overall length of waves and where (Xrays) that are used in imaging show up in the overall length of waves. We experience the sensation of color in shorter to medium length light waves.

There is nothing inherent in the particular wavelengths that allows us to see visible colors. Like the "backwards" eye design, these particular wavelengths are what we ended up with. Color and wavelengths have no special inherent quality. Any color (except the color white) can be produced by visible light of a single wavelength (pure spectral or monochromatic colors). White is a mixture of various wavelengths. Any color (except white) can be produced by a single wavelength or a mixture of various wavelengths of light. The numerical distance in nanometers of the wavelengths of light that cause the sensation of color in our human eyes have no connection with physical, objective characteristics of the waves and the sensations they produce.

The randomness of our Visible Light Spectrum (as it is called) to produce the sensation of sight and color does not support an infinite designer or god. We could have gotten the sensation of color through different frequencies of light waves. We could have gotten the sensation of color through sound waves or a sense of smell. We could have not gotten the sensation of color at all. Again, this lack of design or lack of inherent quality does not support an infinite designer or god.

The sensation of color supports an evolutionary origin. Primates have varied color recognition with Howler Monkeys having an identical color palette as humans. Primates with color recognition or wider color recognition (some primates have no color recognition) use their color recognition to choose leaves that had the highest amount of protein for the least amount of toughness. Mammals that have color recognition have three proteins versus two proteins. The three proteins that allow us to see colors are duplicates of the two earlier proteins seen in other mammals (Neil Shubin *The Universe Within*).

As Richard Dawkins in *The Blind Watchmaker* explains

How did ears get their start? Any piece of
skin can detect vibrations if they come in
contact with vibrating objects. This is a
natural outgrowth of the sense of touch.
Natural selection could have enhanced this
faculty by gradual degrees until it was sensitive enough to pick up very slight contact
vibrations. At this point it would automatically have been sensitive enough to pick up
airborne vibrations of sufficient loudness
and/or sufficient nearness of origin.

Dawkins, in the same book also explained that evolution by cumulative natural selection is the only way to
explain the organized complexity of our existence. Injecting
a god into the mix is a postulation without an explanation
of the origin and progression of the complexity of this god.
A simple postulation such as god "is and always was" is a
postulation not an explanation from known facts or actual
experience.

Millions of evolutionary divergences began with the
chance separation of two sub-populations of a species sepa-
rated by geographical barriers. Some of the mechanisms that
natural selection uses would include speciation, where geography and natural barriers created new species, an "arms
race" where predator and prey evolved better ways to kill
and avoid being killed, sexual mating preferences or males
attracting females, natural selection for favorable changes,
cell multiplication and separation (long ago) and eventually
cell multiplication and cells bonding or sticking together.
Natural selection shows up in intermediate forms found in

different locations geographically in the fossil record due to speciation. This was a mere listing without explanation. The explanations are found in Dawkins book and a huge myriad of books supporting natural selection.

There is great scientific proof against a recent creation. If you discuss starlight from billions of light years away then Christian apologists create a fiction that god made starlight instantly appear or travel at an infinitely faster speed around the time of creation (Dennis R. Petersen *Unlocking the Mysteries of Creation*). If you discuss the fossils then you run into Christian apologists speaking to the small percentage of fossils in reverse order. If you talk about dendrochronology and trees that are older than the young earth or a clonal colony of trees with root systems aging back tens of thousands of years then you get Christian arguments of tree rings that occur faster than a year. There are some occurrences of tree rings of less than a year old. That fact can be scientific, but, a colony of trees would be likely to have "improper" dating methods or other such problems to a Christian apologist.

THE FLOOD AND OTHER MYTHS

Many discussions about science and the Bible are pointless. For example, you could scientifically prove the impossibility of Noah's Ark. A Christian discussion involves many miracles and defying logic, history, science and reason. Instead of millions of kinds of animals needed to fill the Ark, we are usually left with a few thousand? All of these animals were miraculously transported as juveniles? Even juvenile dinosaurs of many dinosaur species would be enormous. Animals from all across the world are just teleported or something to the desert of the Middle East? All the animals, predators and prey just "get along" and receive the proper food and ventilation that they need for 40 days? The fish and other aquatic mammals and reptiles, I imagine, were left to fend for themselves?

The highest mountain, Mount Everest, is around 5.5 miles high. The average ocean depth is about 2 miles deep. So, you would need to add over 3.5 miles of fresh water (rainwater) to the salt water (oceans). You would have both fresh water and saltwater which would kill both fresh water and saltwater animals. There are a few animals that might survive both freshwater and saltwater or a mix of both. The salt and fresh water combination, temperature, oxygen levels and contaminants from the earth's surface that is now being submerged would be a deadly cocktail for fish and aquatic life. How much rain would you need per minute to get around 3.5 miles of water? Let's keep the math simpler and just cover the earth in 3 miles of water. There is 5,280 feet in a mile and 63,360 inches in a mile. 3 miles * 63,360 = 190,080 inches. 190,080 inches / 40 days = 4,752 inches per day. 4,752 inches per day / 24 hours in a day = 198 inches in an hour. 198 inches in an hour / 60 minutes in an hour = 3.3 inches per minute. 3 inches in an hour has rarely been done, 3 inches a minute would be quite a miracle.

The bigger miracle is what is the source of this water? You could not add 3.5 miles of rain water with 2 miles of average ocean water depth. We search the whole galaxy and find very little liquid water outside of planet earth. That extraterrestrial water is still light years away. How did it get here to give us a global flood? Plants would not survive the saline mixture, seed destruction, germination prevention, and pressure and current from being around submerged for miles.

You cannot say that the Christian apologist does not have imagination. Some sources have cited that the water receded by god changing the topography by mountains rising and valleys sinking (Psalms 104:6-8 RSV). This creativity takes care of two problems. First, you can decrease the amount of water needed for a global flood because the mountains were not as high. Second, you can explain where all the water went (it never left). I want to table my response to this argument until the New Testament section of this chapter where I will talk about Psalms 104.

There have been hoaxes of the Ark on Mount Arafat. Let's say for arguments sake, that there was an Ark on Mt. Arafat. That would prove, at best, that an Ark was built. A few animals may or may not have been included. It does not prove a great flood with millions of land animals aboard this "small" wooden boat. "Small" in the sense that it was supposed to carry millions of animals. "Large" in the sense that a wooden boat of that size with that weight load and stress has not been proven to be an engineering possibility without steel or other supports.

Something may have actually occurred regarding flooding. One possibility is that there was flooding from the Mediterranean Sea to the Black Sea. Columbia scientists William Ryan and Walter Pitman have proposed that the sealed Bosporus strait which acted as a dam between the Mediterranean and Black Seas broke open when climatic warming at the close of the last glacial period caused icecaps to melt, raising the global sea level. This event may be the catalyst for the Epic of Gilgamesh and the biblical story of Noah's Ark that followed.

Proving anything short of a worldwide flood would be very damaging to the case of creationism. A local flood would show that Noah never had a conversation with an omniscient god. An omniscient god might have told Noah where the flood was going to occur and when to leave the lands. Of course, an omnipotent god could have prevented a flood, but, where is the lesson in that? We constantly need to be murdered to teach us a lesson in morality? A local flood would clearly show an uninspired false Bible as Genesis 6:7 (RSV) stated

> So the LORD said, "I will blot out man whom I have created from the face of the ground, man and beast and creeping things and birds of the air, for I am sorry that I have made them" and Genesis 6:17 (RSV) said "For behold, I will bring a flood of waters upon the earth, to destroy all flesh in which is the breath of life from under heaven; everything that is on earth shall die."

Any flooding was localized. The civilizations in China, Egypt, Babylon and Mesopotamia exist uninterrupted. There are writings before and after the time that the great, worldwide flood was supposed to have occurred. There are descendants and lineage from these civilizations. There is growing awareness and study of concurrent cities along the

Amazon basin and parts of the Andes that existed, but, were not included in the monotheistic Bible myth.

The irony is that we are supposed to believe in the omniscience and especially omnipotence of a god here in the story of Noah's ark. It would take miracle stacked on miracle to pull even half of this off. When we deal with the murder, abortion and infanticide and contradictions and morality of the Bible then we are suddenly dealing with fallible and limited knowledge and power. The story of Noah's Ark likely involves the drowning deaths of children, infants and unborn children. Noah's Ark is just one story or a small part of the millions that died in the Old Testament at the hand of a god who is supposed to be omnibenevolent.

Instead, Noah's Ark is logically impossible even with the help of an alleged omnipotent god whose unlimited power should have been able to fill all the holes in bad story telling. This story is so badly told that even an omnipotent god could not fix it. For instance, each animal "kind" had to be "born" to exist and be identified as a species. This implies a certain minimum size that an animal could start at birth. Again, it is a logical impossibility. A cannot be A and Not A at the same time. You cannot shrink all the millions of animals that exist AND distinguish them as a breeding "kind" that was supposed to be fruitful and multiply and fill the earth (Genesis 9:1 RSV)

The Bible myth is a hodge-podge of myths and stories from different authors patched together. One example is the Book of Genesis story of Cain. When Cain killed his brother Abel, there was only supposed to be his immediate family that existed at this time. Yet, we see that Cain needed a "mark" from god to protect him. Who did Cain need this protection from? What could this "mark" be that everyone must be familiar with? At this same time that Cain supposedly has a mark, Cain has a wife and is building a city (Genesis 4:15-17 RSV). This of course begs the question of where all these unnamed people came from that had to exist at the same time as Adam? If so, then how could Adam and Eve be the parents of all existing humans?

Biblical writers were unaware of real dinosaurs or their fossils, but, had a slew of mythological creatures such as the Satyrs (Isaiah 13:21 RSV, Isaiah 34:14 RSV), Night Hags (Isaiah 34:14 RSV), Fiery Serpents (Deut. 8:15 RSV), Flying Serpents (Isaiah 14:29 RSV, Isaiah 30:6 RSV). Unicorns and Dragons are so numerously mentioned that it becomes overly redundant to list all the numerous biblical passages. In the next section, New Testament, we will examine the giant Nephilim (The Book of Enoch 7:12, Genesis 6:4 RSV, Numbers 13:33 RSV). People of the ancient world believed in so many mythological creatures that it is no surprise some of them ended up in Bible mythology. It should be no surprise that no fossilized remains of these mythical creatures have been uncovered.

We are left to believe that two of every kind of animal repopulated the earth? How did predator animals live without eating the last of the prey species? With only two of each species, most of the animal species would have become extinct through starvation or being eaten.

NEW TESTAMENT

How about the New Testament? Humans make mistakes, but, over time usually improve their knowledge and understanding. An alleged omniscient and omnipotent being does not have the luxury of making mistakes. This should especially be true in the course of setting up a plan of salvation for his alleged creation, man, who in god's likeness is just below the status of the angels. An allegedly inspired book such as the Bible should be spot on perfect.

Again, let's start with murder. While the New Testament doesn't have the sheer number of murdered people as the Old Testament, it does have the same absurdity. The New Testament actually exceeds the Old Testament in prophecy of future murders as we shall see. The New Testament is thought by most, in large part, to deal with the future and a second coming of Christ. So, future New Testament murders should be appropriate to catalogue. The New Testament certainly does not deny or vilify the record of past or future murders of the Old Testament, in fact, it adds to future murder.

First, let's look at past murder in the New Testament. Ananias and Sapphira were murdered for not making a large enough monetary contribution to god (Acts 5:1-10 RSV). King Herod Aggripa was murdered for giving a powerful oration that listeners believed came from a god not a man. God was not pleased with his speech and an angel came down and immediately murdered him on the spot (Acts 12:21-23 RSV). What is interesting to me if you read the whole chapter of Acts 12 is the timing of the murder. King Herod had killed some who belonged to the church. He then had James the brother of John killed and had arrested and imprisoned Peter. It wasn't until Herod's speech *did not give God the glory* in verse 23 that Herod was struck down as verse 23 states "Immediately an angel of the Lord smote him, because he did not give God the glory; and he was eaten by worms and died."

The New Testament speaks of a flat earth in Revelations 7:1 (RSV) it says "After this I saw four angels standing at the four corners of the earth..." In Jude 1:14-15 (RSV) "It was of these also that Enoch in the seventh generation from Adam prophesied, saying "Behold, the Lord came with his holy myriads, to execute judgment on all, and to convict all the ungodly of all their deeds of ungodliness which they have committed in such an ungodly way, and of all the harsh things which ungodly sinners have spoken against him." The book of Enoch 1:9 has the wording a little different: "And behold! He cometh with ten thousands of His Saints To execute judgment upon all, And to destroy all the ungodly: And to convict all flesh Of all the works of their ungodliness which they have ungodly committed, And of all the hard things which ungodly sinners have spoken against Him." Old Testament Deuteronomy 33:2 may be the source of these New Testament passages. In Deuteronomy 33:2 (RSV) it states, "The LORD came from Sinai, and dawned from Seir upon us; he shone forth from Mount Paran, he came from the ten thousands of holy ones, with flaming fire at his right hand."

Why do I bring up several passages regarding Enoch? Christians only want to see angels in a certain way in the fictional story of the Bible. Good angels can supposedly stand on the four corners of a flat earth. Bad angels are supposed to stay in hell as 2 Peter 2:4 (RSV) says, "For if God did not spare the angels when they sinned, but cast them into hell and committed them to pits of nether gloom to be kept until the judgment." Jude 1:6 (RSV) also confirms, "And the angels that did not keep their own position but left their proper dwelling have been kept by him in eternal chains in the nether gloom until the judgment of the great day." In typical contradictory fashion the leader of the bad angels, Satan, has already been released on the earth (Revelations 20 RSV). An angel coming down from heaven to earth would not be newly binding Satan for a thousand years (Revelations 20 RSV) if Satan was not already on the earth. If Satan was already on the earth and did not keep his own position and *left his proper dwelling* (heaven) then Satan should have already been bound until judgment day. (2 Peter 2:4 RSV and Jude 1:6 RSV) If Satan had already been bound until judgment day then Satan would already be bound when an angel descended from heaven in Revelations 20 (RSV). The Book of Enoch discusses angels who have fallen from heaven. These angels mate with female humans and produce giant Nephilim (children of fallen angels). These Nephilim have been described in the Book of Enoch as being 450 feet tall (three hundred cubits) in Enoch 7:12. Three hundred cubits (450 feet) just happens to be the length of Noah's ark. Popular number in fictional storytelling I guess.

Nephilim are mentioned in the Bible also Genesis 6:4 (RSV) says, "The Nephilim were on the earth in those days, and also afterward, when the sons of God came in to the daughters of men, and they bore children to them." Numbers

13:33 (RSV) says, "And there we saw the Nephilim (the sons of Anak, who come from the Nephilim) and we seemed to ourselves like grasshoppers, and so we seemed to them." A grasshopper stands at less than a half-inch, you need more than 2 grasshoppers per inch. An average man might stand at 6 foot tall or 72 inches. So, 2 grasshoppers per inch times 72 inches equals 144. That would make the biblical Nephilim 144 times taller than a 6 foot man or 864 feet tall.

This is where the Christian apologist might say not to take things so literally. He was making a size comparison and used the word "like" a grasshopper. Alright, perhaps. If you don't want to be literal here with an 864 foot tall half-man half-angel then why be literal in Psalms 104:8 (RSV). The mere mention of mountains rising and valleys sinking must literally be related to the Great Flood of Noah? There is not even a specific reference to the Great Flood of Noah. Noah is not named. The earth was set on its foundations and water fled and took flight (Psalms 104:5-7 RSV). Are these literal to the flood also? Did the Great Flood myth discuss setting the earth on its foundations and having water take flight? Receding water to me is not water taking flight in some airborne fashion. At least, with the Nephilim we are talking about Nephilim.

You could argue that the description of the biblical Nephilim is embellished to prevent having to fight the sons of Anak (Nephilim) and steal their lands. The description might have been embellished in an "evil report" that describes men of great stature (Number 13:32 RSV). Before any "evil report" or embellishment we still see a strong Nephilim as Numbers 13:28 (RSV) "Yet the people who dwell in the land are strong, and cities are well fortified and very large; and besides, we saw the descendants of Anak there." The way that this describes *and besides, we saw the descendants of Anak there* surely describes a possible or alleged familiarity there for its audience that the Bible myth is being told to at that time. The audience had likely been told of the Nephilim myth before. That familiarity of this myth appears to be one of special fear of a strong and possible very large people. Was this special fear describing a larger people that were half human and half angel or was this an embellished story (more embellished than previous biblical myths of that time). Or was the story of the Nephilim supposed to lie in between the extremes.

Whatever the case may be, the story of the "evil report" ended as most Bible stories end, with the death of the faithless who gave the evil report and didn't want to steal the lands that others were occupying and the survival of the two men who had faith in god and wanted to massacre the people who had lands that they wanted to steal. Same story repeated over and over again. Have faith and murder. The exact details of the Nephilim is just a fictional distraction to the message of faith whatever the cost may be.

Without even having to dig deeper in the Book of Enoch raises questions to me. In the Bible, Jesus and the apostles were known to cast out demons. Were these demons fallen angels? Regardless of the answer that that can be given, why were demons invading human hosts and when, if ever, was it said to stop? Fallen angels are supposed to be contained to the nether gloom of hell according to 2 Peter 2:4 (RSV). How were they inhabiting humans or even mating with them? If demons are not fallen angels then how did they inhabit humans and when, if ever, did that stop? Of course, demons and fallen angels never started in the first place because they don't exist in the first place.

Jesus and the New Testament did not chronicle the end of demons or evil spirits. If one verse of the Book of Enoch is inspired by Christian thought then how can you decide inspiration at that point? There were many people possessed by demons and exorcising demons in Jesus's time according to the Bible myth. There are dozens of references to demons alone, add in uncleans spirits and other such references and the number continues to climb. With no clear answer on demons and angels "living among us?" how do we know if angels and demons can inhabit the earth? How do we know if demon possession is possible?

The books by the apostles, Matthew, Mark, Luke and John have so many contradictions of the same events. I am not going to give chapter and verse for every contradiction. I will expand on some of the contradictions with chapter, verse and/or explanation. This list of New Testament contradictions is far from complete. There are many more scriptural contradictions. There are also many historical contradictions that don't fit the time, places and events that I omitted entirely. I give a few contradictions outside of the four listed apostles. The named apostles in this paragraph contradict themselves regarding the birthplace of Jesus, dates of Jesus's birth, Joseph's genealogy, Jesus's entry into Jerusalem, Judas's death, Barabbas's crime, people who found Jesus's tomb, what was found at the tomb, Jesus being the son of David, the time and place of Jesus's ascension after his resurrection. Jesus could have committed a sufficient fake martyrdom by his own death by suicide. Instead, Jesus wanted death by heretic and any guilt and shame from the people who would carry out his crucifixion.

Paul Carlson in New Testament Contradictions (1995, *TheSecularWeb*) states:

> There are several passages in the gospels where Jesus says he will return in the disciples' lifetime (Mark 13:30, Matthew 10:23, 16:28, 24:34, Luke 21:32, etc.).

> The same expectation held during the period the apostle Paul wrote his letters. In 1 Corinthians 7:29-31 Paul says that the time is so short that believers should drastically change the way that they live. But Paul had a problem - some believers had died, so what would happen to them when Jesus returned?

> Paul's answer in 1 Thessalonians 4:13-18 shows that Paul expected that at least some of those he was writing to would be alive when Jesus returned - "we who are alive, and remain..." The same passage also indicates that Paul believed that those believers who had died remained "asleep in Jesus" until he returned. However, as the delay in Jesus' return grew longer, the location of Jesus' kingdom shifted from earth to heaven and we later find Paul indicating that when

believers die they will immediately "depart
and be with Christ" (Philippians 1:23).

It is quite obvious that Jesus never intended
to start any type of church structure since
he believed he would return very shortly to
rule his kingdom in person. It is also quite
obvious that Jesus was wrong about when
he was coming back.

Regardless of whether these passages are related to the
fall of Jerusalem around A.D. 70 or some failed second coming is probably relatively irrelevant to the big picture. The
big picture being that any alleged inspiration and authority
either passed (A.D. 70) or was never delivered (Jesus's return
to start his church). The bigger picture is that there never
was inspiration and authority because it was a myth in the
first place. The Bible is a work of fiction.

The New Testament is a gateway to government. A
belief in New Testament churches is a gateway to the political federal and state governments. Just replace the Messiah
with a president and congressional leadership. Just take the
authority of the church and replace it with majority rule or
democracy.

Here are some New Testament contradictions from
evilBible.com that I edited, condensed, italicized and put in
Revised Standard Version (RSV) wording:

Christ *is* equal with God (John 10:30 RSV)
Christ *is not* equal with God (John 14:28 RSV)

Jesus *was* all-powerful (Matt 28:18 RSV, John 3:35 RSV)

Jesus *was not* all-powerful (Mark 6:5 RSV)

The law *was* abolished (Ephesians 2:15
    RSV, Rom 7:6 RSV)

The law *was not* abolished (Matt 5:17-19 RSV)

Christ's witness of himself is *true* (John 8:17-18 RSV)

Christ's witness of himself is *not true* (John 5:31 RSV)

It *was lawful* for the Jews to put Christ
    to death (John 19:7 RSV)

It *was not lawful* for the Jews to put Christ or
    any man to death (John 18:31 RSV)

Man *is justified* by faith alone (Rom 3:20 RSV,
    Gal 2:16 RSV, Gal 3:11-14 RSV)

Man *is not justified* by faith alone (James
    2:20-22 RSV, Rom 2:13 RSV)

It *is impossible* to fall from grace (John
    10:28 RSV, Rom 8:31-39 RSV)

It *is possible* to fall from grace (Hebrews
    6:4-6 RSV, 2 Pet 2:20-21 RSV)

No man is without sin (Rom 3:10 RSV)

Baptized Christians are sinless (1 John 3:9 RSV)

Worldly prosperity a *reward* of righteousness
    and a blessing (Mark 10:29-30 RSV)

Worldly prosperity a *curse* and a bar to fu-
    ture reward (Luke 6:20-24 RSV, Matt
    6:19-21 RSV, Matt 19:24 RSV)

The Christian yoke is *easy* (Matt 11:30 RSV)

The Christian yoke is *not easy* (2 Tim 3:12 RSV)

Temptation *to be desired* (James 1:2 RSV)

Temptation *not* to be desired (Matt 6:13 RSV)

Elijah went up to heaven (Old Testament—2
    Kings 2:11 RSV)

None but Christ ever ascended into
    heaven (John 3:13 RSV)

Good works *to be seen* of men (Matt 5:16 RSV)

Good works *not* to be seen of men (Matt 6:1 RSV)

Judging of others *forbidden* (Matt 7:1-2 RSV)

Judging of others *approved* (1 Cor 6:3
    RSV, 1 Cor 5:12 RSV)

The wearing of long hair by men *sanctioned* (Old
    Testament—Judges 13:5 RSV, Num 6:5 RSV)

The wearing of long hair by men *con-
    demned* (1 Cor 11:14 RSV)

Circumcision *instituted* (Old Testament—Gen 17:10 RSV)

Circumcision *condemned* (Gal 5:2 RSV)

Taking of oaths *sanctioned* (Heb 6:17 RSV)

Taking of oaths *forbidden* (Matt 5:34-37 RSV)

It *is* our duty to obey our rulers (Rom 13:1-7 RSV)

It is *not* our duty to obey rulers (Acts
    4:26 RSV, Luke 23:35 RSV)

Women's rights *denied* (1 Tim 2:12 RSV, 1
  Cor 14:34 RSV, 1 Pet 3:5 RSV)

Women's rights *affirmed* (Acts 21:9 RSV, Luke 2:36 RSV)

Obedience to *masters* enjoined (Col
  3:22 RSV, 1 Pet 2:18 RSV

Obedience due to *God only* (Matt 4:10 RSV, 1
  Cor 7:22-23 RSV, Matt 23:10 RSV)

There *is* an unpardonable sin (Mark 3:29 RSV)

There is *not* unpardonable sin (Acts 13:39 RSV)

Before we leave this section, I wanted to return to Enoch and try to sum up faith's part in the destruction of individualism and reason. Enoch was supposed to be a good faithful man according to Hebrews 11:5 (RSV) "By Faith Enoch was taken up so that he should not see death; and he was not found, because God had taken him. Now before he was taken he was attested as having pleased God." Faith is the catalyst to save the faithful Christian. Have enough faith like Enoch and you might get fast-tracked to heaven and avoid death entirely. It is amazing how one book, the Bible, is alleged to be inspired, other books are non-canonical and other books are said to be fictional. Why not apply reason across all these works? Reason could have been applied to make divisions among these works, but, where reason becomes troublesome; faith steps in. With outcomes like we have discussed, that is a whole "boatload" of faith. If you reference faith, faithful, faithfulness, faithless in the Bible, you will find that faith is probably most used word in Bible followed by death. Faith and death. Faith and death are the two main ingredients in the Bible. How many more humans will die at the hands of other humans in the name of faith? Faith infiltrates many country's governments and prevents individualism. I hope it is becoming clear why I have focused on how faith poisons individualism and reason.

ADDITION OR SUBTRACTION

I used to believe that you had creation through addition. An infinite god created or added something from nothing. I now believe the opposite, in most respects. Infinite space can subtract a finite universe or a finite planet. Under the right matter and circumstances, further subtraction can evolve a very small fraction of life. Richard Dawkins in *The Blind Watchmaker* said, "Given infinite time, or infinite opportunities, anything is possible."

Who wants to believe that they will no longer exist? People might say that they no longer want to exist. These people most likely want a better or different existence or to hit "restart" and start their existence over. A lack of an afterlife is a huge obstacle to overcome. I understand this. Still, to cling to faith and continue murdering in the name of faith and ignoring reason and individualism is a modern day version of a witch hunt. You can kill, demonize or create myth to defend your faith. Anything not in your faith can be a witch or an infidel or an apostate or heretic, etc. to be destroyed and murdered as was done for centuries and in many parts of the Middle East and other Islamic areas continues to be done to this day.

The Bible is a fictional story without an ending. We know the story of the beginning, we know of the resurrection.

What really happens after the resurrection? The four horsemen of the apocalypse come riding when things are really bad? So, when things get bad to a certain point, we need a Great Flood or a Second Coming of Christ to wipe us out, again? Or did the "end" already occur as Matthew 16:28 (RSV) seems to show "Truly, I say to you, there are some standing here who will not taste death before they see the Son of man coming in his kingdom." My parents, Steve and Debra Wallace, in *The End Times Hoax* showed that the "end times ended" with the fall of Jerusalem around A.D. 70. My parents omitted many, many Bible verses they found in an effort to have the reader "discover" evidence on their own. Even with these deliberate omissions, their book still contains a very thorough discussion on the topic.

How do these Bible endings affect our time in the present tense? How much inspiration do we believe or require? Inspired men? Jesus had twelve apostles and two of his apostles, Judas and Peter, betrayed Jesus to some degree or other. Some religions argue inspiration and authority. The authority, they argue comes from genealogy or from religious texts. Blood or Bible gives certain men authority they argue. Some people even take it farther and claim inspiration from god to take a new different path such as cult leaders Joseph Smith, David Koresh, etc. and papal leaders such as the Pope. These alleged inspired men are authorized to change the "law" of the Bible. They are the law as prophets and popes.

What is the critical mass for faith today? An inspired cult leader or pope? An ordinary man with a certain genealogy or bloodline to an ancient past of some biblical figure? Are these "special" men like Judas, Peter, Joseph Smith,

Brigham Young, David Koresh or others any better than you or I? Do they have special authority or knowledge inherent in their blood?

Representation in prisons show that Christians are no less represented in prison populations than non-Christians. If there are special men with special authority with the power to perform miracles then I have not witnessed it. If there are no special men of faith then inspiration and authority fall to the wayside. Without special men then the Christian can try to fall back to the Bible. On balance, Christians are not inherently or demonstrably better people. Unless, Christians wants to follow the morality of murder, rape and incest; they will abandon or ignore the Old Testament and even the New Testament.

Creation by addition needs supernatural processes that do not occur in nature. Creation by addition "gaps up" to animal and human-animal kind or species. Evolution or creation by subtraction relies on natural processes of nature that have evolved through billions of years. Some of these evolved processes are amazing. Take reproduction for example, we can take a teaspoon full of goo—sperm and egg and create maybe an eight pound human baby or a multi-ton whale (maybe a couple teaspoons of goo needed here) several months later. When you examine things like the evolution of the eye, you see that it takes many steps over a very long period of time to evolve into complex natural processes. Those steps and processes are not perfect as we saw from our examination of the human eye. People born today may assume that the complexity of the eye must come from a supernatural origin.

As far as the afterlife, it may be attractive to be on the "supernatural" side or team. You can falsely believe that god can place you in heaven after your death. Sometimes, in the pain of the death of loved ones we may only imagine the very best for loved ones after death. The thought of no supernatural afterlife is too much to bear. The biological and physical sciences are advancing their understanding of the Laws of Nature. These scientists are building the knowledge or preliminary steps that other scientists can follow. Even failures can help point scientists in a different direction or return to the past failure in the future and make it a success with different understanding. This knowledge may eventually progress to a point where an afterlife could be constructed. We will discuss this more in the Conclusion of the book. If faith or cosmic events do not destroy us—the "natural" team will use science, subtraction and natural laws to increase our knowledge and understanding. One day, this knowledge and understanding may progress to a point where an afterlife might be constructed from all this "natural work by subtraction." We have come a long way even in the last few hundred years. If mankind's existence could match the lifetime of our earth of around four billion years (versus a few thousand years for mankind on earth) then we could really accomplish something if we allow ourselves to.

MORALITY AND FREE WILL

Let's start with arguments for there being no room for free will according to determinism. Does self-determination requires knowledge of the process and set of variables by which we can self-determine? Some have called this origination instead of self-determination. The knowledge of the process and set of variables by which we can self-determine requires knowledge of the previous process and set of variables required to self-determine. On and on we regress... Does self-determination requires knowledge of every regression even past the "first process and set of variables" which might be believed to be design or cosmic events? Even knowledge of the "first process" might require knowledge of what caused the first process. From what we know about physics and determinism, everything has already been determined. Every process has been determined from the process that preceded it. Even life itself is a process that has been determined according to determinism.

Does it all come down to matter or nature? John Searle in *Minds, Brains and Science* states

> the causal relations bounce entirely along the bottom, that is, they are entirely a matter of neurons and neurons firings at synapses, etc. As long as we accept this conception of how nature works then it doesn't seem that there is any scope for the freedom of the will because on this conception the mind can only affect nature in so far as it is a part of nature. But if so, then like the rest of nature, its features are determined at the basic micro-levels of physics.

Searle appears to be saying that we cannot stand outside of nature as a supernatural being that can originate free will independent of nature.

Are things predetermined as to what is going to happen in the future? Is determinism and free will compatible as compatibilism states? The Compatibilist will often hold both Causal Determinism (all effects have causes) and Logical Determinism (the future is already determined) to be present or absent in situations for reasons that have nothing to do with metaphysics?

Ted Honderich in *The Consequences of Determinism* states

> Our circumstance is not either that a determinism leaves moral approval and disapproval untouched, or that it destroys it. To suppose that it destroys it, as Incompatibilists do, is to ignore our attitudes which issue in intransigence. To suppose that a determinism leaves moral approval and disapproval untouched as Compatibilists do, is to ignore our attitudes which issue in dismay. Compatibilism and Incompatibilism are as mistaken in other respects, not least in offering what are very nearly absurd explanations of the persistence of the consequences of determinism.

Ted Honderich explains his view that the mistake of compatibilism is to assert that nothing changes as a consequence of determinism, when clearly we have lost the life-hope of origination.

Now let's see if there is room for free will? How much origination, if any, can we have? How far back do we need to go? How many regressions do we need to go back? Genetics or environmental impacts from childhood? Is there a point where determined causes become minimal or meaningless? Is there a point where the impacts of past determination become absurd or meaningless? I believe that it may also turn out to be a mistake to believe that consciousness and the ability to attempt to choose an *ought* from an *is* can be entirely pre-determined from prior causes as Honderich would have us believe.

Michael Shermer in *The Moral Arc* speaks of modular or compartmentalized brain functions. Shermer states that

> Accepting a determined universe, however, does not preclude retaining free will and moral responsibility.
>
> We are a collection of distinct but interacting modules that are often at odds with one another, and the decision-making process often happens unconsciously, so it seems as if choices are being made for us from we know not where.

Shermer defines *free won't* as the power to veto one impulse in favor of another. Shermer cites a study (Marcel Brass and Patrick Haggard 2007) that showed a control structure of the human brain network for self-initiated inhibition or withholding of intended actions. Inhibiting neural networks are higher up than initial decision-making networks which means those impulses and early decisions can be overridden.

How have these ideas held up scientifically? Haggard

in effect later nullifies this 2007 study in a 2013 research article titled *There Is No Free Wont: Antecedent Brain Activity Predicts Decisions to Inhibit*. Haggard concludes "conscious decisions to check and delay our actions may themselves be consequences of specific brain mechanisms linked to action preparation and action monitoring." Modularity of mind seems to have both support and criticism.

Determinism still provides the causes that affect impulses, but, free won't decides which impulses to inhibit? While modularity of mind and free wont might be in question, they both bring up some interesting reasoning. It can be possible for a single cause to have many psychological effects. These effects can come in the form of contradictory impulses and mental states. A single cause might give impulses for sobriety and abstinence while simultaneously or near simultaneously giving impulses for getting drunk, taking drugs and having sex. With contradictory impulses it may be easy to get contradictory mental states such as happiness, sadness, contentment, discontentment, anger, frustration and disappointment. These impulses and mental states could vary in scale and intensity from minute to minute or second to second or to milliseconds.

I gave many different effects of either impulses or mental states. Can all these effects move forward in a deterministic causal chain? Would these effects move forward or would some of these effects be left behind (assuming that at least one of these effects were acted upon—even if it's merely a change of mood or mental state)? Would any abandoned effects cause a gap in the deterministic causal chain? Could we return later and reclaim these abandoned gaps?

These effects seem to be part of our subconscious and conscious mind. A part of our experience regardless of how well we can access, remember or are even aware of all of these effects. The set of choices that we have can be influenced by knowledge and experience. The other alternative is that knowledge and experience play no part in our freedom to choose. The other alternative is an *a priori* (before experience) deterministic "master cause" that was the determining cause that determines all causes to follow. Any knowledge, experience and choice that follows that master cause is irrelevant to the determinism that was already set in motion according to this view.

It is hard to imagine everyday tasks such as getting up every day, driving to work every day and performing daily work tasks without control over our thoughts. I have thought that it would be nice not to set my alarm, not to drive my vehicle to work and not perform my daily work tasks. If free will is an illusion and some "master cause" is at work then even if I decided to try to "fool" the master cause by toggling contradictory thoughts, ideas and action then that would still be determined by the master cause? The knowledge of a master cause determined your contradictory thoughts, ideas and actions according to this view?

If our thoughts are born or influenced by impulses then it becomes clear that many impulses go unfulfilled. If every impulse and mental state is determined then how do some continue forward to action where others do not? How many unfulfilled impulses and mental states can a person accumulate in a lifetime? How many effects can come from a single cause? If we had a million causes, but, ten million effects then can we really call this a deterministic causal chain? To me, a deterministic causal chain would be a 1:1 ratio not a 1:10 ratio.

Where I see unfulfilled impulses and mental states as evidence of more control over which ones I choose to accept or decline, others such as Sam Harris in *Free Will* appear to see it in a different way. I appreciate Harris's work in other topics as you can see from this chapter. Freewill may not have a clean definitive answer like other topics at least at this point in time. Science may help us understand this topic more as time marches on. One day, Harris and I may have similar views on free will. That day is not this day, so, let's move on. Harris discussed his lack of free will in choosing either coffee or tea to drink. His subconscious mind chose one over the other he claims. For Harris, these particular drink choices may have inconsequential differences. For me, I would have to see if the tea contained sugar and therefore had extra carbs or calories. I am on a 2,000 calorie diet. Despite foods that I would enjoy more, I still try to pick low carb foods and try to stay under 2,000 calories for the day. I have been doing this for years.

Later, Harris actually talks about a diet and states "The soul that allows you to stay on your diet is just as mysterious as the one that tempts you to eat cherry pie for breakfast." Harris's requirement for free will appears to be that you are aware and can control all the factors that determine your thoughts and actions. Harris would likely argue that thoughts, impulses and desires can mysteriously arise from the subconscious, therefore, we are not in conscious control. I would argue that we are not helpless victims to our subconscious. We can initiate a diet and consistently lose weight. I lost over 30 pounds and have kept those pounds off for years.

Smokers have stopped smoking and never smoked again for decades to the end of their life. We apparently have the power to change. I would not attribute all of the changes in our lives to the subconscious mind or determinism. Shermer stated in the same book that

> The argument that we are not free to choose because an unconscious part of a brain tells a conscious part of a brain what has been decided is, at best, based on dodgy interpretation of the neuroscience.

Harris's mysterious subconscious commands seem to fit this quote.

Harris queried why today and not yesterday or tomorrow? While the timing of things may just seem to "arise" as Harris likes to put it, does that support determinism or freedom of thought? Harris argued that the mysterious timing of certain events such as starting a diet or taking up martial arts supports a lack of free will. I will argue that in addition to determinism such a mysterious timing could also be an incremental gain of knowledge and experience that reached a tipping point at that particular time.

Many discussions I have read about free will include regression as a reason against free will. They argue that the knowledge that we lack from each regression is proof of the lack of free will. I will argue that each cause and effect regression is also a *progression*. We gain knowledge and experience from each causal chain cycle. Even if the choice or outcome remains the same, the progression occurs. Our knowledge from experience grows unless we were in a coma or other state that might not allow knowledge and experience in the normal sense. Our knowledge from experience can either help affirm or invalidate prior actions, choices and thoughts. While we might carry unknown subconscious wants and desires, we also might build a progression that can temper, alter or eliminate or instead intensify our subconscious wants and desires.

We can control each conscious progression. We can usually choose the environment and situations that we place ourselves in; which can affect our wants and desires? Let us assume for the moment that we can choose both the environment and situations that we place ourselves in. We can evaluate the consequences from this assumption first and then later evaluate other possibilities. So, given this assumption of choice of environment and situations, between conscious progression and choice of environment, we have a strong free will. We don't have an absolute free will that we can have absolute control of our choice of environment, wants, desires and subconscious mind. We cannot absolutely control what we don't know (knowledge) from each regression. We are not omniscient creatures in the first place nor will likely ever be. We don't have absolute control over what is in our subconscious mind. We have experience, knowledge, wants and desires that we are unable to access on a conscious level at all times or at all. We are also not omnipotent, we don't have absolute control over our brain function.

We don't have to have the knowledge and power of a god or prime mover to have free will. We can build years of experience and knowledge. We have memories that can span decades or lifetimes. If we could only retain knowledge and experience for a few days and had an infantile understanding then I would say that free will is an illusion. In an infantile state of understanding, our lack of knowledge does affect our free will. It takes time to develop concepts of right and wrong or to develop a concept that there is no right and wrong. At this stage of infantile knowledge, we are controlled almost exclusively by our wants and desires.

Would we say that a baby has free will? I would imagine the answer to be no. A baby has wants and desires that overwhelm any reason. The desire for food, shelter, warmth, clean diapers, attention from others. As our knowledge and experience grow over time, our level of free will grows also. Our knowledge and experience will never be omniscient or infinite, though we can still have free will. There is a threshold where we have the knowledge, experience and ability to reason (whether we use that ability is a free will choice at that point). It is somewhere around this threshold that free will engages.

Harris appears to apply this determinism to morality. If we exercise morality then we were determined to do so. If we don't exercise morality then were determined to do so. This level of determinism leaves no room for responsibility. Wherever we are morally or immorally that is where determinism put us according to what appears to be Harris's argument.

Moral responsibility was one of the reasons I wrote on

free will. Determinism doesn't negate moral responsibility. The current justice system recognizes different levels of responsibility based on circumstances and capacity. Capacity referring to age (experience), mental and physical causes and other variables. Any Voluntary State should not be undermined by anyone seeking to diminish moral responsibility by denying that we have the ability to be morally responsible.

In what you might call the extreme empathy position, supporters of illusionary free will and non-responsible criminality, believe that if we have no free will and no control over our genetic composition then anyone put in the entirety of a criminal's genes and experiences would do the identical actions of the criminal. Therefore, with this view, punishment is replaced with public safety. If you believe that there is no free will and no control then punishment may not be appropriate. The criminal might only be detained to the point that might affect public safety. Punishment and retribution are not included in this type of criminal assessment.

Any "filter" to sort incoming causes will be entirely deterministic based on previous causes and experiences. The behavior of a computer program seems more like causation than reasoning. Any human choice without free will seems more like causation than reasoning. Any rehabilitated "causes" that make a convict appear "safe" can be undone by other future causes since there is no free will or control involved?

Without a free will "filter," the courts can only try to control possible causes such as the environments that a criminal might be exposed to. Outside of prisons, the courts can lose control of the causes that a convict might be exposed to. The best "exposure" for most criminals is imprisonment. Since the convict has no freewill and no control then we cannot count on any filtered judgement or rehabilitated judgement to control the actions of the convict?

If we do not have free will then it might be believed that our morality is left to chance or luck. If morality is just luck then criminals can never be accused of anything more than bad luck. They are just victims to whatever arose in the mind and "forced" them to act upon it. We are responsible for our own moral code. Our moral code is not left up to chance. Our progressions are a powerful tool in growing our knowledge and experience and our ability of free will.

How strong is that determinism? Does every deterministic causal chain have the same level of influence? Obviously not. So, do we have any control over the environment or the situations that we find ourselves in? Obviously, we cannot choose our birth parents. We usually cannot choose most of the people that our parents have put around us. We usually cannot choose any rules or morals that our parents may or may not give us. It takes a while to develop an ability to choose freely in a broad sense of the word. At some point, we choose the influences we wish to have. The determining regressions no longer overpower the progressions that we choose.

Can a regression get so weak that it is no longer, by any practical means, determined? I believe that we can combine this question with causal and logical determinism. The future is not one event. The future is not even a million or a billion or a quadrillion different events. The future is larger than that.

There are differing strengths of regression and number of regressions. How many progressions do we need as a child grows up to overcome the influence of parental regressions? At what point is a man or woman making his or her own decisions without parental regression? Does a parent have to raise and support their offspring until the day that the parent dies because there might be some speck or hint of determinism that lingers?

How does evolution fit into the picture of free will? Views for and against free will have both claimed that evolution works or has worked or will work in their favor. It has been argued that we evolved the illusion of free will. It has also been argued that free will is an evolutionary step. Some views both for and against free will have both claimed that free will or the illusion of free will is a physical necessity. These views both for and against free will appear to believe that science will further validate and support their views. Can views both for and against free will be right or is one side wrong?

Science, to an extent, should support views for and against free will. How is that possible or what do I mean by that? I believe science will add to our knowledge of materialism at the lower level such as biochemistry, hormones, blood sugar, physiology and genetic tendencies while at the same time adding to our knowledge of self-control, language, concept formation, consciousness, choice of impulses and psychological states at the higher levels—freewill.

Will future developments in science increase or decrease

the responsibility of the criminal offender? Many believe that science will support determinism and lack of responsibility of the criminal offender as the offender could not have done otherwise. I believe that there will be more responsibility over time. In most cases, the criminal offender could surely have done otherwise. We have culturally and perhaps even genetically evolved over time. To, perhaps, oversimplify—myths such as the Bible helped keep sexual reproduction, family, kinship and other grouping characteristics channeled into a local area or tribe for protection, survival and reproduction. Tribes of religious people went to war in the same manner as competing herds, prides and packs of animals might fight over territory and mating rights.

We have curbed our violence and impulses over time and developed more complex and peaceful ways to survive and reproduce. A purely deterministic viewpoint that dismisses free will may argue that natural selection is not appreciated enough to see that free will is an illusion. I would argue that a purely deterministic viewpoint doesn't see *enough* natural selection. Natural selection would favor traits that enhance survival and reproduction. Free will as an evolutionary step or process involves complex decision making in a socially cultural setting. Free will can help us not have to lock horns or tusks or kill the offspring of a rival for the right to reproduce. Instead of growing large horns or tusks, natural selection has "grown" human free will, consciousness, reason, logic, planning, strategy and other tools to survive and reproduce. I believe it is more probable over time for natural selection to develop actual horns, tusks or free will versus illusionary horns, tusks and free will. I know that nature has bluffs and disguises in the animal world. Consciousness was a huge evolutionary investment for the human brain. The evidence and probabilities, to me, favor natural selection to have developed an actual free will.

While time marches forward sequentially into the future, it may not always be this way. Time (and space) may bend forward as Einstein theorized. With more than a quadrillion different causal chains going with so many past regressions over 13 billion years, is the future entirely determined? Can a human being with the ability to recognize ought and subject have any non-determined future events on any almost infinitely regressed causal chain of determinism? Is the day of your death determined on the day of your birth? Or, do we know that there will be a future where you will die by a succession of age (a causal chain where one day passed on to the next to the next...), but, the exact day can be determined or influenced by choices made by the agent or human being?

Where do physicists fall into the free will picture? Newton, Einstein and Hawkins appear to believe that free will is an illusion. Kaku and Stenger believe that free will is possible. For Kaku, the Heisenberg uncertainty principle makes our future choices uncertain. For Stenger, the Heisenberg uncertainty principle also applies, but, Stenger adds more to the equation. Stenger in *GOD And The Folly Of Faith* states

> Every decision we make is the result of a complex calculation made by our individual conscious and unconscious brains working together. That calculation relies on

input from our immediate circumstances
and our past experiences. So the decision is
uniquely ours, based on our specific knowledge, experience, and abilities. That seems
pretty free to me.

Some might dismiss uncertainty or indeterminacy because it happened at the subatomic level and does not affect
free will of complex life and objects. The problem with this
belief is that determinism was at the subatomic level at the
time of the Big Bang.

Immanuel Kant argues that, while all empirical phe-
nomena must result from determining causes, human
thought introduces something seemingly not found elsewhere in nature—the ability to conceive of the world in
terms of how it ought to be, or how it might otherwise be.
For Kant, subjective reasoning is necessarily distinct from
how the world is empirically. Kant argues that because of
reason's capacity to distinguish *is* from *ought*, reasoning can
'spontaneously' originate new events without being itself determined by what already exists. Kant proposes that taking,
what we now call the compatibilist view, involves denying
the distinctly subjective capacity to re-think an intended
course of action in terms of what ought to happen.

So how does this discussion on free will end? How did
similar discussions on free will end for other philosophers
and writers? For Ted Honderich, on the last page, he gives
us a philosophy that we can create and develop. It must have
slipped his mind to mention this philosophy on the previous
700 plus pages of his two volume work. Sam Harris gives a

free will experiment where he writes random thoughts about a rabbit and an elephant.

I had hoped to be more conclusive or at least humorous in ending my discussion of free will and morality. Moral responsibility is not an all or nothing event. There can be degrees in between. While determinism can be as direct and relevant as having a gun pointed at your face, it can also be as irrelevant to moral choice as a Big Bang explosion over 13 billion years ago. A "list" for determinism would consist of a vacuum or a closed system where any chance, uncertainty, uncaused causes, indeterminism or any human experience, mental state or action does not rise to the level of affecting any determined outcome.

There are many reasons that we have partial or complete free will. I have alphabetized a list. While a person may discount one or two of these reasons from the list, I think to discount the entire list and declare that free will is an illusion would be a grievous error.

Chance

Evolution

Free Wont

Forced to choose as if we had free will

Heisenberg Uncertainty

Indeterminism

Mental States

Natural Selection

Ought from is—consciousness

Psychological impulses

Progression—knowledge from experience increases

Uncaused Causes

PARTICIPATION OF GOD

If this life is a "test" of faith then how much will god participate or test us? If life is a test then where does this test come from? Our imagination or the Bible? The Bible has stories of temptation such as the Garden of Eden, Lot and Jesus in the desert. When I was a Christian, suffering was described, by church preachers, as a test of faith. If I kept my faith despite suffering or the suffering of others then my faith is said to grow stronger. If this "test" thinking were true then god only needed to do two things—create human life and create knowledge of the parameters of the test such as the Bible.

To my knowledge, there are no direct assertions in the Bible that your life on earth is a test of faith that requires a certain mandated amount of suffering and physical or mental pain. There are things that you can do to be said to be "saved" (to heaven) in the Bible. I don't know of any mandated suffering that is part of our individual "test." If there is no mandated suffering then god is free to intervene and save lives and reduce suffering.

Christians assign themselves mental tests in addition to any assigned physical tests. When science does not have definitive proof for something, it can be called a theory. When Christians do not have definitive proof (or any proof) it is called faith. There can be no proof for the virgin birth of Christ. There can be no proof of the resurrection of Christ.

These supernatural events might be considered tests of faith for the faithful Christian. These supernatural events can never be proven. In no particular order or inclusiveness of testable issues; the murder, rape, infanticide, homophobia, mythical stories, mythical creatures, logical contradiction and animal sacrifice and a myriad of other issues should be a mental test for any reasonable person. Of course, it is less of a test or no test at all depending on your mental aptitude, ability and use and/or level of religious indoctrination.

When there is a god you need theodicy or rationalizations without proof to explain why any supposed omnibenevolent, omnipotent and omniscient god would not intervene to save lives and reduce suffering. An omniscient god could think up a way to save innocent life and reduce suffering. Of course, Christians that can defend the moral atrocity that calls itself the Old Testament can defend god's absence of intervention. Some Christians might say that it is not for me to second guess the mind of god. God's wisdom and logic may not be known (or make sense) to me as a fallible sinful creature (that is just lower than the angels according to Bible myth). Omnibenevolent and Omniscient ability apparently can mean contradiction, suffering and murder if it comes from the hand of god.

While there are "tests" and temptations in this fictional Bible myth, there is supposed to be some participation by this god. Throughout the Bible, prayer is a commandment and an example. Unless prayer is wholly a function of redemption of sin then prayer should serve some other function? Is prayer talking to god? If so, then there could be some expectation that god is listening and might participate in answering prayers? If there is a chance that god might participate then shouldn't this god save innocent lives or reduce suffering? Or, do you have to know of your murder and suffering beforehand and then ask for god's help in prayer? Answered prayers have been claimed from probably every faith that exists. Yet, millions of babies and children die despite the prayers of their parents.

There is an excuse or rationalization for god not saving innocent life. Christians posit that god did the innocent a favor by allowing their lives to be taken. By having an innocent status such as babies, young children and the faithful, god has "locked in" their salvation and everlasting life in heaven. If innocent babies and children were going to be sinful, raping, molesting and murdering criminals as adults then did god do any alleged future inhabitants of heaven a favor? God may have inadvertently helped victims on earth, but, did heaven no favor? If innocent babies and children were going to be helpful, productive members of society as adults then did god do the innocent or earth a favor? God's omnibenevolent nature is imagined in his lack of action and allowing people to suffer and die. Omniscient and omnibenevolent status implies the knowledge and desire to think out a way to avoid suffering and murder. Omnipotence implies the power to achieve any conceivable way to avoid innocent suffering and murder.

CHAPTER 5
HISTORY AND IDENTITY

For the most part, we might be able to trace the origins of the influences of the Founding Fathers back to the Age of Enlightenment or Reason. So far, we have discussed individualism and collectivism mostly in terms of ideas and thought. Individualism and collectivism exists or is absent in varying, subtle degrees in groups, communities and institutions. Our own identity of how we relate to our self and others reflect an identity. This identity is influenced by many threads running through history often at the same time.

Leonard Peikoff in *The Ominous Parallels* wrote

> Since men cannot live or act without some kind of basic guidance, the issues of philosophy in some form necessarily affect every man, in every social group and class. Most men, however, do not consider such issues in explicit terms. They absorb their Ideas— implicitly, eclectically, and with many contradictions—from the cultural atmosphere around them, building into their souls without identifying it the various ideological vibrations emanating from school and church and arts and media and mores.

It can take a lot of effort to examine all the implicit atmosphere that surrounds us and "convert" that into explicit
terms.

HIERARCHAL IDENTITY

For instance, take our Pledge of Allegiance that we
recited at school on a daily basis? I recited the Pledge so
many times as a child in school that even decades later it
is still burned in my memory that I can effortlessly recite it
below: "I pledge allegiance to the Flag of the United States
of America, and to the Republic for which it stands, one
Nation, under God, indivisible, with liberty and justice
for all." The Pledge was adopted by the US Congress with
the name Pledge of Allegiance with the above wording in
1954 (the wording was slightly different and didn't have
an official name before 1954). Congressional sessions open
with the recital of the Pledge. School teachers taught us that
before we recite the pledge we are supposed to put our hand
on our heart. I guess this is to "feel" our allegiance. We
are also supposed to "see" the flag as we recite the pledge.
Schoolrooms often have flags hanging in them. Now that we
have the "proper" visual and emotional cues, we are ready
to recite the Pledge.

Looking critically at the Pledge I see many issues. What
are we pledging allegiance to? Allegiance can be defined as
loyalty. What are we supposed to be loyal to? A nation? A
state? A nation and a state? Many states have their own state
flags and their own state pledges that may be recited after
the national pledge is recited. This conditions us to pledge
loyalty to our state and nation as an "all or nothing" pledge.

There are no conditions to our loyalty. There are no choices as to what we are loyal to. If we are born in the United States, we have implicitly signed an all or nothing "social contract" whether we want to or not. With our implicit social contract, we have the explicit all or nothing pledge of loyalty to our nation. Under this pledge, our nation is said to be a republic. A republic is governed by laws. Which laws am I supposed to be loyal to? All laws? Even laws that I am opposed to?

According to the Pledge, the republic of the United States is one nation under god, indivisible. Where should I start first? An indivisible single nation or under god? Let's start with an indivisible single nation. Why is it indivisible? Do we have a right to secede as an individual, group or individual state? Our nation originally believed in a right to secede as the American Revolution attested. Eleven southern states believed they had a similar right to secede as the Civil War attested. At what point did our nation become indivisible? At what point did we lose our right to secede as we did from Great Britain? When Lincoln decided it should be so? When the Supreme Court decided so in Texas v. White (1869)? The Pledge never answers this question. For me, it is not a legal question of laws before or after the Civil War or some "defining moment." It was an extra-legal affair regarding America and Great Britain. The most compelling arguments for me are extra-legal arguments versus legal arguments before and after the Constitution, Articles of Confederation, Declaration of Independence, Supreme Court cases or whatever document(s) you wish to pin the question of legality to.

As far as the *under God* portion of the Pledge, what does being under god mean from a moral or legal perspective? What is or isn't being done as a nation to be under god? What can the Pledge do? It can condition you to all or nothing choice and loyalty. It can take the absolute rule of kings and the church and replace it with a near absolute rule of the democratic state. When you make an all or nothing Pledge it may seem like a great freedom to make a single choice as to your president (king). The great power of democracy is the illusion of freedom of choice while being under near absolute rule.

This national sovereignty of the Pledge can be taken to different levels with slogans. There is the slogan *God Bless America*. The slogan *God Bless America* is very exclusive to the area that god is supposed to bless? Should god bless everyone, everywhere or just Americans? This exclusiveness to race and geography is similar to the sovereignty that is (was) given to kings, royalty and other privilege of birth. I believe that the Pledge of Allegiance and the slogan *God Bless America* should be avoided entirely.

The Pledge of Allegiance serves the trifecta of absolute submission of god, king and country. How badly is this submission wanted? Pretty badly, I believe. We all subsidize public education through taxes. The only way to use this subsidy is through public schools. There is no voucher or refund for using a private school.

God, king and country have been helping each other out for a long period of history. The church would sanction the rule of the king while the king defended the church in return. Kings and churches needed divine authority to continue their rule. To continue their rule they needed a belief that authority is passed through lineage. Kings needed princes and noblemen, churches needed popes and priests. Today many still have the belief that certain men have the divine authority to run church government as popes, priests or other leaders despite the fact that they cannot show divine inspiration through miracles or other inspired actions.

So where do we stand today? Absolute rule of kings have been replaced by a near absolute rule or representative democracy of one king (congressman) for around a million people. To my knowledge, no king ever ruled over a million people. Instead of birthright we have an all or nothing democracy that allows a choice of one king over another king in the form of a congressman or congresswoman. The church no longer executes people for heresy or witchcraft or goes on Crusades to kill in the name of god. A huge improvement here. Though, we still have many people who still believe in a divine authority that rests in certain men through lineage or otherwise (such as digging up some golden tablets—Joseph Smith) that allows them to rule in the name of god. Many still believe that the Bible, Book of Mormon and other religious texts are complete, unaltered inspired works of god that provide a moral code to live life on earth and ascend to heaven. We still allow for a small group of kinglike rulers of church and state to rule over us in a hierarchy where we should know our "place." Our place being a preset set of questionable morals as I discussed in the morals section of the Breakdown and Morals chapter. Our place being a preset, nearly deterministic democracy where we use our one choice to determine which king will rule over us for four years. This is the identity that many of us have. Many are proud of this identity and can't wait to go to church or vote and even encourage people to go to church and provide motivation and transportation to go to church or vote.

INDIVIDUAL IDENTITY

The Age of Enlightenment was a monumental shift away from the divine rule of kings and churches. It was an Age where the individual was perceived to have inherent natural rights or value from god. From this fundamental position, we started developing rights to property, social contract theory and the development of ideas surrounding marketplaces and a replacement of the barter system. A hierarchal identity was being challenged by an identity with the ability to reason and choose. In this tradition our nation was founded with many of the ideals of the Enlightenment.

I believe that there have been some threads of individualism and reason that have followed and in some cases improved and developed many of the ideas of the Enlightenment. To me, those threads came from Objectivism (Ayn Rand), Libertarians, Anarcho-Capitalism, Minarchist Libertarians, Austrian School of Economics. It is from this similar thread that many of my views and concepts of this book were derived from. I want to show the threads of individualism and then in later sections of this chapter show threads of thought that are in conflict with these threads of individualism. So, I am not going to try to summarize all the importance and contribution of these threads of individualism since they are reflected throughout this book. I will say that in terms of

measuring the state and how the state interacts with institutions, individuals and markets; the threads of collectivism
are gaining increased traction overall. Unlike the Pledge of
Allegiance that was (is) in perhaps every public school, the
threads of individualism that I have described might exist
with a few professors in a few colleges. The threads of individualism are something that usually have to be sought out
unlike hierarchal and collective threads. You can have an
individualistic identity. There are just some headwinds that
should be faced also such as removing the identity of divine
hierarchy and collectivism.

COLLECTIVE IDENTITY NAZI GERMANY

Most people believe that the rise of Nazi Germany was
based on a sequence of events. For instance, I was taught
in grade school that it was a result of war sanctions by the
Treaty of Versailles. I don't believe that a series of events
could cause a national identity that could sweep across
a majority of German people with all different incomes
and education levels. *Mein Kampf* had been read by over
200,000 people between 1925 and 1932 (Leonard Peikoff
The Ominous Parallels). Hitler was the icing on the cake
on a long line of German philosophers including Kant,
Hegel and Marx. Germany was also influenced by German
Romanticism. There were German philosophers who were
not collectivist thinkers, but, their ideas did not take hold
like the collectivist philosophers named above.

Many individuals experience challenging events in
their lives. Abuse, assault, poverty, low self-esteem, death
of a loved one, depression, etc. How many individuals who

experience these conditions go out and commit murder based on an event in their life? A few perhaps. I would not call it a majority of individuals who experience such events go out in support of murder. Yet, this is what we had in Germany. I believe it took something different than mere events to turn the German people into supporting the German Nazi State.

I believe it was an identity through a succession of ideas that garnered such widespread support through the German people. There may be no stronger historical identity than Nazi Germany. They were able to reach the ultimate end or conclusion of collectivism. They reached the ultimate identity for Germans and Germany. They were able to dehumanize individuals to the point of zero or nothing or object and elevate the German State to the point of the absolute. Individuals had no value as individuals. Only the state had value. Psychopathic murderers are able to accomplish the same thing when they murder others. They can place no value on others and all value on themselves. They treat others as an object. They ignore the sacredness or specialness of existence and self-awareness. An individual's ability to exercise reason, responsibility and emotion.

Leonard Peikoff stated in *The Ominous Parallels*

> To liberate humanity from intelligence, Hitler counted on the doctrines of irrationalism. To rid men of conscience, he counted on the morality of altruism. To free the world of freedom, he counted on the idea of collectivism. These three theories together constitute the essence of the

Nazi philosophy, which never changed
from the start of the movement to its end.

It is not enough that the Nazi must sacrifice himself or herself for the sake of others. Others must learn to sacrifice for others. According to Nazi philosophy, if this sacrifice comes in the form of a sacrificial oven to be burned alive then this is the sacrifice that they must make for others. Hitler believes that the universe is ordered by force and that man is a mere dust particle in that order. He further believes that for man to be moral he must submit and serve that force by his own free choice. Otherwise, force will be used against him.

It was believed by Marx that existence is a social activity that takes all individual action of earning and production and blends that into a social state. Nazism took all this individual action and transformed into an absolute state with supremacy over all other states or nations. The same philosophy that subordinates the individual to the state was now extended to subordinate the world to the German state. They further took the supremacy of the German state to the supremacy of a certain race of German people. They took the supremacy of a certain Aryan race of German people to the supremacy of the Fuhrer over the Aryan race.

Instead of kings and nobleman, we have a Fuhrer and a Third Reich of Aryan brotherhood. Take away all the dressings and trappings and you have the same philosophy repeated in time. This time maybe even a stronger version? At least, the serfs knew of their low station in life and likely would have loved to change their situation if they could. Germans voted in their own serfdom and never had restrictions on foreign travel. Germans were free to leave. They chose their servitude to the state and celebrated their own feeling of supremacy.

COLLECTIVE IDENTITY UNITED STATES

Our colonial beginnings before we founded the United States were marked by a dark, undeserving way that we felt about our identity. Man was believed to be innately depraved and only through the salvation of an omniscient, omnipotent and omnibenevolent god could we find salvation for our soul or any value as a man. This innate depravity may have continued through the Renaissance. For a brief time in the Enlightenment that followed the Renaissance did man view himself better than innately depraved? During this brief time under the influence of the Enlightenment, the United States was founded.

The Founding Fathers supported the primacy of the individual over the collective in most ways. I believe the spirit of much of the Founder's writing was individualist. The more individualistic writings were in books and declarations such as the Declaration of Independence. The specific operation of the state took a collectivist approach by default for lack of a better approach or by design? Checks and balances merely affected the speed of collectivism. Leaving individualism up to majority rule and representative democracy (where one congressman is like a king representing up to a million or more voters) left individualism up to the majority and "kings." In the chapter, Rise of the Individual, I showed some of the rise of Marxism in the last 200 years. Here, I want to show some of the collective influences by less well-known names that have risen much more recently.

An absolute form of collectivism such as Nazi Germany, once created, burned out very quickly within a few years. An absolute form of collectivism exposes its extreme and often violent consequences in dramatic fashion. As the Age of Enlightenment was ending there were new generations of Romantic philosophers from the Age of Romanticism seeking to dismantle every part of the Enlightenment. The Enlightenment focused on reason, reality, truth and logic. Romanticism focused on history, myth, faith, tradition, polylogism, subjectivism, organic wholes, pragmatism, social Darwinism, consequentialism, utilitarianism, etc. The common thread that all of these Romantic themes shared was that knowledge is unknowable, logic and truth are relative and reality is whatever you want it to be.

There are two huge dividing lines that exist from shortly after the founding of our nation to present day. The first is how we feel about our self. For a very short time individualism was the dominant theme in our identity. Now collectivism is the dominant theme in the American identity. Those are two diametrically opposing views of how we view our self as an identity. The other huge dividing line is reality. Whether we believe reality is independent or dependent of our own existence will determine our identity, our institutions and our state.

Romantic writers believed that reality and truth are relative to your purpose, the best utility, the best consequence or your frame of reference. This Romantic thread of thought believes that the reality of an object is derived from the conscious mind of the subject. At the extreme end of subjectivism, the essence of an object is created by the mind of the subject. Objects do not exist independently of the mind according to extreme subjectivism. Under polylogism, truth is relative to race or culture. What is true for one race or culture might not be true for another race or culture. Polylogism falsely holds that since reality and truth are not universal or objective then logic does not have to conform to any universal or objective frame of reference.

In fact, polylogism falsely holds that every race and culture have their own truth and logic specific for them. If reality, truth and knowledge are all relative and unknowable then there is no point of using reason to find them because they cannot be found. The Enlightenment was entirely discarded by Romanticism. Public Education in the United States has followed much of the Romantic and Nazi model of education. Whether or not knowledge is knowable to public education, knowledge is surely not a priority. It's pretty common knowledge that US public schools spend the highest or near the highest per student globally worldwide, but, get near the lowest worldwide in average test scores for public school children. If education was about knowledge and putting out a good product then the government would grant vouchers or refunds to cover or offset the cost of children wanting to go to private schools that, on average, have tested much higher. Instead, parents must subsidize public school and pay out of pocket for private school.

A majority of "kings" passed The Patient Protection and Affordable Care Act or "Obamacare" by a 219-212 vote (even the kings were split) in March 2010. This was a king driven initiative without popular support of the serfdom voters. As Nancy Pelosi is thought to have said, "We have to pass it so we can read it." Obamacare has been evaluated on how many people were added to healthcare and if healthcare cost rose or fell. Obamacare should be evaluated on whether we need increased socialism and selflessness. Obamacare should be evaluated on how many congressional kings use Obamacare and our public school systems. I don't think a single congressional king sends their children to public schools or uses Obamacare. Obamacare should be evaluated on whether Obamacare was a choice of the kings or a voluntary individual choice. It is surely not an individual choice. If you don't pay for healthcare, you will get a tax penalty. You are coerced into buying healthcare whether you want it or not, otherwise, you pay a tax penalty.

How did we get to the point of coercion where you are penalized for not choosing public schools and participating in socialized medicine? The American Identity… The American Identity started with strong values of ethics, rights and social contracts. These were fundamental values that the Founding Fathers founded our nation upon. The end of the state was to promote these fundamental values through democracy and laws of the newly founded Republic of the United States. The Progressives or Progressivism through the Progressive Party (Third Party) which included President Theodore Roosevelt sought reforms from a move from an agricultural based economy to a capitalized industrial economy. Progressives sought a "just" working society. From wages, hours and working conditions, etc.; we moved or progressed to Social Security (retirement),

Medicare (healthcare) and other social reforms by the end of the Democratic presidency of Franklin D. Roosevelt.

John Dewey took democracy and progressivism a step farther. Progress for Dewey was a democracy and philosophy that sought to remove the values the Founding Fathers instilled in the United States as the end of the state. Dewey sought to remove these values he believed were static or obsolete. At the same time, Dewey did not want to promote a nihilistic State with no values. Dewey proposed a dynamic end for the state. Social problems and conflicts are to be solved using the scientific method of Francis Bacon. Dewey has a three-fold technique of observation of facts, construction of hypothesis and testing of consequences. Philosophical problems should be dealt with according to Dewey as a reconstruction of philosophy to deal with societal problems. These problems should, according to Dewey, be current problems that exist or have arisen with the lifetime of the philosopher. Dewey believed that philosophy should not be a "rigid" hierarchy of "fixed" ends.

The end of the state, for Dewey, is to test consequences and find the best result (regardless of the values or timeframes that may be abandoned or added). For Dewey, social justice should be evolutionary, progressive and should grow through time. The "cure," for Dewey, for any perceived problem of democracy is more democracy or better educated or "evolved" majorities of people.

Education in public schools are about the Pledge of Allegiance that we covered earlier, children grouped by grade and age (not ability), yearbooks, student government, gym, physical education, school newspapers, field trips,

Drug Abuse Resistance Education (D.A.R.E.), group projects—with the exception of the Pledge of Allegiance, many of these influences have been credited to Dewey.

When we look at our democracy and our Democratic and Republican parties, what do we see? For the most part, only subtle differences between the two parties. Despite a new Republican majority in the House and Senate, I do not imagine Republicans undoing the education monopoly of the state. Parents who want to send their children to private school will still have to pay for both public and private school. There will be no voucher system that will likely arise. Dewey's socialization of our children in public schools to make loyal citizens out of our children will continue uninterrupted regardless of which party controls the White House.

While there are some outposts of individuals as I mentioned earlier in the Individual Identity section, our ruling political parties and numerical majorities of voters still appear to endorse a sacrificial view of the public and the state in the overall American Identity. So, I wanted to revisit conservatism.

Conservatism is part of our American Identity. Democrats appear to be a more socialistic variant of conservatism than the Republicans. For the most part, a democratic, majority of congressional kings will rule over most every aspect of your life no matter which party you choose. To use the words of Dewey, we are "growing and evolving" our socialistic Marxism while keeping the seeds and root system to grow and spread a totally selfless state such as Nazi Germany with the likely absence of the racist elements of fascism. We have a dangerous catastrophic government foundation while believing we have strong vibrant freedom and democracy.

Our main political parties (Democratic & Republican) follow the Dewey method. They follow consequences and utility. They redistribute wealth and tax and spend according to social goals. The majority or public comes before the private or individual. National debts in the form of domestic and internationally social goals come before avoiding national debt. The creation of the debt is more important than whatever individual consequence to the individual these collective actions incur. As long as the debt is created and the money spent, that is the important thing to the congressional king. Our congressional kings can just kick the can down the road and inflate (steal) the money supply and create more national debt through national budget deficits.

To conservatism, freedom and other individual values can only be thought of within the confines of the institutions that "made" freedom and these other values "possible." To conservatism, we "owe" the institution not the individual for any freedom or other values. While the institution should exist to protect your freedom, it is the individual who chooses not to try to hurt or kill you. The individual chooses a role within the institution. It is akin to saying that the object (institution) is more valuable than the subject (individual) who created and operates the object. If the end is the object or institution instead of the subject or individual then we have idolatry for the institution instead of self-love and self-respect or selfishness.

VICTIM IDENTITY

When is a person a victim? A person is a victim when someone uses aggression against them. The government should not be in the business of delivering aggression. The state has the monopoly of force in some cases, but, the state should not be using that monopoly of force to initiate aggression, collude or participate in aggression. The state should be only using restitution for past aggression (crime—justice and courts) or prevention for future aggression (crime—police, civil and national defense, natural resource protection, etc.). The state uses aggression against non-aggressors. Coercion and aggression is used to "solve" non-aggressive "victimization."

What does the state count as victimization? Is having children victimization? Is not saving for retirement victimization? Is not having healthcare victimization? Is being poor victimization? To the current state, if a person has no healthcare, retirement savings and free education or are poor then they are a victim. The state "solution" of this financial inequality is the aggression of progressive taxation to fund welfare, food stamps, housing assistance, and free education including college, free basic phone coverage, no tax liability and many other "solutions" of the Involuntary State? The state often jumps ahead to "how" we are going to fix or handle this or that without really answering "why." The "why" is more important than the "how" or "what." The "why" is more important than the "how" or "what" non-aggressive victimization they may be "afflicted" with. The identity of what we call a victim is very important. Whether we have individualism, collectivism, the Involuntary State or the

Voluntary State rests on what we identify a victim to be. The Voluntary State has a social safety net that operates without aggression or distinction between non-aggressive victim statuses.

We take away a human life in the name of capital punishment, self-defense and euthanasia. Capital punishment involves extreme physical aggression and usually loss of life against the victim. Self-defense should be an implied, attempted or highly probable threat of aggression. Euthanasia is debatable whether it is aggression to end your life to avoid suffering.

Are there victims? Yes, of course. There are aggressive acts of crime. The state can see and adequately address most acts of aggression committed by others. The acts of aggression that the state commits by its own hand are the ones that it seems unwilling to address. State aggression such as direct aggression in the form of civil asset forfeiture, taxation (The Involuntary State), inflation (increasing the money supply, bonds sold, national debt and other measures that inflate our money) and eminent domain (literally taking your home and/or property for fair market value regardless of the conditions of the housing market, the cost of moving and what might be going on in your life). Indirect or direct aggression by the state for the allowance or weak efforts at fighting aggression in the form of a national debt, lack of better immigration controls, naked shorting, higher cost of government through lack of better immigration controls, higher cost of government through social welfare from the increased population because of the lack of better immigration controls (marriage and/or children of US citizens by illegal immigrants), job victimization (depending on how immigration and natural resources are handled), etc. The state's lack of criminalizing aggressive actions and/or outright participation and/or collusion in aggressive actions such as High Frequency Trading and encouragement of bad banking and monetary policy. The state insuring subprime loans, poor lending standards, etc. through the government agencies Fannie Mae and Freddie Mac in addition to the government bailout of AIG to the tune of around 85 billion dollars (the government had up to an 80 percent stake in AIG) while executives from AIG received up to 450 million in bonuses in a company that had more liabilities than assets. The state's allowance, participation and lack of criminality of the growing derivatives (debt) markets that have more than doubled in size since derivatives helped bring about the 2008 recession. The state is allowing banks and other financial institutions to use aggression against client deposits, the housing and financial markets and the value of our money through a growing derivatives (debt) market which in turn helps cause events such as the 2008 recession.

Again, whether we have individualism, collectivism, the Involuntary State or the Voluntary State rests on what we identify a victim to be.

SUMMARY

While the dangers of extreme selfishness such as theft, rape and murder are well known, the dangers of extreme altruism are not well known. Extreme altruism is more properly called selflessness. I would like to note that the evolution of altruism, reciprocal altruism and premoral activity in the animal kingdom helped make our human moral evolution possible. I believe there could be some debate on many things that are called altruistic are actually selfish in the medium and long term time frames. Any altruistic behavior in animals may be fine, but, when the human animal claims altruism there can be many levels of deception, manipulation and abuse involved in these claims. Identifying with selflessness is a very dangerous road for humans to pursue.

One way to think of identity is in two basic categories *selfish* and *selfless*. If I asked people at random whether it would be better to be selfish or selfless what do you think the response would be? The answer might depend a little on where I asked the question. You can be helpful, giving, and charitable and exhibit many other attributes and still be selfish. You could give your life for another and still be selfish. For instance, if I were dying with a couple months to live and I could give an organ to a family member or friend that I valued as much or more than myself and extend their life by decades then I could give my life selfishly for another.

Is it selfish:

To want to avoid paying for every single government entity?

To want to have privacy in your conversations?

To want to avoid "travel restrictions" and reporting for money sent overseas?

To believe that you should be able to carry cash on your person, auto or home without fear of the government confiscating it through asset or civil forfeitures?

To believe that having cash does not make you a drug dealer, etc.?

To want to avoid wars that have combatants whose religious and political beliefs and actions on both sides will continue regardless of whether we spill American blood and money?

To want to avoid weekly drone strikes where primary and collateral damage occur?

To want to avoid paying Social Security for people who are undisciplined to save on their own?

To imagine that I could do a better job managing my own money than the collective government spends my money?

To believe that I should have primacy over my own money and affairs?

To believe that I should not have to subordinate myself to majorities and representative "one in a million kings" in state and federal congress?

To believe that I have individual rights that take primacy over the collective state?

To believe that any alleged consent or social contract should actually have signed consent and signed contractual basis?

To want self-determination of value?

To want to avoid a deterministic preset value hierarchy based on the value that the state decides that I can have?

To want to make my own decision versus voting majorities and congressional kings?

It is selfless:

To give away every dollar you earn?

To let your children's education become a monopoly of the state where only public education is subsidized by taxpayer money?

To let your children's education prioritize socialization over knowledge?

To allow the majority to decide how to spend your money?

To participate in majority rule every 2-4 years?

To allow your kings in congress to pass laws in your name as a proxy to your majority rule?

To allow the state to keep growing the national debt through The Involuntary State?

To allow the state to devalue the money it allows you to keep through an increasing money supply, stimulus, growing debt and spending; in other words, inflation?

To file taxes and report every financial dealing to the state?

To allow progressive taxation and aim for a social outcome and social result?

To redistribute your income to others who may not have worked as hard or planned as well (or worked or planned at all)?

To socialize retirement through Social Security to help those who may not have developed any discipline or knowledge to save and invest?

To save and invest through Social Security for others retirement and put more into the system than you can get out (your savings and investment is a social exercise for the social benefit of all)?

To possibly losing better health care plans that might save your life by subsidizing healthcare for all (socialized healthcare)?

To sacrifice healthcare to the government (as if the government is better at producing a healthcare product)?

An absolute selfless state such as Nazi Germany is selfish for the king, dictator or Fuhrer and selfless for all others. An absolute ruler, ironically, uses selfishness to set the state's priorities and goals (though the absolute ruler may claim that they are selfless). The absolute ruler is the standard of value in a selfless state. The selfless state seeks to systematically erase your natural or earned advantage. No two people are equal. People are unequal in their skills and abilities. A selfless collective state seeks equality of outcomes at the expense of natural skills and abilities.

Nazi Germany was a selfless state that submitted to the absolute rule of Hitler. Being selfless was no virtue as innocent life was slaughtered at the hands of such selfless citizens of the absolute German State. Absolute value resided in the Fuhrer who gave Germans their only value which was service or murder for the Fuhrer. Take away reason, reality, truth and selfishness and what do you get? A selfless, mindless meat helmet who is a puppet and pawn to the absolute rule of a Fuhrer or dictator such as Hitler.

The ultimate end of selflessness is to value everyone above yourself despite any effort and accomplishments that you make. You are the lowest thing of value that "graces" the earth. The true lowest thing that "graces" the earth is likely to be sitting in a jail somewhere. Is this what I am supposed to aspire to? Under the selfless state, my only value is the value to give to others who have more value.

Could someone argue that the ultimate end of freedom and selfishness is to be in a state of nature free to do as you choose? The answer, of course, is contained in the question. *Free to do as you choose* which means that you could choose to cooperate with others in a voluntary manner. Could you have a state of absolute rule or selflessness where everyone voluntarily exploits everyone else? For a moment, perhaps, it is theoretically possible to have a voluntary, absolute rule. Very quickly that absolute rule becomes involuntary rule for someone who is coerced by his countrymen or foreigners. There were Germans that didn't vote for Hitler and Germans that later became involuntary participants in Nazi absolute rule. Of course, Jews, non-Germans and non-Aryans were coerced from the outset.

The collective US identity is a little selfishness and a lot of selflessness. The average US citizen will not see the philosophical contradiction. He might see some things he would like to see become more selfish and maybe something he would like to see become more selfless. Of course, he will not phrase it in his mind in this way. Majority rule is a perfect tool to create selflessness not individual selfishness. The majority can just wish it and any minority of people have to go along.

If things are done in the name of god, the church, the king, the Fuhrer, the congressional king or the democratic majority then the individual can try to avoid responsibility for the coercion that is used. It isn't the individual, it is the absolute ruler or majority that is tightening the noose. The individual can entirely avoid reason or truth under collective rule. If the individual has to explain the reasons and justification for his actions as an individual then the odds increase that reason or truth might present itself. The absolute ruler wants to put all actions under the name and authority of the absolute ruler. Any thought, explanation or discretion regarding the individual's freedom from coercion can show doubt of the absoluteness of the absolute ruler. If the explanation gets any longer than "the Fuhrer said so" then reason or truth might creep in.

There are two huge dividing lines that exist from shortly after the founding of our nation to present day. The first dividing line is how we feel about our self. For a very short time individualism was the dominant theme in our identity. Now collectivism is the dominant theme in the American identity. Those are diametrically opposing views of how we view our self as an identity. The other huge dividing line is reality. Whether we believe reality is independent or dependent of our own existence will determine our identity, our institutions and our state. It is a huge encompassing statement.

The way that man views himself is a determining factor in the condition that man lives. This view or identity is determined by a few building blocks which include reality, justice and how man places himself in the world as an individual or part of a collective and how man chooses ends and means.

Identity plays a major part in the direction that a state follows. This can be seen throughout history. Identities that we think are good can often be bad even evil. In the morality section of the chapter Breakdown and Morals, I showed how moral code from an absolute value setter such as the concept of god through the Bible has some huge problems. History has demonstrated that when we place a higher value on men in churches, men in governments, absolute dictators, absolute Fuhrers, men that constitute a majority than the value we place on our self then we run into disastrous consequences resulting in coercion and death.

The ultimate identity is the individual. Leonard Peikoff in *The Ominous Parallels* writes

> A man cannot think if he places something—
> anything—above his perception of reality.
>
> Reason is an attribute of the individual.
> Thought is a process performed not by men,
> but by man—in the singular.

Christians place a god above reality as a supernatural force. Christians also place a god above any reason because god holds primacy for them. Nazi Germany merely placed a Fuhrer in the place of a god. Socialism, communism, democracy merely place reason as a collective attribute. An attribute to be decided by a majority or a select group of "kings" that rule in a congressional, socialist or communistic party. A proper Voluntary State allows the individual the opportunity to perceive reality and reason as a singular being.

A proper Voluntary State may only be realized if gods, tyrants, despots, democracies, congressional kings, institutions and any collective identity are discarded. Our individual identity cannot be diminished or abandoned in the name of compromise or selflessness or collectivism, etc. Many want individualism, but, want to compromise and marginalize any individualism with democracy and collectivism. Individualism with democracy is not individualism it is collectivism.

CHAPTER 6
THE INVOLUNTARY STATE

Here is a partial list of some of the federal departments, agencies and other entities that you pay for. If you
could voluntarily pick and choose then which ones, if any,
would you choose to pay for? Has the Federal Interagency
Committee for the Management of Noxious and Exotic
Weeds caught your eye? Would you like to purchase that
one out of pocket? Can I interest you in the Commission
on International Religious Freedom? Atheists enjoy paying
for mythical religious freedom across the world? How about
the Federal Voting Assistance Program? Voters might need
assistance in their effort to coerce the minority to their will.
Maybe you would like to throw a party for our politicians by
ordering the Joint Congressional Committee on Inaugural
Ceremonies? There are so many to choose from...

Every federal department, agency or entity in this list
should have represented a voluntary choice. We should have
had the voluntary choice over whether we wanted to directly
finance these federal departments, agencies and entities and
the level of control, if any, they can exercise. This, of course,
is a federal list. There are many duplications and even some
additions at the state and local level. There are, of course,
fifty states each with a myriad of their own bureaucracy. I do
not want to provide a list for every state in the union. I want

to note the difference in size between the Involuntary State list and the list in the Voluntary State chapter of the book.

As you peruse the list, consider that financial consequences are only one part of the damage of the Involuntary State. Physical consequences can result from the Involuntary State. Many of the government entities of the Involuntary State enforce many non-aggressive, victimless "crimes" that are on the law books. There are many victims who suffer and sometimes die due to lethal enforcement for non-aggressive crime—overcriminalization.

AbilityOne Commission
Access Board
Administration for Children and Families (ACF)
Administration for Native Americans
Administration on Aging (AoA)
Administration on Developmental Disabilities
Administration for Children and Families
Administrative Conference of the United States
Administrative Office of the US Courts
Administrative Review Board
Advisory Commission on Accessible Instructional
    Materials in Postsecondary Education
    for Students with Disabilities
Advisory Council on Historic Preservation
African Development Foundation
Agency for Healthcare Research and Quality (AHRQ)
Agency for International Development (USAID)
Agency for Toxic Substances and Disease Registry
Agricultural Marketing Service
Agricultural Research Service

Agriculture Department (USDA)
Air Force
Air Force Reserve
Alcohol and Tobacco Tax and Trade Bureau
Alcohol, Tobacco, Firearms, and Explosives Bureau
AmeriCorps
American Battle Monuments Commission
American Samoa
Amtrak (AMTRAK)
Animal and Plant Health Inspection Service
Antitrust Division
Architect of the Capitol
Archives (National Archives and Records
    Administration) (NARA)
Arctic Research Commission
Armed Forces Retirement Home
Arms Control and International Security
Army
Army Corps of Engineers
Arthritis and Musculoskeletal Interagency
    Coordinating Committee
Asset Forfeiture Program

Bankruptcy Courts
Barry M. Goldwater Scholarship and
    Excellence in Education Program
Benefits Review Board
Bonneville Power Administration
Botanic Garden
Broadcasting Board of Governors
Bureau of Administration

Bureau of African Affairs
Bureau of Alcohol and Tobacco Tax and Trade
Bureau of Alcohol, Tobacco, Firearms, and Explosives
Bureau of Arms Control, Verification and Compliance
Bureau of Consular Affairs
Bureau of Consumer Financial Protection
Bureau of Democracy, Human Rights and Labor
Bureau of Diplomatic Security
Bureau of Economic Analysis (BEA)
Bureau of Economic, Energy and Business Affairs
Bureau of Educational and Cultural Affairs
Bureau of East Asian and Pacific Affairs
Bureau of Engraving and Printing
Bureau of European and Eurasian Affairs
Bureau of Fiscal Service
Bureau of Human Resources
Bureau of Indian Affairs
Bureau of Industry and Security
Bureau of Intelligence and Research
Bureau of International Information Programs
Bureau for International Narcotics and
    Law Enforcement Affairs
Bureau of International Organizational Affairs
Bureau of International Labor Affairs
Bureau of International Security and Nonproliferation
Bureau of Justice Statistics
Bureau of Labor Statistics
Bureau of Land Management (BLM)
Bureau of Legislative Affairs
Bureau of Near Eastern Affairs

Bureau of Ocean Energy Management (BOEM)
Bureau of Oceans and International
     Environmental and Scientific Affairs
Bureau of Overseas Buildings Operations
Bureau of Political-Military Affairs
Bureau of Population, Refugees and Migration
Bureau of Prisons
Bureau of Public Affairs
Bureau of Reclamation
Bureau of Resource Management
Bureau of Safety and Environmental Enforcement (BSEE)
Bureau of South and Central Asian Affairs
Bureau of Transportation Statistics
Bureau of Western Hemisphere Affairs
Bureau of the Census
Bureau of the Fiscal Service
Bureau of the Public Debt

Capitol Police
Capitol Visitor Center
Census Bureau
Center for Food Safety and Applied Nutrition
Centers for Disease Control and Prevention (CDC)
Centers for Medicare and Medicaid Services (CMS)
Center for Women Veterans
Central Intelligence Agency (CIA)
Chemical Safety and Hazard Investigation Board
Chief Acquisition Officers Council
Chief Financial Officers Council
Chief Human Capital Officers Council
Chief Information Officers Council

Citizens' Stamp Advisory Committee
Citizenship and Immigration Services
Coast Guard
Commerce Department (DOC)
Commission of Fine Arts
Commission on Civil Rights
Commission on International Religious Freedom
Commission on Security and Cooperation
    in Europe (Helsinki Commission)
Committee for the Implementation of Textile Agreements
Committee on Foreign Investment in the United States
Commodity Futures Trading Commission
Community Oriented Policing Services (COPS)
Community Planning and Development
Compliance, Office of
Computer Emergency Readiness Team (US CERT)
Congress—U.S. House of Representatives
Congress—U.S. Senate
Congressional Budget Office (CBO)
Congressional Research Service
Consular Affairs, Bureau of
Consumer Financial Protection Bureau
Consumer Product Safety Commission (CPSC)
Coordinating Council on Juvenile Justice
    and Delinquency Prevention
Copyright Office
Corporation for National and Community Service
Corporation for Public Broadcasting
Corps of Engineers
Council of Economic Advisers

Council of the Inspectors General on
    Integrity and Efficiency
Council on Environmental Quality
Court Services and Offender Supervision Agency
Court of Appeals for Veterans Claims
Court of Appeals for the Armed Forces
Court of Appeals for the Federal Circuit
Court of Federal Claims
Court of International Trade
Customs and Border Protection

Defense Acquisition University
Defense Advanced Research Projects Agency (DARPA)
Defense Commissary Agency
Defense Contract Audit Agency (DCAA)
Defense Contract Management Agency
Defense Field Activities
Defense Finance and Accounting Service (DFAS)
Defense Finance and Accounting Service Out-
    of-Service Debt Management Center
Defense Information Systems Agency (DISA)
Defense Intelligence Agency (DIA)
Defense Legal Services Agency
Defense Nuclear Safety Board
Defense Security Cooperation Agency (DSCA)
Defense Security Service (DSS)
Defense Technical Information Center
Defense Threat Reduction Agency (DTRA)
Delaware River Basin Commission
Denali Commission
Department of Agriculture (USDA)

Department of Commerce (DOC)
Department of Defense
Department of Education (ED)
Department of Energy (DOE)
Department of Health and Human Services (HHS)
Department of Homeland Security (DHS)
Department of Housing and Urban Development (HUD)
Department of Justice (DOJ)
Department of Labor (DOL)
Department of State (DOS)
Department of Transportation (DOT)
Department of Veterans Affairs (VA)
Department of the Interior (DOI)
Department of the Treasury
Diplomatic Security Service
Director of National Intelligence, Office of
Domestic Policy Council
Drug Enforcement Administration
Dwight D. Eisenhower School for National
    Security and Resource Strategy

Economic Adjustment Office
Economic Analysis, Bureau of (BEA)
Economic Development Administration (EDA)
Economic Research Service
Economic, Business and Agricultural Affairs
Economics and Statistics Administration
Education Department (ED)
Education Resources Information Center (ERIC)
Election Assistance Commission (EAC)
Elementary and Secondary Education, Office of (OESE)

Employee Benefits Security Administration (EBSA)
Employment and Training Administration
Endangered Species Program
Energy Department (DOE)
Energy Information Administration
English Language Acquisition Office
Environmental Management (Energy department)
Environmental Protection Agency (EPA)
Equal Employment Opportunity Commission (EEOC)
European Command
Executive Office for Immigration Review

Fair Housing and Equal Opportunity (FHEO)
Fannie Mae
Farm Credit Administration
Farm Credit System Insurance Corporation
Farm Service Agency
Federal Accounting Standards Advisory Board
Federal Aviation Administration (FAA)
Federal Bureau of Investigation (FBI)
Federal Bureau of Prisons
Federal Citizen Information Center
Federal Communications Commission (FCC)
Federal Consulting Group
Federal Deposit Insurance Corporation (FDIC)
Federal Election Commission
Federal Emergency Management Agency (FEMA)
Federal Energy Regulatory Commission
Federal Executive Boards
Federal Financial Institutions Examination Council
Federal Financing Bank

Federal Geographic Data Committee
Federal Highway Administration
Federal Home Loan Mortgage Corporation (Freddie Mac)
Federal Housing Administration (FHA)
Federal Housing Finance Agency
Federal Interagency Committee for the
    Management of Noxious and Exotic Weeds
Federal Interagency Committee on Education
Federal Interagency Council on Statistical Policy
Federal Judicial Center
Federal Labor Relations Authority
Federal Laboratory Consortium for Technology Transfer
Federal Law Enforcement Training Center
Federal Library and Information Center Committee
Federal Maritime Commission
Federal Mediation and Conciliation Service
Federal Mine Safety and Health Review Commission
Federal Motor Carrier Safety Administration (FMCSA)
Federal National Mortgage Association (Fannie Mae)
Federal Protective Service
Federal Railroad Administration (FRA)
Federal Register
Federal Reserve System
Federal Retirement Thrift Investment Board
Federal Student Aid Information Center
Federal Trade Commission (FTC)
Federal Transit Administration (FTA)
Federal Voting Assistance Program
Financial Management Service
Fiscal Responsibility and Reform Commission

Fiscal Service, Bureau of
Fish and Wildlife Service (FWS)
Food Safety and Inspection Service
Food and Drug Administration (FDA)
Foreign Agricultural Service
Foreign Claims Settlement Commission
Foreign Service Institute
Forest Service
Fossil Energy
Fulbright Foreign Scholarship Board

General Services Administration (GSA)
Geological Survey (USGS)
Global Affairs (State Department)
Government Accountability Office (GAO)
Government Ethics, Office of
Government National Mortgage Association (Ginnie Mae)
Government Publishing Office
Grain Inspection, Packers and Stockyards Administration

Harry S. Truman Scholarship Foundation
Health Resources and Services Administration
Health and Human Services Department (HHS)
Healthy Homes and Lead Hazard Control Office
Helsinki Commission
Holocaust Memorial Museum
Homeland Security Department (DHS)
House Office of Inspector General
House Office of the Clerk
House of Representatives
Housing Office

Immigration and Citizenship Services
Immigration and Customs Enforcement
Indian Affairs
Indian Arts and Crafts Board
Indian Health Service
Industrial College of the Armed Forces
Industry and Security, Bureau of
Information Resource Management College
Information Resources Center (ERIC)
Innovation and Improvement Office
Inspectors General
Institute of Education Sciences
Institute of Museum and Library Services
Institute of Peace
Inter-American Foundation
Interagency Alternative Dispute
    Resolution Working Group
Interagency Council on Homelessness
Interior Department (DOI)
Internal Revenue Service (IRS)
International Labor Affairs, Bureau of
International Trade Administration (ITA)
International Trade Commission

James Madison Memorial Fellowship Foundation
Japan-United States Friendship Commission
Job Corps
John F. Kennedy Center for the Performing Arts
Joint Board for the Enrollment of Actuaries
Joint Chiefs of Staff
Joint Congressional Committee on Inaugural Ceremonies

Joint Fire Science Program
Joint Forces Command
Joint Forces Staff College
Joint Military Intelligence College
Judicial Circuit Courts of Appeal
Judicial Panel on Multidistrict Litigation
Justice Department (DOJ)
Justice Programs, Office of
Justice Statistics, Bureau of

Labor Department (DOL)
Labor Statistics, Bureau of
Land Management, Bureau of (BLM)
Legal Services Corporation
Library of Congress (LOC)

Marine Mammal Commission
Maritime Administration (MARAD)
Marketing and Regulatory Programs
    (Agriculture Department)
Marshals Service
Mediation and Conciliation Service
Medicaid (CMS)
Medicaid and CHIP Payment and Access Commission
Medicare Payment Advisory Commission
Merit Systems Protection Board
Migratory Bird Conservation Commission
Military Postal Service Agency
Millennium Challenge Corporation
Mine Safety and Health Administration
Minor Outlying Islands

Minority Business Development Agency
Missile Defense Agency (MDA)
Mississippi River Commission
Morris K. Udall and Stewart L. Udall Foundation
Multifamily Housing Office

NOAA Fisheries
National Advisory Council on Indian Education (NACIE)
National AIDS Policy Office
National Aeronautics and Space Administration (NASA)
National Agricultural Statistics Service
National Archives and Records Administration (NARA)
National Assessment Governing Board (NAGB)
National Bipartisan Commission on
    the Future of Medicare
National Board for Education Sciences
National Board of the Fund for the Improvement
    of Postsecondary Education (FIPSE)
National Capital Planning Commission
National Cemetery Administration
National Commission on Fiscal
    Responsibility and Reform
National Constitution Center
National Council on Disability (NCD)
National Council for the Traditional Arts
National Counterintelligence Executive, Office of
National Credit Union Administration
National Crime Information Center
National Criminal Justice Reference Service
National Defense University
National Defense University iCollege

National Drug Intelligence Center
National Economic Council
National Endowment for the Arts
National Endowment for the Humanities
National Environmental Satellite, Data
    and Information Service
National Flood Insurance Program (NFIP)
National Gallery of Art
National Geospatial-Intelligence Agency
National Guard
National Health Information Center (NHIC)
National Highway Traffic Safety Administration
National Indian Gaming Commission
National Institute of Corrections
National Institute of Food and Agriculture
National Institute of Justice
National Institute of Mental Health (NIMH)
National Institute of Occupational Safety and Health
National Institute of Standards and Technology (NIST)
National Institutes of Health (NIH)
National Intelligence University
National Interagency Fire Center
National Labor Relations Board (NLRB)
National Laboratories (Energy Department)
National Marine Fisheries Service
National Mediation Board
National Nuclear Security Administration
National Ocean Service
National Oceanic and Atmospheric
    Administration (NOAA)

National Park Foundation
National Park Service
National Passport Information Center (NPIC)
National Railroad Passenger Corporation (AMTRAK)
National Reconnaissance Office
National Science Foundation (NSF)
National Security Agency (NSA)
National Security Council
National Security Division
National Technical Information Service
National Telecommunications and
　　Information Administration
National Transportation Safety Board
National War College
National Weather Service (NOAA)
Nations Human Settlements Programme
Natural Resources Conservation Service
Natural Resources Revenue, Office of
Northern Command
Northwest Power Planning Council
Northwest Power and Conservation Council
Nuclear Energy, Science and Technology
Nuclear Regulatory Commission (NRC)
Nuclear Waste Technical Review Board

Oak Ridge National Laboratory
Occupational Safety and Health Administration (OSHA)
Occupational Safety and Health Review Commission
Ocean Energy Management, Bureau of (BOEM)
Office for Civil Rights, Department of Education
Office of Administration

Office of Administrative Law Judges
Office of Advisory Committee Management
Office of the Assistant Secretary for Administration
Office of the Assistant Secretary for Policy
Office of the Associate Attorney General
Office of the Attorney Recruitment and Management
Office of the Chief Financial Officer
Office of the Chief Information Officer
Office of the Chief of Protocol
Office for Civil Rights
Office of the Coordinator for Counterterrorism
Office of Communication and Outreach (OCO)
Office of Community Planning and Development
Office of the Comptroller of the Currency
Office of Congressional and Intergovernmental Relations
Office of Compliance
Office of Cybersecurity and Communications
Office of the Deputy Secretary (ODS)
Office of Disability Employment Policy
Office of Deputy Attorney General
Office of the Director of National Intelligence
Office of Dispute Resolution
Office of Domestic Finance
Office of Economic Policy
Office of Elementary and Secondary Education (OESE)
Office of Educational Technology (OET)
Office of Emergency Communications
Office of Employment Discrimination
      Compliant Adjudication
Office of Equal Employment Opportunity

Office of Fair Housing and Equal Opportunity
Office of Faith-Based and Neighborhood Partnerships
Office of Federal Contract Compliance Programs
Office of the Federal Coordinator, Alaska
    Natural Gas Transportation Projects
Office of Federal Detention Trustee
Office of Field Policy and Management
Office of English Language Acquisition, Language
    Enhancement and Academic Achievement for
    Limited English Proficient Students (OELA)
Office of the Federal Register
Office of Federal Student Aid
Office of Financial Stability
Office of the First Lady
Office of Foreign Missions
Office of Fossil Energy
Office of General Counsel (OGC)
Office of Government Ethics
Office of Global Criminal Justice
Office of Healthy Homes and Lead Hazard Control
Office of Hearings and Appeals
Office of the Historian
Office of Housing
Office of Infrastructure Protection
Office of Information Policy
Office of Intergovernmental and Public Liaison
Office of Inspector General
Office of Innovation and Improvement (OII)
Office of Insular Affairs
Office of Intelligence and Analysis

Office of Intelligence, Security and Emergency Response
Office of International Affairs
Office of Justice Programs
Office of Labor-Management Standards
Office of Labor Relations
Office of the Legal Adviser
Office of Legal Counsel
Office of Legal Policy
Office of Legislation and Congressional Affairs (OLCA)
Office of Legislative Affairs
Office of Management and Budget (OMB)
Office of Management Policy, Rightsizing and Innovation
Office of Medical Readiness
Office to Monitor and Combat Trafficking in Persons
Office of National Drug Control Policy (ONDCP)
Office of Natural Resources Revenue
Office of National AIDS policy
Office of National Laboratories
Office of Nuclear Energy (Department of Energy)
Office of Operations Coordination
Office of Overseas Citizens Services
Office of the Pardon Attorney
Office of Policy
Office of Policy Development and Research
Office of Personnel Management (OPM)
Office of Planning, Evaluation and Policy Development
Office of Postsecondary Education
Office of Privacy and Civil Liberties
Office of Presidential Correspondence
Office of Probation and Pretrial Services

Office of Professional Responsibility
Office of Public Affairs
Office of Public and Indian Housing
Office of Public Engagement and
    Intergovernmental Affairs
Office of Refugee Resettlement
Office of Research
Office of Risk Management and Analysis
Office of the Secretary (OS)
Office of Science and Technology Policy
Office of Scientific and Technical Information
Office of Servicemember Affairs
Office of Sex Offender Sentencing, Monitoring,
    Apprehending, Registering and Tracking
Office of Social Innovation and Civic Participation
Office of Small and Disadvantaged Business Utilization
Office of the Solicitor
Office of the Solicitor General
Office of Special Counsel
Office of Special Education and
    Rehabilitative Services (OSERS)
Office of the Staff Secretary
Office of Surface Mining
Office of Survivors Assistance
Office of Special Counsel
Office of Sustainable Housing and Communities
Office of Tax Policy
Office of Terrorism and Financial Intelligence
Office of Thrift Supervision
Office of Transition

Office of Tribal Justice
Office of the United States Global AIDS Coordinator
Office of University Programs
Office of the Vice President
Office of Vocational and Adult Education (OVAE)
Office on Violence Against Women
Office of Weapons of Mass Destruction and Biodefense
Office of Weapons Removal and Abatement
Office of the Comptroller of the Currency (OCC)
Office of the Director of National Intelligence
Office of the Federal Register
Office of the Pardon Attorney
Office of the Under Secretary (OUS)
Office of Urban Affairs
Office of the Worker's Compensation Program
Open World Leadership Center
Out-of-Service Debt Management Center
Overseas Private Investment Corporation
Overseas Security Advisory Council

Patent and Trademark Office
Pacific Command
Pacific Northwest Electric Power and
     Conservation Planning Council
Pardon Attorney, Office of
Parole Commission (Justice Department)
Pension Benefit Guaranty Corporation (PBGC)
Pentagon Force Protection Agency
Pipeline and Hazardous Materials Safety Administration
Policy Development and Research (HUD)
Political Affairs (State Department)

Postal Regulatory Commission
Postal Service (USPS)
Power Administrations
President's Advisory Board on Tribal Colleges
    and Universities (WHITCU)
President's Advisory Board on Historically Black
    Colleges and Universities (WHIHBCU)
President's Council on Physical Fitness and Sports
President's Intelligence Advisory Board
President's Intelligence Oversight Board
Presidio Trust
Prisoner of War/Missing Personnel Office
Privacy and Civil Liberties Oversight Board (PCLOB)
Professional Responsibility Advisory Office
Public Diplomacy and Public Affairs (State Department)
Public and Indian Housing

Radio Free Asia (RFA)
Radio Free Europe/Radio Liberty (RFE/RL)
Radio and TV Marti
Railroad Retirement Board (RRB)
Reclamation, Bureau of
Refugee Resettlement, Office of
Regulatory Information Service Center
Rehabilitation Services Administration
    (Education Department)
Research and Innovative Technology Administration
Risk Management Agency (Agriculture Department)
Rural Business and Cooperative Programs
Rural Development
Rural Housing Service

Rural Utilities Service

Safety and Environmental Enforcement, Bureau of (BSEE)
Saint Lawrence Seaway Development Corporation
Science Office (Energy Department)
Science and Technology Policy, Office of
Scientific and Technical Information, Office of
Secret Service
Securities and Exchange Commission (SEC)
Securities Investor Protection Agency
Selective Service System (SSS)
Senate
Small Business Administration (SBA)
Smithsonian Institution
Social Security Administration (SSA)
Social Security Advisory Board
Southeastern Power Administration
Southern Command
Southwestern Power Administration
Special Forces Operations Command
State Department (DOS)
State Justice Institute
Stennis Center for Public Service
Strategic Command
Substance Abuse and Mental Health Services
    Administration (SAMHSA)
Supreme Court of the United States
Surface Mining, Reclamation and Enforcement
Surface Transportation Board
Susquehanna River Basin Commission

TRICARE Management
Tax Court
Taxpayer Advocacy Panel
Tennessee Valley Authority
Trade and Development Agency
Transportation Command
Transportation Department (DOT)
Transportation Security Administration (TSA)
Transportation Statistics, Bureau of
Treasury Department
Trustee Program

US AbilityOne Commission
US Access Board
US Agency for International Development (USAID)
US Air Force
US Air Force Reserve Command
US Arctic Research Commission
US Army
US Army Corps of Engineers
US Botanic Garden
US Capitol Police
US Capitol Visitor Center
US Central Command (CENTCOM)
US Circuit Courts of Appeal
US Citizenship and Immigration Services
US Coast Guard
US Commission of Fine Arts
US Commission of Fish and Fisheries
US Commission on International Religious Freedom
US Commodity Futures Trading Commission (CFTC)

US Court of Appeals for Veterans Claims
US Customs and Border Protection
US Department of Agriculture (USDA)
US Department of Commerce (DOC)
US Department of Health and Human Services (HHS)
US Department of the Treasury
US Election Assistance Commission (EAC)
US Fleet Forces Command
US Geological Survey (USGS)
US House of Representatives
US Immigration and Customs Enforcement
US International Trade Commission
US Marine Corps
US Military Academy, West Point
United States Agency for International Development
United States Mission to the African Union
United States Mission to ASEAN
United States Mission to the Arab League
United States Mission to the Council of Europe
    (and to all other European Agencies)
United States Mission to International
    Organizations in Vienna
United States Mission to the European Union
United States Mission to the International
    Civil Aviation Organization
United States Mission to the North
    Atlantic Treaty Organization
United States Mission to the Organization for
    Economic Co-operation and Development

United States Mission to the Organization
    of American States
United States Mission to the Organization for
    Security and Cooperation in Europe
United States Mission to the United Nations
United States Mission to the UN Agencies in Rome
United States Mission to the United Nations Office
    and Other International Organizations in Geneva
United States Mission to the United Nations
    Environment Program and the United
    Nations Human Settlements Programme
United States Observer Mission to the United Nations
    Educational, Scientific, and Cultural Organization
US National Central Bureau - Interpol
US Navy
US Patent and Trademark Office
US Postal Service (USPS)
US Senate
US Sentencing Commission
US Trade Representative
US Trade and Development Agency
US Trustee Program
US-CERT (US CERT)
Unified Combatant Commands (Defense Department)
Uniformed Services University of the Health Sciences
United States Antarctic Program
United States Arctic Program
United States Mint
United States Postal Inspection Service

Veterans Affairs Department (VA)
Veterans Benefits Administration
Veterans Day National Committee
Veterans Employment and Training Service (VETS)
Veterans' Employment and Training Service
Vietnam Education Foundation
Voice of America

Washington Headquarters Services
Weather Service (NOAA)
Weights and Measures Division
West Point (Army)
Western Area Power Administration
White House
White House Commission on Presidential Scholars
White House Office of Administration
Women's Bureau (Labor Department)
Woodrow Wilson International Center for Scholars

CHAPTER 7
A VOLUNTARY STATE

FORMING A VOLUNTARY STATE

A republic bound by laws is the best form of the state. The Founding Fathers had that part right. You need law. Most of the law should not have any wiggle room. While some parts of our constitutional republic do not give any wiggle room, other parts give so much wiggle room that the spirit of the republic has been undermined. What do I mean by the "spirit of the republic?" Natural rights were a fundamental theme of individual rights to our Founding Fathers. The individual is often coerced with tools of collectivism. Majority rule, majority voting, and the addition of hundreds of thousands of laws (if not more) that are collectivist versus individualist.

The two major components of a Voluntary State are its formation and its protection. Our focus now will be the formation of a Voluntary State. A Voluntary State is an individualistic state. An individualistic state is a non-aggression state. A non-aggressive state does not use aggression to the individual. Is there goods that are not aggressive to others? Yes, public goods. A public good is a good that is both non-excludable and non-rivalrous in that individuals cannot be effectively excluded from use and where use by one individual does not reduce availability to others.

One of the big debates on any move to a voluntary, individual economy might be how many checks a person has to write. The collectivist would love to continue to have one amount automatically deducted from your paycheck every week. If you were to deny automatic payroll deductions and taxes and let individuals voluntarily choose, you would get a different result. You would increase choices. I don't believe that people would want to write hundreds of checks for every agency and department. That is my point, really. Currently, we have an all or nothing choice for government departments and agencies. That is the government's point, really.

Currently, we have an annual date that taxes are due which is typically around April 15. The time you would normally spend trying to comply with a coercive tax code could be spent deciding your voluntary choices for the government that you want to see. You could simply use a computerized program that shows the prices for each government good or service or department or agency. You can click either yes or no. Any "no" answer might contain an "acknowledge waiver" or something that might have a partial list of possible out of pocket costs for declining to be "insured or covered." I would consider giving people a 3 month grace period of non-payment before an individual is considered uninsured for the government good or service or department or agency in question. There could be something equivalent to gap insurance for government goods and services. The gap insurance would cover you for government goods and services that you might be uninsured for. The cost of the gap insurance might vary on how many goods and services that you have. The more that you cover, the less that gap insurance has to potentially cover, thereby lowering cost. Payments for government services could be paid monthly over the internet, mail or through automatic payroll deductions.

Having any government is a risk to an individual's personal freedom and productivity. I do not take this lightly. It is of paramount importance. I choose to have a government only to preserve my personal safety, property and help resolve conflict with others. My choice of government is hardly a fair choice. It is an all or nothing choice. You can either choose to be a US citizen or renounce your citizenship. There is no middle ground.

Every day private insurance covers home, auto, life and other policy protections. We choose the coverage that we want. Enough people voluntarily choose these protections to safeguard their property that the cost of production is low. Granted, the government requires basic liability insurance for autos, but, in almost all cases comprehensive and collision insurance is also purchased to safeguard your property. If you don't have insurance then you have to pay the full amount of the damages.

PROPERTY

Property is one of the most important concepts of any state. Roger Scruton in *Modern Philosophy* stated that

> It is always necessary to remember that a right of private property is composite. It may involve one or some or all of the following: a right to use; a right to exclude

others from use; a right to sell, barter or
give; a right to hold without using; a right
to accumulate; and a right to destroy. A
philosophical argument might justify one
of those rights without justifying the others.

There are also *duties* and *constraints* associated with
property. No two pieces of land are exactly the same. We
have swamps, beaches, mountains, plains, valleys, etc. You
cannot divide that diverse land in any fair or reasonable way
that I am aware of. Rights, duties and constraints associated
with property are, perhaps, impossibly indivisible.

Let's look at the following example, if A has land and B
does not then by what right does A impose an obligation,
duty or constraint on B to not trespass, violate, vandalize,
use, etc. A's land? B has no land. A has no obligations,
duties or constraints because B has no land. B has a duty
while A has no duty or A has a right while B has a duty.
This relationship is contradictory. Another example, A&B
both have land, but, A has a much larger piece of land with
rivers, lakes, underground aquifers and roads that B needs
for transportation and water needs. It is much more difficult
for B to transport himself around A's property without going
through it and provide himself with water from extended
distances. A&B both have land, but, unequal duty? Another
example, imagine C has no land, but, has the duty not to
aggress against A&B's lands. What does C get in exchange
for his duty not to violate A&B's property rights? Again, we
have a contradictory relationship with C having only duties,
obligations and constraints and A&B having only rights.

In the examples from the previous paragraph, the state

or collective gets money from A&B to buy the land. The state or collective gets property taxes every year from A&B. What does C get directly? What direct exchange took place between C and A, B or the state? None. The state did not directly enrich C in some way. In fact, the state might have spent money from the purchase of the land and the annual property taxes of the land on things that C was directly opposed to.

I am going to start with the premise that land has value. I am also going to go with the premise that we are owners of the land. So, if land has value and we are owners of the land then we have rights to some value of that ownership. Land is currently zoned for commercial, residential, agricultural, etc. Generally, it takes more land to produce agricultural products. Property taxes are lower in agricultural zones. Property taxes are high in commercial zones. It takes only so much space to reside or live in residential areas. If you need more space then you need to provide more production. Property taxes are high in residential areas.

The premises of land having value and that we own the land have to go together. If we say that the land has no value or that we do not own the land then we are led to some ridiculous conclusions. Imagine if one person claimed the whole world as his own and made us all trespassers? If no one owned the land and the land had no value then the one person claiming the world could claim the world and owe us nothing.

Currently, the state determines what is public and what is private property. They collect money as an initial sale and annual taxes on the property. This money is supposed to go to some collective "good." Again, like the examples of A, B and C; there will be unequal rights and duties.

Buying houses or other property that goes on land is a voluntary choice. Land is a limited commodity that has value. We are owners of the land. The more land that you buy and use, the more production in the form of money that needs to be paid to the owners of the land which is the public. How do you pay the public for their land? Annual property fees in a similar fashion to what we have currently. Private property owners usually implicitly or explicitly demand the obligation or duty that we do not trespass, use the resources from their land or violate or destroy the land they have bought from us. We give them the right to use the land and the duty for us not to use the land unless they grant us the right to do so. This is an exchange. An exchange of value for value. Land for money. It is a voluntary exchange.

There has to be something that reflects the value of land and the ownership of the land. I would propose a fee system structured in a similar manner as property taxes. The difference would be the recipient of the fees. Instead of some collective good, (that is a private good, in most cases), the fees would go to the individual owners as an annual check or could be credited against any annual purchases of services of the state. Property owners would be both payer and recipient. As both payer and recipient of property fees, the size and number of properties would determine whether you pay more than you receive.

If you fell on hard times or wanted to sell your property for any reason then you could simply sell and no longer pay property fees and be only a recipient of property fees.

People that we consider citizens would be property owners in the land. They would be eligible to become a recipient of property fees. The more people that are considered citizens eligible for receipt of property fees, the lower the average property fee payment may be. Of course, these added citizens may become property owners themselves and may or may not offset their added numbers with added property fee payers and payments and rising land prices (which could cause other problems such as higher costs of housing, food and other production).

Land is one extreme that can be a private good or a collective good. There are a few things that are *a priori*. For instance, land and water exist without man's production. Food is largely produced by man. Without man-made production of food, we would deplete every land based food item within a year? While objects exist without man's production, we should make some distinctions based on survival. While we might value gold, every ounce of gold could be held by one person in a survival sense. If one person held or could control every gallon of water, that control could be detrimental to the world's survival if the one person in control of the water wanted it to be detrimental. Obviously, we can survive without gold, but, not survive without water.

So, we should have a right to our own income and production. Private property encompasses possibly every man-made object that doesn't violate the equal property rights of others. Where those violations can intersect such as land and water, private property becomes a public matter.

Monopoly of Force

What are the implicit premises with a monopoly of force? A monopoly of force can imply that there could be a need for third party resolution when two or more people have a dispute that may not be able to be resolved by the two or more parties involved. A monopoly of force can imply that there are some issues that have a moral hazard that is so great that intervention is needed. To have a monopoly of force you implicitly suggest that you can improve on the state of nature. I don't believe that we really have any good record of what the state of nature was. We can only assume and suppose based on perceived behaviors and incentives that man may or may not have had in the state of nature.

Any monopoly of force should be based on the premise that no better solutions to the problem(s) exist that we are aware of. We can assume, for instance, that an individual may not feel "safe." A state of nature has no agreed upon rights or laws. There may be implicit "moral crimes," but, no explicit crime because there are no rules, order or law. In this type of environment anything can "go" or be allowed explicitly. We may or may not assume that man can and may exercise this explicit allowance to do anything he wishes. While man may be able to try to do anything he wishes explicitly, his choices and/or outcomes may not be desirable in many cases. To protect one man from another, man began to form groups under rules of conduct.

Majority rule was thought, by the Founding Fathers, to be a necessary solution in the absence of better solutions? I am attempting to show that majority rule is no longer (or ever was) a necessary solution in the absence of better solutions. Monopoly of force appears to be a necessary solution at this time. Monopoly of force over a geographic area seems to occur whether we want it to or not. The basic inequality of man appears to equate into a basic inequality of rule in a state of nature. Since no two people are equal, no two people may have equal "rule" under a state of nature. It is only through agreement that any type of equality of rule can occur. This agreement can come at a cost. That cost can be an agreement over the monopoly of force over a geographic area. No single man that I am aware of ever rose to power without the agreement of other men.

The inequality of man and the moral hazard of man appear to be forces that may never be overcome without some agreement or monopoly of force. Where I am offering a "viable" solution to majority rule over 200 years after the Founding Fathers put it into place, perhaps, 200 years later someone can offer a "viable" solution to monopoly of force. I say "viable" as the rule of kings and dictators or collectivism or other forms of coercion are not "viable" to me. While monopoly of force may be better than "competition of lawless force," (or private protection agencies dispensing their own law or rule) there may be a better solution in the future. There may also be the possibility of the "monopoly of force ruler" operating under bad laws or no laws at all.

Democracy and majority rule seem, to me, to be "worshipped" or revered as a "great" thing. Everyone is told to "vote" and to exercise his "rule." If an individual doesn't vote, many people argue that we will lose some of the "power" of democracy and that a "worse" form of "rule" could step into the void. The monopoly of force should have no "reverence."

If we can increase freedom and preserve property and limited resources without a monopoly of force then let's examine that possibility. I wish that we could all have total freedom of security, safety, property, limited resources, etc. without a monopoly of force.

Monopoly of force departments might start with the assumption that 30 percent of Voluntary State citizens will go "naked" and not voluntarily participate. They would have to base their revenue models on a 70 percent participation rate. This might mean that monopoly of force service providers might ask for a higher price for services per person because of the estimated loss of naked choosers. Monopoly of force allows the ability to assess fees and penalties if monopoly of force service providers are asked or forced to provide services to naked choosers. The naked choosers must pay for the cost of services that they used in fees and a penalty for raising the cost that paying customers had to pay for monopoly of force service providers to provide service. Monopoly of force service providers can also collect fines for people who break the law. Usage fees, fines and penalties might close some or all of the gap lost to the assumption of 30 percent non-participation rate. If the gap is mostly getting filled then the next year the asking price per person should be lowered.

The naked chooser could also get hit three times for not having coverage for basic government services. In the previous paragraph, a naked chooser could pay usage fees and penalties for not having police service coverage. If the naked chooser finds himself in court then he will have to pay court fees and penalties for not having court service coverage. The courts can base their revenue models on the same 70 percent participation rate and similar monopoly of force revenue income from usage, fines and penalties.

Since the monopoly of force appears to be the best solution, we should at least constrain the power of this monopoly of force. The monopoly of force should be based on the non-aggression premise of not aggressing against non-aggressors. Law enforcement is supposed to help reduce aggression. They are often referred to as peace officers that "keep the peace." They are supposed to help provide the means to live in a non-coercive state. They are not supposed to define what an individual's end should be. In the same manner, government entities can provide the means to own or use property without violating others rights to own or use property. It might be nice if philosophy had solved the problem of property? We have unequal property or land and wildlife and unequal use of property, land and wildlife. The federal government and individual states own the lands by default. I say "by default" because we have not divided the United States between around 320 million pieces for each individual citizen. Despite ownership in "common" or "collective," this ownership by the federal government and individual states is not absolute. We are all owners, whatever that means, and should, I believe, have access and ownership to this property, land and wildlife. For example, if all salmon and trout were harvested to extinction by windfall profits that, would be aggression towards the people who could never enjoy a salmon or trout again. The victims of this aggression never received any financial benefit from their ownerships rights of the salmon or trout and could never enjoy any non-financial enjoyment that the fish might provide as a sportsman or otherwise.

Ayn Rand believed that the police, army and the courts are the only justifiable monopoly of force as she stated in *For The New Intellectual*

> The only proper functions of a government are: the police, to protect you from criminals; the army, to protect you from foreign invaders; and the courts, to protect your property and contracts from breach or fraud by others, to settle disputes by rational rules, according to objective law.

The police, army and courts are divided into many departments and agencies. It would be "cleaner" to leave the police, army and the courts as Rand defined it. Though, I believe it is important to try to define in more detail the limits that they should operate. Police, for instance, should be trying to protect the individual rights of individuals and reducing coercion and aggression. Instead, many law enforcement agencies are enforcing collectivist laws on objects themselves. The objects commit the crimes in asset forfeiture or civil forfeiture. The assets are taken because they have committed a crime. Individuals are rarely charged with a crime, but, the assets who committed the crime are confiscated. The absurdity of an object committing a crime is obvious. Still, it continues in law enforcement. Objects such as money, alcohol, tobacco, firearms, drugs, homes, cars, planes, etc. commit crimes and are confiscated or regulated. The regulation and confiscation of objects for crimes or their potential "danger" is still ongoing. Shotguns that were a fraction of an inch "too short" were the catalyst for the death of four people in Ruby Ridge, Idaho.

While it may be preferable for some departments and agencies to have a monopoly of force there is no need or preference for other departments and agencies. The Department of Social Services gives money away as a social safety net. Under coercion, everyone is forced to participate or pay. Any participation would be voluntary under a voluntary government. There would be no monopoly of force. The Department of Social Services would become a charity that voluntarily accepts donations like any other charity does.

The Department of Labor which handles unemployment could pay out an annuity or lump sum based on what you paid into unemployment to date. Or you could forgo these payments and continue with either a "fully-funded" or "Ponzi Scheme" as unemployment could be kept alive on a voluntary basis. Who knows how that would turn out? That's why I say "fully-funded" or "Ponzi Scheme" because who knows how that would turn out. Anyone who voluntarily participated in the Department of Labor might be very risk averse towards handling money in a responsible way or very socialistic or some craziness in between.

The same could be said of the Social Security Administration which handles Social Security. The Social Security Administration would be also be voluntary and have no monopoly of force. Again, people who still want to participate in Social Security would be very risk averse towards money or very Social-istic (pun intended).

Some departments would cease to exist instantly under

a voluntary system such as the Department of Revenue and the Internal Revenue Service. To date, there are around 51 Departments of Social Services for the federal government and every state of the union. The Department of Labor likely has around 51 different departments.

There are hundreds of government departments, agencies, administrations, etc. just on the Federal Level. Each state has hundreds of departments, and with all fifty states, that is a lot of bureaucracy. There will be a few government entities that may need monopoly of force in a Voluntary State. There will be a few government entities that everyone consumes and everyone should pay.

Unfortunately, we have swung the door way open in regards to public goods. We have one man, a literal king, who decides for over 320 million people to declare war or declare a National State of Emergency. We have had a National State of Emergency for over 100 years. Due process, juries, trials can be suspended at will. Martial law, accusations and sentencing of instant "enemies of the state" can be declared. A National State of Emergency retains these powers.

What is the optimal cost and efficacy of our national defense? This takes consensus and cooperation to answer. Our wars and conflicts should have consensus and cooperation, but, often does not.

While virtually every law enforcement agency may have its own atrocities in their history, at least, some agencies have a legitimate scope of operations that can protect individual rights. Later I will provide a list of government entities that if operated in their proper scope could protect individual rights. While there might be something to add as I am not a law enforcement expert or a resource conservation expert; you need to prove it should have a monopoly of force. The list of government entities contained in this chapter are the ones that I can defend in theory if they do not abuse their proper scope of force.

David Friedman in *The Machinery of Freedom* seems, to me, to promote an idea that private protection associations could spontaneously arrive at a supremacy of force relative to local areas. There are also other associations that spontaneously arrive at supremacy of force relative to local areas; they are called street gangs. He doesn't believe that a preexisting monopoly of force is a preferable method of force. A spontaneous supremacy of force or a preexisting monopoly of force can both succeed or fail, I believe. There are so many possible outcomes and so many degrees of success or failure.

I prefer a preexisting monopoly of force in most cases. To me, there is always the hope that we can arrive at a body of rights, duties, morals, law and justice that can guide us to individualism. I feel more uncomfortable leaving things up to private protection associations. It should not be up to the discretion of the private protection associations to accept or ignore a body of law that would exist under a Voluntary State. Which brings justice, under Friedman's model, to arbitration if there is no workable agreement under the private protection associations. Which, to me, begs the question of an evolution of law for private protection associations. If arbitration, under Friedman's anarcho-capitalism, creates guidelines to settle disputes between private protection associations then wouldn't these precedents at some point precede future disputes between private protection associations?

Would arbitrators learn about the precedents of other arbitrators? Would these precedents affect their decisions at
all? Would there be different precedents and guidelines for
different arbitrators? Would rulings be random depending
on the arbitrator? Since each arbitrator is different, each
ruling may be different?

Justice under anarcho-capitalism or apparent limited or
lawless society appears to be a more spontaneous or random
decision to be decided at the moment. This spontaneity can
be a good or bad thing depending on the moment and who is
deciding. Justice under laws and a Voluntary State can reach
an optimal point of justice at least from an individualistic
viewpoint. That justice under a Voluntary State could grow
past the optimal point of individualism to collectivism?
Individualism could be marginalized through loopholes
or incremental collectivist measures? The Voluntary State
can theoretically "lock-in" an optimal set of laws. Private
protection agencies can vary with the people operating the
agencies and the people arbitrating for the agencies.

When your "product" is protection and your tools are
firearms and force, keeping costs down and profits up may
not always be an exercise in clever diplomacy. It could be
an exercise in fear and brutality for people outside of your
agency. The fear and brutality may act as a deterrent against
crime and serve as an impetus to join the locally dominant
private protection agency bully. It may be thought, by some,
to be better to join the bully than be bullied. Isn't majority
rule a bully or be bullied situation? Your income, through
taxes, are determined by a majority. Better to bully through
majority vote than be bullied as a losing voter? Third parties

represent far more than 1-2 percent of voter opinion. Voters don't want to lose in an election even if their views are not represented well or even hardly at all?

Competing private protection agencies would likely have mob and cartel influences as these activities could be profitable for a few well-armed individuals to divide the power and profits even after they might provide "protection" to their paying "constituents." The Voluntary State might have politician influence as politicians might try to work their way into the remaining government agencies that are voluntarily supported. Politicians might try to get or create jobs as consultants or publicists for government agencies. Politicians might try to expand the influence and money coming into the remaining government agencies. Without taxation, damage from politicians, should be greatly muted as it should be more difficult to abuse and corrupt a government agency that is voluntary and may be competing against other government agencies for voluntary funds.

Areas of conflict that should inevitably lead to a spontaneous arbitration under anarchy are better served, I believe, by a preexisting monopoly of force. If monopoly of force outgrows an "optimal" state then there are a few things that we can do as I describe in the Move To The Voluntary State chapter. Under anarcho-capitalism even if we "reset" back to a lawless or conditional state of nature, we could be subject to more and more increasing arbitrary and absolute decisions by arbitrators and private protection associations. You could have a situation where you have a near state of nature and have a near state of rule similar to a king or a dictator. You could be "obeying" the nature of anarchy and have a virtual dictatorship. Under laws and a Voluntary State, to achieve a virtual dictatorship you would have to break the law or change the law and have an Involuntary State to achieve a virtual dictatorship. Under anarcho-capitalism you would only have to ignore voluntary market forces. I like the fact that a preexisting monopoly of force can allow you to define an optimal point of individualism through laws and justice. Under anarcho-capitalism, you could define a marginal point of voluntary market forces, but, you could not define an optimal point of laws or justice to secure or define those voluntary market forces under a lawless state of anarcho-capitalism.

How is the possible abuse of force in a democracy, anarcho-capitalism and the Voluntary State put in check? The short answer is that power can be abused and cannot be entirely put in check. The profit motive has potential problems in an anarcho-capitalist government. A lack of courts, laws, and prisons are problems concerning peace and justice. A lack of management for non-profitable land and wildlife and a lack of resource conservation and management are problems concerning our natural resources and environment. Competing private protection associations may not play by a fair set of rules. These associations may even play by a dangerous set of rules especially if there are no preset laws and arbitrators that can be paid off. While you can pay off judges in democracy or the Voluntary State, judges still have laws and judicial review that monitor and guide what the judge is supposed to do. Arbitrators have free reign and discretion under anarcho-capitalism. While arbitrators could be agreed upon by both sides, a strong bully association might not agree to a mutual arbitrator. A strong, bully association might have their own paid or pet arbitrators. These bully associations may have the power to force others to use their arbitrator(s). Under anarcho-capitalism, without any courts or laws that can be enforced by a central authority, might makes right as they say. The Voluntary State can have potential problems as fines and fees can be beyond "reasonable." Though, the profit motive may not protect against fraud, theft and guilty verdicts of justice influenced or perpetrated by stronger bully associations.

Here is a list of government entities that could have a proper scope if they do not abuse this monopoly of force power.

Law Enforcement:
Police Departments
Fire Departments
National Defense (Army, Air Force, Navy, Marines)
Border Patrol
Coast Guard
US Immigration and Customs
Department of Agriculture
Center for Disease Control

Limited Resources or Property Protection:
Fish & Wildlife
Forest Service
National Park Service
Department of Transportation

Justice:
Courts

Bureau of Prisons
Patents & Copyrights
Cash Redemption Department (it would be a new
    department)

Regulation:
Federal Aviation Administration
Department of Motor Vehicles
Department of Transportation's National Highway Traffic
    Safety Administration

MONOPOLY OF FORCE LAW ENFORCEMENT

The police handle the interior security. The Border Patrol handles our border with Mexico and Canada. The Coast Guard handles our coastal waters. The Navy handles longer range waters. The Air Force handles the air. We are covering the geographical perimeters and interior. It is basic security with most of the listed agencies. Some of these agencies could be used for an "offensive defense." In this case, you are "defensive," but, you are not fighting over your own soil. I also included US Immigration and Customs and the Department of Agriculture. The reason for this is because threats to security can come in the form of disease, firearms, fruit or other potentially dangerous objects. Unlike the BATF or the DEA who might go after alcohol or marijuana (in much of the country), I am talking about objects and their placement. Tainted fruit in non-native areas. Firearms on an airplane. There is a huge distinction in terms of practicality and individual rights. The placement of an object can be the difference between an imminent threat and basic freedom.

Police and fire departments are monopoly of force allowances for good reason. You usually want to limit the amount of people waving guns around or people who could get trapped in a burning building. Also, there is redundancy or extra cost of having multiple police and fire departments. Also, jurisdiction and assessing any costs would be complications. We are trying to reduce the size and cost of government, not create more government.

There is some free rider effect for "naked" choosers who didn't pay for police services, but, got a deterrent effect that might have helped the "naked" choosers stay safe. The "naked" free riders will likely need police services at some point and will have to pay a large fees and penalties when they do use police services. Free riders may also get their home or property saved from fire because of other "paying customers" so to speak. Free riders may not be so lucky if their house or property starts a fire and they have to pay out of pocket costs, fees and any possible court costs.

Defense is a difficult case. Defense cannot be excluded in its use. Everyone is using it whether they want to or not. Property ownership is a choice as I explained earlier in the property section of this chapter. Providers of defense do not have a choice. They would be coerced to provide a service to free riders that they could not easily individually charge for when it is used. Most goods and services can be individually consumed. The individual consumption can be measured and priced. Individual consumption cannot be measured and priced in regards to defense. It cannot be excluded. How do you price an F-16 flying over Wisconsin? Do Wisconsin people pay because of the flight over their land? If the threat is nationwide then having only Wisconsin pay does not seem fair. If an enemy launched a missile at us, would we charge those who might have been hit by the missile? Do we guess where an enemy might have attacked and charge those people? It would become ever more complicated as you have variable population distributions and variable threat levels across the state and the rest of the world.

You can exclude yourself from the roads (driving). You can hope and pray that you never have to use police or fire. With enough effort, risk and luck you can exclude yourself from almost everything. You can choose to buy almost every state service. National defense is one thing that you cannot exclude yourself from. Can you classify national defense as self-defense? Self-defense allows you to purchase firearms and other defensive weapons and deterrents. The actual threat may be self-defense. National defense may not have an immediate or imminent threat at the time you prepare for it.

National defense (Army, Air Force, Navy, Marines, Border Patrol, Coast Guard, National Guard, US Immigration and Customs, Department of Agriculture, Center for Disease Control) governmental entities could be argued as self-defense in part of their functions. There are many threats from bullets, bombs, chemical agents, biological terrorism, imported foods and fruits that could come across our national borders.

Anarcho-capitalist national defense has a small possibility of working. A certain number of people might voluntarily pay for local defense in their local area. Local areas could contract with other local areas until a national size defense was attained. On the other hand, people may not voluntarily pay for local defense. Local defense agencies might not ever patch together a viable national defense.

Does my right to self-defense or national defense have primacy over another person's right to his own income? Self-defense has primacy. First, my life could be put in jeopardy without a proper defense. Second, for my own safety, I could have forced emigration to a safer country because of a lack of national defense. This emigration would be a harm that is much greater in cost per person than the cost per person for a national defense. Third, remember that National defense is something that cannot be excluded. The inability to exclude makes national defense a unique, singular case. Primacy of self-defense is not an open door to exploit the right to income by any numerical majority or congressional king. The right to income is one of our most basic and strongest rights. Only self-defense and our own life has primacy over the right to income.

I have argued why that there will be coercion involved no matter what we do. Whether we have national defense or do not have national defense might be coercion for some people on either side of the argument. The inability to avoid coercion is why I can still talk of mandatory costs or fees in a Voluntary State and not sound oxymoronic about it.

There is a distinction between the CDC and the FDA. The CDC might be facing an imminent threat of epidemic or pandemic proportions. The CDC can be a part of our national defense from international manmade biological weapons and terrorism. Are lives lost during drug trials? The government does make exceptions, at times, for life and death urgent need before the end of the drug trial. Could life be saved if these life and death circumstances were left to the doctor and patient to weigh the risks instead of the FDA? The FDA might be a "wash" at best. How many drugs were not developed because they would be created at a loss because of FDA trials and patent issues?

Ideas can be measurable for an idea such as a "brand" that may have many ideas surrounding its concept(s) and founding. When a brand is copied or sold under a false identity, the sales can be tracked to show the sales results based on the "branded idea(s)." Measurable sales can also be tracked around copyrights and patents. Developing an idea which can translate into a product can involve billions of dollars if the idea and product development is beneficial enough. There can be billions of dollars at stake if some ideas and products were copied or stolen. If stealing ideas and products are theft then there is aggression involved in their theft. If aggression is involved then justice needs to step in on behalf of the victims of aggression.

Justice can be a difficult task. Judging aggression in the world of ideas is not real easy. On one hand, ideas can be protected so that we have an incentive to generate a greater number of beneficially developed ideas and products. On the other hand, we can cause aggression by protecting or attempting to protect ideas and product development. If we prevent in part or in whole, an idea and/or product from being copied then we might see aggression in the way of higher prices in a possible monopoly type environment.

These higher monopoly prices can have more possible aggression if this idea/product is a vital part of other products that have no known replacement or, at least, very high priced replacement.

Yet, isn't the point of developing ideas and products—to become irreplaceable? To develop ideas and products that are better in some way than other ideas and products. To make money on these ideas and products.

Still, if a product is being protected and the protectors pay a higher price as a result of providing the protection then is the higher price of the product aggression also? Do we want to make obligations and create rights? Rights and justice may have to sort some things out regarding ideas and products. Patents, copyrights, etc. should exist in the Voluntary State if we rightly see the importance of obligations, rights and laws surrounding ideas.

I believe that we should have rights around patents, copyrights, etc. Patent rights should be rights that have a lifespan that pertains to the people who had the ideas. Patented ideas should not have protection that extends many generations like kings and royal bloodlines. If a person or business wants to continue to succeed they might have to continue to improve their ideas or come up with new ideas. Henry Ford was one of the first creators of early automobiles with the Model T Ford. What if Ford had a monopoly on the automobile and everyone could only drive a Model T Ford. Of course, to keep Fords on the road a lot of new ideas and new vehicles had to occur over the last hundred years or so.

Copyrights may have longer protection than patents,

but, the protection for copyrights may be minimal from day one. Some copyrights may only involve citing the source of the work that you copied, paraphrased or were influenced by.

I believe that there should be a patent for "development" for, say, 10 years. A patent monopoly of "sales" of 15 years from any date of FDA approval could follow the "development" patent. Currently, we lump the development, sales and approval together as a single patent. So, if the FDA rejects the drug multiple times then there might be only a couple years left of patent monopoly protection until competitors can make generic versions of the same drug. The successful completion of drug approval should be rewarded or incentivized with 15 years from the date of approval. This would vastly increase the profitability of creating more drugs and more chances to save lives.

The FDA could still exist as a voluntary entity. It would add credibility to a drug's release and sales. The FDA could have market prices for its services offering up different plans such as a "decision" plan or "consultation" plans. A decision plan could involve where the FDA helps lay out the drug trials that it wants to see such as Phase 1, Phase 2, Phase 3, etc. After the conclusion of the trials, the FDA will give a decision on whether the drug is approved or not approved by the FDA. Consultation plans might be food and drugs that had some "consultation" from the FDA. These plans would raise upfront costs of getting a drug approved, but, if patents were granted for 15 years *after* FDA approval then these costs would really pay off well over the extra years of exclusive sales.

On the other hand, we don't want drug companies

sitting on patents that others could use to save lives or improve the quality of life. So, if there is no FDA approval after 10 years then there is no 15 year extension after any approval which keeps the whole process under a 25 year maximum patent life. If it takes longer than 10 years to get FDA approval or there is no attempt at FDA approval then you would be limited to 15 years total which would leave you with less than 5 years of exclusive sales after any approval. These measures provide incentives to develop the patented drug and get FDA approval.

The FDA might have "proxy" monopoly of force in certain instances. If the police or the courts determined that there were food or drug safety issues then the police or the courts could *initiate* the entry of the FDA. The FDA could then use "proxy" monopoly of force that was *initiated* from the police or the courts. The police or the courts are likely acting on indirect aggression such as complaints, injury, illness and death regarding the safety of food and drugs with any initiation of entry of the FDA.

MONOPOLY OF FORCE LIMITED RESOURCES

Here again, we run into unsolved philosophical problems. Who owns the land? How is use of land determined? No two pieces of land are exactly the same. Obviously, land varies greatly between mountains, deserts, lakes, rivers, plains, valleys, etc. We have different prices for different pieces of land. We even zone the land in different ways. We have agricultural, commercial and residential zoning as a few examples. We acknowledge different value and different usage for different plots of land. Obviously, it takes more land to feed a family for a year than provide housing for a family for a year especially with any varied diet. Agriculture should get some different consideration. Instead, we often charge grazing fees as an example. Wild animals can eat for free, but, ranchers trying to grow food must pay a fee to the government. If ranchers have to pay grazing fees to graze their cattle, then, this adds to the cost of meat. Would I rather pay less per pound for meat or have the Bureau of Land Management have nicer toys and power?

The "example" from the previous paragraph, if you guessed, is at the heart of the Bundy Standoff where the Bureau of Land Management tried to confiscate around 300 head of cattle for past due grazing fees. Is the Bureau of Land Management protecting the means of cattle usage? Are they preventing extinction of a species? No and No.

The more difficult cases are ones where you run into the free rider problem and other obstacles. Roads are a tough one where you run into the property obstacle. Who owns the roads? Do you have private roads paid by private individuals? If you have private roads by private individuals you create a huge problem. You are giving these private individuals a monopoly of force in many cases. In many towns and cities roads are very limited. There isn't land and space to have "competing" roads. There is often one road possible to certain areas. If a private individual or group owns the road then they can gain a private gain on toll charges for what should be a public road. They can gain many multiples of cost and charge whatever they want for as long as they want. Any deviation would be a violation of the individual rights of the owner. On the other hand, it is a violation of other people's individual rights to pay a coerced toll charge.

We could leave the roads to the Voluntary State and have the Department of Transportation as a sort of non-profit monopoly for roads. If the free rider problem became a problem then the Department of Transportation could install checkpoint scanners or booths like private toll roads do now. The registration tags that currently validate registration could validate payment to the state for transportation. Violators would pay much more than if they had, say, an annual pass like we do for registration tags.

Some people might believe that we should just make payment for roads mandatory or force people to pay and skip the checkpoints and tags that could be scanned at speed as you pass through the checkpoints. We have an individual right to our own income. Some people just use public transportation, others may be blind, aged or otherwise hindered from operating a motor vehicle. Some people may have suspended driving licenses or choose to walk or use non-motorized transportation. If we don't allow people the choice to pay then we have violated their right to choose and their right to their own income.

I do believe that people would voluntarily create a social safety net to prevent widespread starvation in the United States. We already provide this assistance outside of our borders internationally through voluntary charities. Animals on the other hand, are a different story. We have already proven that we can fish and hunt animals to extinction or near extinction. Our human species has caused the extinction of 322 animals according to the journal *Science*.

How do we handle a public good such as clean air? If a producer that is producing has the right to produce, but, affected individuals nearby have a right to clean air then how do we handle these conflicting rights? How about things that are limited resources, but, not public goods such as water, mineral and land rights?

If an area or nation has an advantage against other areas, it can often be a short-term advantage. The United States had a technological advantage for a few decades? We "imported" over 20 million immigrants through lax security, enforcement and naturalization. For a while the economy had a relative equilibrium with very low unemployment. Jobs could be had relatively easily. Companies located manufacturing hubs overseas for products with little or no transportation costs relative to a percentage of their cost. Examples include, telecommunication, phone and internet customer service, manufacturing phones and electronics. Over time, the competition learned our methods and technology and even developed their own. With their higher populations, the competitors could reduce labor costs.

What did the United States do with this technological advantage? We created a 17 plus trillion dollar national debt, bought bigger homes, second homes, boats, second cars, etc. Very few saved money and very few kept their bigger homes and toys. Very few saw our technological advantage was a short term thing. As investors, these macro events are all around us with most of the answers or at least most of the clues in plain sight. We hit a technological zenith around the year 2000 when prices of stocks were over one hundred dollars a share with no earnings. I pulled all my meager savings out of the stock market because of the price to earnings ratios. I was a year early, but, I still avoided a 25-50 percent or more loss.

In 2008, like most people, I noticed housing prices rising rapidly and easier credit flowing like cheap wine. Despite this warning sign, I believed that houses were "too big to fail" and housing prices might flatten out eventually after a while. Unlike price to earnings ratios that are easily and readily available, derivatives were sort of a hidden shadow banking activity hidden from the public. After the 2008 banking and housing crisis, private and public websites and agencies started tracking and distributing derivatives data and information. Articles, government reports, etc. started discussing and explaining derivatives.

Who pays for the imported labor of 20 million immigrants? Who pays for the lower wages that Americans now experience? Greater supply of labor lowers the price demand or wage of labor. Economics 101—price, supply, equilibrium. Now it might be argued that higher wage jobs were created to manage or help low wage jobs such as managers, technicians, etc. It could even be argued that jobs were created to service the additional influx of immigrant labor. Some of these jobs could have survived the 2008 housing crisis. Out of those surviving jobs, how many people lost their homes due to lower hours worked, loss of spouse job, etc.?

We are left with over 17 trillion dollars in debt. We have rising healthcare and education costs as some believe we have an obligation to provide free healthcare and education in a public goods or other type of argument. The additional

20 million "imported" people to help fuel our technological advantage are now a rising debt obligation. Healthcare, education, Social Security, Medicare, etc. are now to be provided to our "imports" whether they are employed or not. Are the companies who benefitted from the importation of labor going to pay for the added cost or the loss of our jobs or homes? No. The correlation between the companies who benefitted from the "imports" and the taxpayers who pay for their services goes mostly unnoticed by the general public.

The real "unseasonally adjusted" unemployment numbers include workers that haven't found work after 6-12 months. If a person hasn't found work after unemployment runs out than the person is labelled "stopped looking for work." The government no longer counts this person. If we include seasonal adjustment, underemployment and the people whose unemployment runs out then you get what the Bureau of Labor Statistics call the "U-6." The main headline number is the "U-3" number which is much lower. The U-6 rate is often double the rate of the U-3 number.

The starting point of the economy is recognition of limited resources, limits to any advantages or innovation and limited time to use any resource or advantage. As investors, our job is to recognize the supply and demand of resources and how this will affect the price over varying time frames. Resources can be commodities, knowledge, processes, capital, land, labor etc. Remember, equilibrium is one point in time and one supply and demand "intersection." Equilibrium is dynamic and always changing.

Monopoly of force and property are obstacles. If you decline to fund and support a government agency or department, are you still bound by the government agency or department? If you didn't choose the Fish & Game Department does that mean that you can hunt and fish all that you want? Should the Fish & Game Department have the monopoly of force for all fish and game? At this point, the government and states own the land. Individual people or businesses can buy land from the state or government. In fact, we currently pay property taxes on the "right" or "privilege" to use the lands. The city, state or federal government can decide that they would like to use your property in a different way than you are. They can use eminent domain and, perhaps after paying you a "fair market" price, take your land.

There is a profit motive for beekeeping, zoo keeping, fish hatcheries, keeping cattle, sheep, goats, etc. There are many more fish and wildlife that could be kept for a profit motive. An anarcho-capitalist might argue that natural resources are protected by the profit motive. An anarcho-capitalist might implicitly be stating that limited resources that need to be saved will be saved by the profit motive. Is there a profit motive to stop poaching in vast wilderness expanses, rivers, lakes and vast oceans? Poaching is not a crime under a true anarcho-capitalist view? A true anarcho-capitalist would not give the state the monopoly of force for limited natural resources. The Voluntary State monopoly of force government agencies are anarcho-capitalist in the sense that no one is taxed or forced to pay for their existence. These monopoly of force government agencies become "state-like" when someone voluntarily commits a crime and poaches or takes limited natural resources. We could debate what might be considered poaching or a crime. We could debate the number or type of fish and animals that can be harvested or hunted or the price or amount of water or other commodities that can be used. We can debate the amount of commodities that could be exported to other countries. While we can debate quantities of harvest, hunting and exports, we should not be debating whether poaching or outstripping limited natural resources could be a crime.

It is your choice to buy services through the Fish & Wildlife, Forest Service, National Park Service and the Department of Transportation. These governmental agencies have a monopoly of force. Hunters, fishermen, sportsmen, etc. would likely be better off voluntarily paying beforehand instead of waiting to get caught violating these department's fish or wildlife quotas and guidelines.

MONOPOLY OF FORCE JUSTICE

I think it is important to have some discussion around justice. There is what might be called state justice and market justice. First, let's look at state justice. The state is an agent of society for the punishment of crime. Even some of the most ardent minimal government thinkers advocate courts or third party arbitration of some manner. Implicitly this implies that there is a value(s) that have primacy over freedom and the right to our own income? We might imply that these value(s) include self-defense and justice. Self-defense in the sense that some criminals pose a proven threat to the general public. Justice in the sense of revenge or retribution for the crime they are convicted of. Imprisonment implies that there is a higher value than freedom, otherwise, we could never take away someone's freedom?

Next, let's look at market justice. Andrew J. Galambos in *Sic Itur Ad Astra* has a market version of imprisonment. He envisions a society where money is in the form of credit. Criminals are ostracized from the free exchange of money or credit with other people. The criminal's credit is shut down. There is no prison in the normal sense. Just an ostracism from society. Morris and Linda Tannehill in *The Market for Liberty* call prisons a "'school for crime,' where he'll learn to do the job of robbing you more successfully next time." Market justice is not interested in revenge or rehabilitation. It is interested in retribution or repayment for injuries. Judges and juries are replaced with arbitrators whose livelihood depends on accuracy and reputation via the profit motive.

Market justice can only compensate victims monetarily after the fact. In stalking cases, the same victim may be repeatedly victimized. Market justice might argue that market justice can prevent crime better than state justice. For new criminal offenders market justice prevention superiority may or may not be true. For repeat offenders market justice prevention superiority is clearly false. Once an offender is convicted under state justice, he is incarcerated in an actual prison. He is not allowed to repeat his theft, murder or rape for many years or ever again.

Under market justice we allow repeat thieves, rapists and murders to roam the streets (or in a hopeful Galambos exile) without putting them in prison. This is unconscionable to me. The main concern to the Tannehills appears to be whether the criminal is employed so that he can provide a monetary retribution to the victim. After the criminal settlement for the crime, the criminal can seek a better job or a second job to pay for his future repeated criminal activities of assault, rape, stalking and murder or other offenses. This is a ridiculous possibility.

If a victim wants monetary retribution then the victim can sue in civil court under the state justice system. A victim usually wants criminal retribution that is non-monetary. It takes very little imagination or thought to see that monetary retribution is insufficient in almost every case. I would love to have a conclusion where we don't need the state. I won't advocate allowing people to be repeatedly robbed, raped and murdered to achieve that end.

If you have an ostracized criminal as Galambos proposes that is cut off from society then what are some of the more likely scenarios that could unfold? Will the criminal just meekly curl up in a ball in the fetal position and calmly wait to starve to death? Will he seek an alliance with a gang or group of criminals who are either self-sufficient past criminals or future criminals in the making? Will he find a way to kidnap a person in a less technically secure setting than Galambos's technically creative home defense? Galambos assumption of safety as a superior defense may have its flaws. For example, what might be considered the most important defense system in the United States is purposely decades behind current technology. Our missile defense system is based on non-computerized analog technology so that it cannot be defeated by hackers in a computerized attack.

I think it is clear that ostracized criminals will not

meekly await death and their criminal activity will increase and intensify. It is common knowledge that an animal is most dangerous when they are cornered. Ostracizing criminals is like cornering a dangerous animal.

Someone might argue that freedom is the highest value, but, you somehow can "lose" your freedom by acts of crime, violence or murder. I would think it might be better to say that freedom was superseded or that self-defense and justice have primacy over freedom. Market justice has freedom superseded or lost. It is permissible to have criminals make monetary retribution under market justice. Monetary retribution is a loss of freedom. You give up your time or refrain or abstain from certain goods or services because of loss of money due to market justice monetary retribution. So, in essence, according to market justice it is OK to give up a little or some freedom for committing crime, but, not your complete time and freedom as state justice and being incarcerated in a prison would demand.

What is considered a strength by market justice advocates can also be a weakness when it comes to the profit motive. An arbitrator usually decides a market justice case when two opposing associations cannot agree to a settlement. The arbitrator might get paid a percentage of any guilty monetary settlement or verdict. There could be a monetary profit motive to have guilty verdicts for the arbitrator. Without a state justice courtroom or jury, a market justice arbitrator can avoid a jury and might get a percentage of any monetary settlement or verdict without anyone such as a jury to oppose him. Even if there is no formal percentage monetary settlement, it is easier to commit fraud in market justice with only one person (arbitrator) involved than in state justice with a judge and a jury of 12 people and laws and judicial review. Under state justice, the judge and jury are not paid a settlement percentage to influence guilty verdicts. State justice judges and juries are inclined to let the facts of the case dictate the verdict and are more resistant than market justice to fraud.

Market justice breaches freedom, but, not to the point that it will allow the state to enter. Market justice would rather allow thieves, rapists and murderers to roam the streets than give the state any possible chance to exist or grow. If denying the existence or growth of the state was the standard of value or supreme value in a value hierarchy for Galambos or the Tannehills then they should have just stated that clearly and tried to defend it.

It becomes clear that there are conditions where you can lose freedom or where freedom is conditional or subordinate. By allowing criminals a free pass to repeat their crimes, market justice is sanctioning coercion in an obscenely negligent way.

The Bureau of Prisons needs a monopoly of force to imprison court determined criminals. There has to be a monopoly of the way that crime is handled. If a crime is committed then the accused person is either innocent or guilty. The accused is either set free or imprisoned. We could make prisoners pay for the cost of the Bureau of Prisons if it were at all possible. Prisoners, for the most part, cannot earn income unless we want to set them free to roam the streets to repeat their crimes and earn an income as in the market justice model.

If we agree that the Bureau of Prisons is necessary and cannot be excluded then the courts are a necessary part of the prison system. Entry and egress will be based on the courts. I think this is pretty self-explanatory. What I want to focus on now would be a newly created department called the Cash Redemption Department or something along that line.

Currently, we have money that is fiat and has no parity linked to any specific backing. Money is production. It is a promise of actual production. One way to make money have more productive value is to have money come from a productive source. If people voluntarily pay for government services from their own productive income then the government funding comes from a productive source. People had to produce something to earn the money that they give to the government. Another way to make money have more productive value is to have money backed by gold and other commodities. For example, gold can set the parity that other commodities follow. The parity value could be held in gold, silver, platinum, copper, oil or natural gas. As long as the value of the dollars correlate to the commodities held in reserve. Currently, government can simply raise the debt ceiling on our national debt and create money without producing anything in return or create "non-produced money."

The Cash Redemption Department would exist to stabilize the money supply. The mandate of the Cash Redemption Department would be different than, say, the Federal Reserve. The Federal Reserve, which is a band of thieves that need to become extinct in their use, has a dual mandate. The Federal Reserve has a 2 percent inflation (theft) target and about a 5.5 percent unemployment target. Under a healthy economy, prices and inflation should head down or deflate. The Federal Reserve and the growth of the money supply has turned deflation into inflation and pocketed much of the difference in the hands of the elite and the 1 to 5 percent who have around 40 percent or more of the wealth in our country. Of course, not all of the elite 1 to 5 percent have used some of the market manipulations in the Market chapter of the book or exploited the excess labor market through immigration.

The Cash Redemption Department would oversee the money supply. Their mandate is zero percent money supply growth or decline. They are to maintain a static money supply. They are replacing lost or destroyed coin and currency in circulation. They can specialize in helping catch criminal counterfeit rings and set security standards for our money. They would oversee the Mints that print money and decide if they need to be reduced or eliminated in size and function. Like derivatives, only a small percentage of cash actually changes hands. The Federal Reserve and the government has manipulated how and what they count as price inflation. The Cash Redemption Department would audit the gold used to back our currency and the cash in circulation. They would maintain a static zero percent money supply growth or decline—prices would either inflate or deflate. Most of the time, there would be price deflation. The Federal Reserve has tried to train everyone that inflation is the norm. There still will be price bubbles, but, they will be shortened and less severe than the Federal Reserve debt and money supply fueled bubbles.

Anything that we do with the money supply that does not involve inflation could easily cause stock prices to go down in the short-term. Many economists and politicians do most of their work, it seems, trying to improve the stock market versus the economy. We may never be able to improve the value of money without a short-term dive in prices. As long as we measure most things by rising stock prices then we may have an impossible time making a positive long term improvement in the value of money.

What happens to the auto, housing and personal loan and other credit markets without "free money" from the Federal Reserve to be repaid at around 1 percent? Currently, banks get a government monopoly in the form of "free money" from the government. The Federal Reserve Discount Window has three rates; primary (0.75 percent), secondary (1.25 percent) and seasonal (0.15 percent). The Federal Reserve Target Rate of zero to 0.25 percent. Private Citizens or investors cannot get free money from the government in these windows. If this bank monopoly were broken then investors could enter the market with increased numbers of investors and potential profitability. Investors could invest in REITs (Real Estate Investment Trusts), mortgage pools, funds or companies that could lend money to home buyers. Without the Federal Reserve "fronting" all the risk, interest rates (on loans and credit) would likely rise if investors were to take on this role. The interest rate on money is supposed to stay at a non-inflationary zero percent target in our current Involuntary State. The interest rate that investors, funds, and now banks operating on any of their own cash reserves would again likely be higher in the Voluntary State as the Federal Reserve is not putting credit markets awash in "cash liquidity" or diminished risk. Interest rates will likely rise as there is more risk to everyone involved in the credit markets. Higher interest rates and the removal of bank monopoly can create higher potential profitability for investors to create new classes of ETFs (Exchange Traded Funds), REITs, etc. for different grades or credit statuses. Deflation, a reduced governmental cost based on the voluntary choice to pay for fewer government departments and higher interest on retirement type investments such as bonds, certificates of deposit, etc. should vastly outweigh any higher costs for loans based on any higher interest rates.

Another impact to markets would be the non-payment of the national debt. The Voluntary State would not be paying off the national debt as voluntary cooperation and donations would be unlikely. This would cause a backlash and hurt the markets initially in the short run. In the long run the world would have to come to an understanding. An understanding that, hopefully, involves the end of drone strikes and democracy for the United States. The United States will, hopefully, not be the policeman and father figure to the rest of the world. We can admit the error of our ways and apologize for not paying the national debt. We can state that we are no longer a democratic nation that borrows from other countries. We, hypocritically believed we should impose our way of government and way of life through wars, drone strikes, sanctions, etc. on others. If we had been the perfect democratic nation then we would not have borrowed money in the first place. We could stress to the world that we will no longer have national debt in the Voluntary State.

By definition, national debt should not be possible in the Voluntary State. There would be no government bonds to sell in exchange for debt. Government bonds should no longer exist in a Voluntary State. We can state to countries that our dollar and markets are more stable because they are not fueled by inflation and debt. Countries might use some of the same tools against us that we have, ironically, used against them, namely, sanctions. We would have short-term pains, but, long term prosperity with no national debt, no taxes and a strong national currency (without high inflation) as I will show in the next couple paragraphs.

So, again, if we agree that the Bureau of Prisons is necessary and cannot be excluded then the courts are a necessary part of the prison system. The Cash Redemption Department deals with theft which is a court matter. The theft of our money. From 1914 through 2014 or 100 years, we had a 3.34 percent average inflation rate (100 Years of Inflation, *LBB Magazine*, April 8 2014). Or if you prefer you could use 3.22 percent average inflation over 100 years (Tim McMahon, Long Term U.S. Inflation, *Inflationdata. com*, April 1 2014). If you prefer government numbers, you could try to crunch some numbers and should still come up with a number in the 3 percent range (One hundred years of price change: the Consumer Price Index and the American inflation experience, Bureau of Labor Statistics, United States Department of Labor, April 2014). I will use 2X the 3.34 percent which equals 6.68 percent or just round up to 7 percent. *Price deflation, compounding* and *masking* would easily give us the 6.68 percent that I rounded up to 7 percent for a rounder number. I feel justified in rounding up because if you look at the excluded items like cars, oil, seasonal items and other excluded or ignored items I am likely very conservative for rounding up to 7 percent. Most importantly, perhaps, is to remember that the 3.34 percent average interest rate *compounds* every year. If we take ten thousand dollars and multiply it by 3.34 then we would get 33,400 or thirty three thousand four hundred dollars. If we *compound* the 3.34 percent average interest rate then we get 267,205 or two hundred sixty seven thousand two hundred five dollars. The compounding effect is a multiple of 8 times more money or 8 times the price increase because of compounding.

This is still not enough to show the price increases that we see over 100 years. Even if we take the simple 3.34 over 100 years which equals 334 percent and add in a multiple of 8 which equal 800 percent, we still *only* get a 1,134 percent increase. McMahon, in the article from the last paragraph, stated that we get 2,275 percent inflation. The 2,275 percent inflation is just over double the amount of our 1,134 percent increase. So, again, if we double 3.34 percent, we get 6.68 percent and can round up to 7 percent. An uncompounded 7 percent figure is still conservative based on the prices of some goods that have seen price increase multiples of between 38 to 75 (3,800 percent to 7,500 percent) in even less than 100 years based on home, auto, bread, meat, etc. prices (Comparison Of Prices Over 70 Years, *thepeoplehistory.com*, December 2015) (Comparing the inflated cost of living today from 1938 to 2013: How the US Dollar has lost incredible purchasing power since 1938, *mybudget360.com*, December 2015)

I have shown that the prisons, courts and money could
tie together. If we accept state justice then we need prisons.
If we need prisons then we need courts for entry and egress
from prisons. Theft is a court matter which brings in the
Cash Redemption Department as the Cash Redemption
Department would protect the value of money from coun-
terfeiting and inflation. Criminals cannot be both free and
imprisoned at the same time (parole and house arrest are still
forms of imprisonment). There is either state justice or market justice. There might be coercion depending on which
side that you are on. There might be coercion depending
on which side of the "money side" you are on. Some might
believe that the Cash Redemption Department should be
a voluntary decision through the Voluntary State. I believe
that theft is occurring and that we need protection of our
money through gold backing. The gold held to back the
currency needs to be audited. Most people do not know or
understand the theft that occurs through the inflation of
our money. Their ignorance does not make the theft any
less real.

The Courts, Bureau of Prisons and the Cash Redemption
Department should be bundled as one mandatory payment.
The cost of mandatory justice would be far, far less than the
7 percent that is stolen through inflation of money unless
you are unemployed or far under the poverty line. If the cost
of mandatory justice is more than 7 percent of your income
then you have much bigger things to worry about such as
basic survival. Thankfully, the safety net of property fees
will sustain you.

Patents and copyrights can just be funded by the people

who use them. The cost of patents and copyrights would likely rise as patents and copyrights are no longer subsidized by the entire taxpayer base. Just people who need patents and copyrights will pay for them. Patents and copyrights have a monopoly of force as patents and copyrights need to be acknowledged and enforced by the state.

MONOPOLY OF FORCE REGULATION AND BEYOND

If an individual deliberately murders someone with intent then that person can be jailed or executed. What happens when people are killed in an airplane? In the case of an airplane, there can be many people involved in the design, maintenance and use of the airplane. Usually, no one even goes to jail over the deaths of people killed in airplanes. No one is usually found criminally negligent as an individual. Instead, the specific airline or the entire airline industry receives the "punishment" for any negligence, flaws or problems. Airplane deaths might range from nearly unforeseeable or improbable to highly foreseeable and highly probable. If the deaths are "too" highly probable then they would be criminally negligent deaths.

When a person is convicted of a crime they serve a sentence for their past crime. The convict can also be assessed on the probability that they might pose a danger to society in the future if they were to be released from prison. There might be an assessment as to whether the convict is "rehabilitated." An airline or the airline industry might be assessed for the present and future threat that they might pose. Around 1,000 people, give or take, die from airplanes every year. How does an airline or airline industry even try to account for these deaths and attain any sort of justice? Justice demands that something is done for the deaths of airplane passengers and crew. In most cases, where there is no criminal negligence then we seem to be left trying to prevent the "accident" or "event" from happening again in the future. An airline or airline industry loses its "right" to be wholly self-regulating when innocent passengers died because of their planes. They are now subject to regulation by the state. Under socialism, we have "socialized" the cost of airline regulation across all taxpayers. Under a Voluntary State, the airline industry will pay for their own regulation by paying for the cost of the FAA (Federal Aviation Administration) who should have the monopoly of force. Flight costs will go up without the "socialized subsidy" of taxpayers paying for airline regulation. Added ticket costs can be offset by the absence of having to pay for the regulation of the airline industry and if you choose less government services than all the coerced services you were forced to pay under an Involuntary State.

Does this line of reasoning apply to firearms? No, almost all firearm deaths are due to the *use* of the firearm (people choosing to shoot other people). Firearm recalls can be handled through the manufacturers, the courts and any voluntary departments or groups that are watchdogging the firearm industry.

From 1966 to 2014, there have been more than 390 million vehicle recalls according to the NHTSA (National Highway Traffic Safety Administration). Some of those 390 million vehicle recalls involved injury or death that precipitated the recall. The actual injury and death and the potential injury and death do not make recalls a voluntary market decision left entirely to the vehicle industry. The NHTSA would continue to oversee vehicle recalls in a Voluntary State. That is too big a number, I believe, to try to handle through the courts alone.

The Department of Motor Vehicles or DMV could be voluntarily funded by people seeking new vehicle licenses or restoring their old suspended or revoked vehicle licenses. The NHTSA could be funded by fines imposed on the vehicle industry who refuse to voluntarily recall unsafe vehicles.

LAW

In a properly defined Voluntary State, there should be some changes to laws under a new Constitutional Convention. A new Constitution would still likely have most of the criminal law from before the new Constitution (assuming criminal laws don't drastically change after the release of this book). Necessary changes at a new Convention would include legalizing objects that might be illegal now such as "excess" cash, marijuana and certain weapons. The general population should carry more weapons and more powerful weapons. The local police should not have militarized vehicles and other instruments of militarization. We should end Civil Asset Forfeiture at the Convention. A new Constitution should establish an individual right to his own income. The individual right to your own income can take away the national debt, the massive Involuntary State and so much more… The individual right to income can only be subordinated if we voluntarily break a criminal law, choose to own property (land), or cause harm to others.

STABILITY

Without democracy, there would be no more elected officials. Theoretically, the one in a million representation of the congressional kings is supposed to direct the actions, in some way, of government workers toward some will of a voting majority? It seems clear to me that for every positive measure that might be undertaken, there might be ten others that will make things worse. The one positive measure might simply be a reversal of one of the ten negative measures from the last "cycle" of measures. So, effectively, you can get nowhere fast.

Let's say for the sake of argument that there is some measure that is non-coercive or self-defense against coercion. What then? Will a congressmen elected every two to four years help you in this case? Will a congressmen be helpful if someone is shot in the back and murdered on the street as policemen Michael Slager shot Walter Scott as captured on video? If foreign aircraft enter US airspace then will your congressman be on call to assess the threat and scramble aircrafts or other defenses? Obviously, your congressman does not respond to immediate threats. Would passing a law change the behavior of the policeman or invading foreign aircraft? Any such laws could be passed by courts instead of congressmen. The court is governed by case law. The case law can be governed by individualism and a proper Voluntary State instead of the personal feelings of the congressmen.

Of course, we can regress and say who governs the courts, military, police, etc.? Who governs these entities under democracy? I would argue that it is not the congressmen. One guess or one part of the temporary equation might be that there is a sort of internal competition. It may seem wrong to use a market term for the state. In any case, competition between cities, states and other branches of government may act as a regulating mechanism to act fairly. This internal regulation may work to an extent, but, I believe that our remaining capitalism provides enough plunder to keep democracy at bay for the time being. As our capitalism becomes more socialistic and government controlled, the opportunity for plunder will diminish and keeping the government from becoming a tyrant will become more difficult.

There may be additional or other explanations for the government being able to avoid armed insurrection and guerilla warfare that we see in other countries. As I will show, it may only be more of a function of time than anything else. Our country is a newcomer with vast natural resources compared to other countries that have existed longer with less resources. While there may be other explanations, they do not involve congressmen as a necessary regulator of courts, military, police, etc. One thing that we can be sure of is that democracy has a natural bias against the individual. The individual is overridden by the majority. The problem gets worse at the congressional level as the congressman doesn't have Social Security, Medicare, "Obamacare," etc. The congressmen has special healthcare and retirement packages. The congressman can pass whatever they want as it doesn't affect them. This indifference and mob rule escalates as socialism grows. The socialism grows until capitalism is eroded and the voting majority has stolen from everyone and all that is left is the very rich and the very poor majority. Even stealing from the rich just buys a little more time as the flaws of socialism or collectivism take hold.

In other words, unless there is a certain level of freedom or individualism the peace that we have seen in democracy will turn into civil war. There is some tipping point of taxation (right to income), theft of banking funds (Cyprus), theft of retirement funds, right to privacy, right to bear arms, right to property, etc. etc. that tips the entire scale. Democracy is not a viable form of government. It is just a new form of government that hasn't totally failed and been replaced yet. Like the brutality of the rule of kings, the brutality of democracy is coming. It is just a matter of time.

CHAPTER 8
MOVING TO THE VOLUNTARY STATE

With a Voluntary State most people might only pay one third of what you pay now to the government. There would be no direct taxation and no sales taxes. There would be no taxes at all. There will be some people who pay a higher percentage of their income to government services. The cost of government services is regressive to income. The more money you make, the lower your cost of government will be. The cost of providing government services does not "care" what your income is. Government services have a cost, they are passing on that cost to you. Currently, government services are progressive to income. The more money you make, the more your percentage of income taxes increases.

There will likely be people who would choose to go "naked" and go without any government services. These "naked" choosers will likely pay a high cost if they ever use government services without coverage. I believe that charitable organizations will help many of the people who are truly in need. The number of charitable organizations nearly rivals the number of government agencies that I listed in the Involuntary State chapter. This charity, I believe, will only go so far. Currently, we have around the same amount of people who take a subsidy check from the government as make a check from actual work and production.

The first generation under a Voluntary State might

struggle with budgeting for their own retirement and health care. Some might overspend and squander the extra money. Some might budget and have a comparable retirement similar to Social Security and Medicare. Some might budget and invest wisely and have much more than they would have had. The same is true of housing and goods. Some might buy huge houses and expensive vehicles and toys with the extra income. Some might buy modest homes and have a better chance of keeping their homes. Instead of money being locked up in a collective Social Security, Medicare, taxes, etc. they can have the extra money to save their homes and the tens of thousands of dollars that might exist as equity. Some may rent as the likely increased housing market of an initial Voluntary State should drive rents lower as more people will buy homes with the extra money most will have in a Voluntary State.

There will be stories of great victory and great tragedy. At first, there will be more unemployment as many people will not want all the services that the government currently coercively provides. People will likely start more businesses as primary and secondary source of income. These business might drive sales domestically and internationally as exports. Unemployment should moderate to normal levels over time. The middle class will start to grow as people will have the opportunity to build businesses with the extra discretionary income from a likely smaller government.

The first generation of the Voluntary State will have some stories of the high cost of going "naked" on government services when they had to use these services, or worse, tried to dispense justice by their own hand and had to pay the consequences of not being authorized by law enforcement.

There are a few ways that we could move to a Voluntary State. Change is most likely at the state government level. Washington and Colorado legalized marijuana in their states. There is some tiny hope that a state could actually eliminate or reduce a state government department or agency. The hope would be that the other states would follow suit clear through to the federal level. Another way is through a Constitutional Convention where the Constitution is revised to subordinate the state under the individual where the state is a limited means that could be voluntary rule. Still, another way is to start moving off of government money. We could create an underground economy with bitcoin and/or an asset or commodity based currency that could be digital or paper based or both.

Our US Declaration of Independence does not approve of standing armies and prescribes well-regulated militias to counter the power of a central or federal standing army. This sentiment or attitude was only partially followed through in the Constitution with the right to bear arms. The government has shown that it has the most powerful standing army or military force in the world. The government has shown that it can declare a National State of Emergency closing in on 100 years. It has shown that it can change the rule of engagement and shoot unarmed citizens through closed doors (Ruby Ridge 1992). It has shown that it can both circumnavigate Posse Comitatus and condense a 52 day standoff into around a single minute of heavily edited footage (Waco 1993). It can also have the most advanced

surveillance in the world, but, cannot show any video footage of what happened to the pentagon at the crucial time
before (alleged plane coming towards the Pentagon), during
(moment of impact of alleged airplane) and just after impact
(black boxes and other meaningful "debris" from alleged
airplane) ("911" 2001).

The September 11, 2001 attacks appears to have provided the reason for the USA Patriot Act (**U**niting and
Strengthening **A**merica by **P**roviding **A**ppropriate **T**ools
Required to **I**ntercept and **O**bstruct **T**errorism) passed a
mere 45 days later on October 26, 2001. The Patriot Act
changed an immense number of Acts as provided:

> Electronic Communications Privacy Act –
> Computer Fraud and Abuse Act – Foreign
> Intelligence Surveillance Act – Family
> Educational Rights and Privacy Act – Money
> Laundering Control Act – Bank Secrecy
> Act – Right to Financial Privacy Act – Fair
> Credit Reporting Act – Immigration and
> Nationality Act – Victims of Crime Act
> of 1984 – Telemarketing and Consumer
> Fraud and Abuse Prevention Act.

The Patriot Act (H R. 3162) is 342 pages long. The
more impressive feat is that each page creates or amends
codes and/or statutes from Acts that I italicized in this paragraph. An incredible and overwhelming amount of work
went into the Patriot Act. It proves how quickly (45 days)
politicians can respond when it comes to your privacy as
the changed Acts detail. When it comes to budgets, debts

or fiscal responsibility we keep raising the debt ceiling and unveiling multi-year plans.

The US government will be financially dangerous and may become a dangerous police state in part because of the financial desperation. It is not a question of if but when. The financial policies of collectivism will fail. They are failing now. I have shown the collective footprint since the founding of our country until now. Our US dollar will collapse. We will be overrun with debt and some form of financial reckoning will occur. At that point, the US might be ready to finally move to a Voluntary State.

SOCIAL SAFETY NET

Many people might believe that only coercion will provide a social safety net. The Voluntary State can provide a social safety net without coercion. I mentioned earlier in the book in the Property section of the A Voluntary State chapter of this book that owning property is a voluntary exchange that will have fees associated with its use. These fees will provide either a net inflow or net outflow to all citizens as owners of the land. These property fees and private charity should provide a social safety net to prevent starvation and have some money to turn things "around." Property owners would be both payer and recipient. As both payer and recipient of property fees, the size and number of properties would determine whether you pay more than you receive. If you fell on hard times or wanted to sell your property for any reason then you could simply sell and no longer pay property fees and be only a recipient of property fees.

A social safety net can be socialized. People that we

consider citizens would be property owners in the land. They would be eligible to become a recipient of property fees. The more people that are considered citizens eligible for receipt of property fees, the lower the average property payment that you may receive. Of course, these added citizens may become property owners themselves and may or may not offset their added numbers with added property fee payers and payments.

How would the Social Safety Net take care of orphans or the physically or mentally challenged? Orphans would have a foster parent or state guardian or state facility or others manage their property fee inflow payments until the orphan is 18 and can manage their own well-being. The physically and mentally challenged might have volunteers or volunteer organizations help them manage their property fee inflow payments and their well-being, otherwise, they will have to pay for this assistance through a private market company or the state will have to step in with a state guardian or facility in more severely challenged situations. I believe that private charity will step in voluntarily and provide additional assistance, but, I wanted to outline some scenarios in the absence of private charity.

I think the biggest problems people will have with the Voluntary State is that many people will struggle with the extra responsibility of having the opportunity of having more money and having a longer term focus because you will be in control of your own money, your own healthcare and your own retirement.

VOTING

Time is the enemy with voting. A tipping point has already been reached. If we collapse quickly in a monetary sense then we can limit the damage done. The longer we fight against rising debt and growing socialism, the greater the eventual abyss that will we will face. For instance, imagine if you had great debt and declared bankruptcy early and changed your spending habits. Imagine, instead, if you waited and sold your cars to pay the interest on the debt and a little of the principal. Next, you sold your home to pay more of the principal. You still have principal and debt. You still declare bankruptcy down the road, but, now you have no home and cars.

As a government we sell Treasury bond debt, print more money thereby making each dollar worth less and likely secretly sell our gold (we haven't had a gold audit since 1953 despite Ron Paul's recent attempts calling for a gold audit). How far will we go? Sell our water rights, raw commodities, public lands, public buildings, roads, national parks, etc. to foreign interests? We help erode our ability to be a reserve currency with each bond sale and printing press dilution of our dollar.

It is hope and false expectations that are hurting us here. We have bought a lot of false hope with the US dollar being the reserve currency for most of the world. We are like a gambler praying on the next pull of the slot machine. We can make it a little better in the short run if we vote and participate in majority rule. There will ALWAYS be one choice that is better than another. Imagine if your choice was one small step to make things more fiscally responsible. How many small steps across how many elections would it take to run a budget surplus? That is assuming the next majority doesn't destroy your small step in subsequent elections?

As futile as a succession of democratic small steps may be, some may believe that the creation of a Voluntary State is an even more futile endeavor. Regardless of any futility, the sooner democracy faces its shortcomings, the sooner we can have another opportunity to choose less government. Currently, each crisis usually is solved by adding more government which creates another crisis (and more government and debt) followed by another crisis (and more government and debt).

While we are on the topic of bankruptcy, have countries had sovereign defaults where they did not pay back all of their debt? According to *CNNWorld, Wikipedia* and Stacey Bumpus *America's Debt Crisis Isn't the First: 10 Nations that Have Defaulted on Debt* many nations have defaulted on their debt partially or in whole. On a personal level, I have never voted in my life and had no agreement or participation in the spending that caused the national debt. How much responsibility do I bear? Do I have more responsibility than the country that was foolish enough to loan our country money in the first place? What did we do with the loans we received from foreign countries? What was the "collateral" used to secure the loans? No collateral I imagine.

Majority rule is an act of aggression. Is there a difference whether 1 percent or 10 percent or 25 percent or 51 percent of the people commit the aggression? Does it make a difference if you are happy with 1 percent or 10 percent or 25 percent or 51 percent of the governments departments and agencies? Does one percentage number make the difference between aggression and nonaggression? Of course not. But, according to majority rule something is right or just or proper when we hit that magic 51 percent. How majority rule should be phrased is, "I going to commit an act of aggression because..."

Most people though cannot wrap their heads around freedom. Though, probably, virtually everyone claims to want freedom, their acts of aggression such as voting say otherwise. Common arguments might be that there would be gaps and free riders. The problem that we have now is the opposite problem. We have over-coverage. It is like having a car worth 20 thousand dollars and insuring the car for 2 billion dollars. You are paying for much more than you need. So much, in fact, you are going in debt. So, is the case of our government? This over-coverage is building up so much debt that it will create gaps of its own when the entire system collapses. We have papered over these gaps with US dollars. The US dollar will collapse and the resulting depression will create an abyss.

If we ever moved to a voluntary based society, any gaps would be played up to epic proportions. The gap(s) would be used as a catalyst to say that we need mandated, compulsory participation in government agencies and departments. Of course, they would find cleverer, friendlier ways to say it using different words, videos, sound bites, etc. Collectivist thinkers will be looking at targeting any voluntary method of government that takes money and power out of their hands. They will do it under the guise of security. It will be under the guise of helping the neediest and the people that cannot help themselves.

Voting is an act of aggression against non-aggressors. Non-aggressors being people who did not vote, people who don't believe in the decision of a majority for many or all things. There is wide division amongst Libertarians as to voting and majority rule. On one side you have Wendy Mcelroy and others who would not vote under any circumstances. She was a cofounder of the Voluntaryists who *seek to reclaim the anti-political heritage of libertarianism* (Vol 1, No. 1 *The Voluntaryist*). On the other side you have the Libertarian Party that runs candidates across the nation on every election. Their biggest presidential candidate in my opinion was Ron Paul who ran for President for the Libertarian Party in 1988 and gathered 431,750 votes. As a Republican candidate in the 2012 primaries, Ron Paul gathered 2,095,795 votes and won state(s) by popular vote, roll call and delegates (*Wikipedia* 1/2015). As I mentioned in the last chapter, third parties represent more than 1 to 2 percent of our views, but, we want to be the bully not the bullied.

The wording of the "non-aggression" moral side constraint has changed over the years, but, the non-aggressive intent has been the same. This non-aggression constraint is often used as a pledge to sign to become a member of the Libertarian Party. As of 1/2015 the membership pledge is worded as "To validate my membership, I certify that I oppose the initiation of force to achieve political or social goals." It was a similar pledge that I signed for a couple years in the late 90s. Even back then I realized that there was never a situation where I could actually reduce the amount of "aggression" by voting (which voting itself is an act of aggression). Any positive reduction of aggression that was hoped to be achieved by voting would be overridden by affirming majority rule. So, I never did vote and never have voted.

The 2014 Libertarian Party Platform Statement of Principles says that

> We hold that all individuals have the right to exercise sole dominion over their own lives, and have the right to live in whatever manner they choose, so long as they do not forcibly interfere with the equal right of others to live in whatever manner they choose.

I would consider that the 2014 version of the "non-aggression moral side constraint." What is *sole dominion*? *Sole dominion* to me includes the right to my own income that I have earned through voluntary exchange. If I vote I am affirming that my own income should be decided by a majority. Even if I vote in an effort to improve my income, I may *interfere* with the *equal right of others* to give part of their income away through social welfare or other programs. The only way to allow sole dominion for the life of the individual is to allow the individual to use their money *in whatever manner they choose*. The only way to allow people to use their money *in whatever manner they choose* is to actually allow them to choose it without voting through majority rule which can constrict or eliminate their choices. How do they choose "it?" They choose what they want voluntarily by their own means which does not *interfere with the equal right of others.* Their own means being the Voluntary State, charity or other direct contributions that do not *interfere with the equal rights of others.* In this way they can *live in whatever manner they choose.*

VOTING V. MONOPOLY OF FORCE

What is the difference between voting and the monopoly of force to *live in whatever manner they choose* (to take some wording from the last section)? Don't they both involve force? Yes, they both involve force. The difference (to take another word from the last section) is the *interference.* As we saw from the Involuntary State chapter, there are thousands of state and federal entities. Individuals do not get to vote on the thousands of individual state and federal entities. For the most part, we get the meager opportunity to vote for one federal president and a couple state and federal representatives to represent your state at the state and federal level. If you wanted a representative to eliminate one state or federal entity out of the thousands that exist, you would have a snowball's chance in hell as they say. That is an incredible amount of interference and gridlock.

Monopoly of force in a Voluntary State should only concern things where interference cannot be avoided. For instance, driving on public roads cannot be avoided unless you have a hoverboard (From the movie series *Back to the Future*) or something. There is no way to avoid possible interference. Collisions, accidents, road repairs, speed limits, construction, etc. etc. involve necessary interference. On the other hand, your retirement, health care and savings does not have to interfere with my retirement, health care and savings. Under majority rule and voting, your retirement, health care and savings are *made* to interfere with my retirement, health care and savings. Majority rule and voting has created a conflict and interference where none should exist. Social Security, Medicare and social welfare are among some of the mandatory unnecessary interference and coercion that exists under voting and majority rule. The Libertarian Party violates its own non-aggression moral side constraint by voting. Maybe the goal is some distant reduction of interference. In the meantime, the hundreds of thousands of Libertarians that vote every year affirm the *interference* of the state and violate the pledge that they signed.

Is the ultimate goal of the Libertarian Party to contradict itself? Imagine if the Libertarian Party were able to use majority rule and voting to enact all of the principles on its 2014 Platform. The Libertarian Party asks you not to interfere with self-ownership, privacy, freedom of expression, consent in personal relationships, abortion, free exchange, property rights, self-defense with personal defense weapons, free market health care and education, etc. etc. Further imagine if the Libertarian Party were able to repeal the income tax, abolish the Internal Revenue Service and all federal programs and services not required under the US Constitution. At this point, you would operating at or close to individual rule. In the very beginning of the Libertarian Party Platform preamble it states

> As Libertarians, we seek a world of liberty;
> a world in which all individuals are sovereign over their own lives and no one is

> forced to sacrifice his or her values for the
> benefit of others.

At this point, should it be left up to majority rule to reinstate the income tax, reinstate the Internal Revenue Service, reinstate all federal programs and services not required under the US Constitution and whether we should interfere with self-ownership, privacy, freedom of expression, consent in personal relationships, abortion, free exchange, property rights, self-defense with personal defense weapons, free market health care and education, etc. etc.? Any honest answer would be that it is not up to the majority. At what point, would the Libertarian Party have the courage to say that these principles should not be left up to majority rule and voting?

THE SECOND STEP

Does this lead to a dilemma? If you were able to somehow use majority rule to attain a near state of individual rule (except for majority rule and voting) then, at the least, you would be faced with a contradiction. Would it be a simple matter of admitting the contradiction of majority rule and moving on? Would every politician give up his or her job? Would everyone who is employed by the machinery of majority rule and voting simply admit that it is wrong and give up their jobs?

What would be the odds of attaining individual rule through majority rule? What would be the odds of the participants of majority rule stepping aside including any elected members of the Libertarian Party? What would be the odds of all of this happening peacefully? Would there be more than persuasion involved? Would it take manipulation or force to fire or remove majority rule and voting from power?

Would manipulation or force to remove majority rule and voting be justified? Yes, majority rule and voting decides what to do with my income through coercion and force. I have not consented to this aggression. I have never voted (in my entire life) nor individually got a choice as to the thousands of state and government entities that my money will go to. I did not agree to the foreign affair policies of this country such as weekly drone strikes in foreign lands. I did not agree to the wars and smaller scale incursions that my money funded. I did not agree to the government debt that we create with my money. I did not agree to the inflation that devalues the money that the majority allows me to keep. I would say that a certain amount of manipulation and force to remove majority rule and voting would be self-defense against the coercion and force that is brought against me.

Majority rule is not peaceful, it is mob rule. We have been in a National State of Emergency closing in on one hundred years. Anyone can be classified as a terrorist or an enemy of the state—even US citizens. Trial by jury and other semblances of freedom can be thrown by the wayside with these laws that sit in the back pocket of our Involuntary State or majority rule. Anyone classified as a terrorist can be shipped off to Guantanamo Bay or some other locale. Just as we cannot assume that majority rule will always be peaceful, overthrowing majority rule may not always be peaceful either. Laws can define boundaries and can be defined in a specific manner. Majority rule can be boundless and arbitrary.

Early Americans might be considered to have seceded from Great Britain. American secession and the Declaration of Independence were not recognized by Great Britain. The American Revolution ensued. The South seceded from the North and declared its independence. Slavery may not have been the central issue in the way that the North liked to portray. In fact, Northern leader Abraham Lincoln's Emancipation Proclamation basically announced that the seceded Confederate States had a little over three months to return their allegiance back to the United States or their slaves would be freed. At the same time, territory controlled by the Northern Union were able to keep their slaves. Up to 80 percent of the Southerners who fought in the Civil War were not slaveowners. The North had their slaves and their issues also. At the Declaration of Independence every state in the United States had slavery. Larry Koger documented blacks owning other blacks in America in his book *Black Slaveowners*. In the most incredible irony, the North became like Great Britain and did not recognize the secession and independence of the South and declared war on the South. This may not be the history lesson that you were taught at school. For more on this subject read *The South Was Right* by John Ronald Kennedy and Walter Donald Kennedy.

A lesson that could be learned here is that any incomplete attempt to secede or declare independence can backfire and lead to even more power and control by the winning party. The power of the state can increase to "protect" against insurrection, terrorism, slavery or other labels that can be falsely applied. Laws and liberties can be ignored, added or changed to "protect" us from these alleged threats. The South had the same right of secession and independence that America claimed against Great Britain. The Northern Union ignored the Constitution of the United States and the right to secede. In terms of legality and effectiveness, the only difference between the United States and the South is that the United States was successful in its secession and independence from Great Britain and the South was unsuccessful in its secession and independence from the United States.

A lesson for the Libertarian Party and supporters of majority rule and voting is to admit that there is a problem and begin to work on possible ways that the problem could be fixed. For instance, the Libertarian Party could state in its platform that it is opposed to majority rule and voting, but, feels that it must work within the system to begin to change it and must use majority rule and voting until that goal can be realized. The next step would be to show how majority rule will be removed once certain goal(s) are realized.

The majority is free to use whatever level of coercion it wishes as a majority regarding the income of others. In effect, there is no individual income, only collective majority income. The fact that we keep a little more money individually if we make a lot more money individually is more of coincidence or discretion of the majority than a right of any individual. An individual has no right to his own income and any good or evil that the majority might wish to exercise with the individual's income. While the Libertarian Party may be opposed to the Internal Revenue Service, it supports majority rule that can support the Internal Revenue Service. While the Libertarian Party may not support the Internal Revenue Service it affirms the Internal Revenue Service by voting for a Libertarian Party candidate and affirming the legitimacy of the government through the voting process and demonstrating the government has the consent of the people through a social compact or democracy. So, logically, by voting, the Libertarian Party supports the Internal Revenue Service.

The second step is the elimination of voting and majority rule. The rights of the individual takes primacy here. It appears that the best the Libertarian Party can do, if it could be done at all, is to gain the wrongful power of the majority and use that wrongful power to destroy the power of the majority. This can be a transparent plan that is part of the party platform or can be a secret subversive plan to be sprung at the most opportune time. Otherwise, it can continue to support the majority indefinitely whatever the majority decides…

The American Civil War shows that secession and independence are deadly and likely ineffective measures. Majority rule, in theory, could bring individualism to a point where we have individualism for everything except voting and the potential for majority rule to change everything back to collectivism. The hope would be to create laws to legislate a final constraint against majority rule. However astronomically unlikely, it is theoretically possible to use majority rule in this way. Majority rule and the state support your effort to pursue this possibility. A vote still shows support for the state despite how the vote is cast.

There is a "diet" version of our support of the government through voting and majority rule. Voter proposed amendments to state constitutions and state statutes in the form of a proposition, referendum, or amendment depending on what they might be referred to by each state could be used. Each state might have different rules, but, generally you need a certain percentage or number of voters to sign in support of the measure. You can usually accomplish the same thing with two thirds state house and senate vote for a measure. In both cases, proposed amendments that meet either threshold can be proposed to state voters to be passed or failed by simple majority vote. A state amendment eliminating state departments or agencies could be an interesting amendment. Another possibility is an amendment for a Constitutional Convention as I will explain in the next paragraph. I imagine that there are ways that states have shielded their own safety by some poison pill or other measure that would prohibit such an amendment from being put on a state ballot. If reduction of state government or support of a Constitutional Convention could be accomplished through a state amendment then voting for a Constitutional Convention could warrant a consideration to vote? I call this a diet version because a vote can be limited to a specific state amendment. It is still a vote and still shows consent of the governed and support of state and federal government overall.

If there is ever a time that we thought we could improve individualism through a Constitutional Convention then voting for a Constitutional Convention might be a consideration. Article V of the US Constitution provides two ways for constitutional amendments to be proposed. One way is a two thirds vote from both the house and senate to approve a resolution to be sent to the individual states for ratification. So far, to my knowledge, all constitutional amendments have been done in this way. Another way is for two thirds of state legislatures to demand a Constitutional Convention meeting. If there were state amendments in most or all states that called for a Constitutional Convention and if two-thirds of the states that had such state amendments passed their amendments then the federal government could initiate a Constitutional Convention. This Constitutional Convention could propose Constitutional Amendments that would need three-fourths ratification by three-fourths of the house and senate vote or three-fourths ratification of all the states legislatures. This might be a case of "be careful what you wish for." Since, I was talking about theoretical possibilities, I wanted to include it. However, trusting politicians with the extra power of constitutional law that could be used for good or evil is a dangerous proposition especially if one goal of the Constitutional Convention was to call for the end of politicians.

CHAPTER 9
GOING ALL IN

I want to provide some practical investment knowledge that a person could start to use right away. I do not want to regurgitate conventional trading tools and techniques. Conventional tools and techniques are important and there are entire books addressing them. What I want to show in this chapter are some dangers of conventional investing and how to protect yourself and, perhaps, to try profiting wildly from these dangers.

People go all in on a fairly regular basis. They pick a stock fund from a small group of preselected funds in their 401(k). They have cash and bank accounts. They go long stocks or long cash. As Cyprus showed, bank accounts can be a risky investment that if banks or governments don't steal from your account directly, your account will not likely keep up with inflation, indirectly. As Greece has shown, when a country is in trouble they (Eurozone governments, in this case, looking for austerity measures) might go right after the pensions among other targets. Greece also showed that governments have no problem declaring bank holidays and limiting cash withdrawals of your money. Having a bank account with all your money in it is going all in. Having only cash is going all in. Having only 401k stock funds whether they are growth, international, small cap, large cap, etc. is going all in stocks. Having only money market 401k funds is going all in cash or interest bearing cash. Having a 401k retirement fund that is supposed to be "balanced" can even be going all in. All the "balanced" positions are LONG positions. There could be situations where ALL long positions could fall at the same time and there is no "balance."

If you say that most people might work 40 years then how many 40 year periods would have been conducive to a buy and hold strategy? Forty years ago there were no ETF (Electronic Traded Funds) that tracked indexes such as the Dow Jones, S&P, NASDAQ or others. There were no leveraged ETFs that paid out multiples of the index. There were no leveraged ways to hold commodities as a Fund. You picked individual stocks. Some stocks had to do with commodities, but, were not designed to reflect the price action of any commodity or index. How many stocks have existed for more than 40 years? In North America that would be a small handful? Kodak (recently filed Bankruptcy), DuPont, the Hudson Bay Company, W. R. Grace, Ford Motor Company and Shell. Could you have bought and sold shares in all those companies 40 years ago?

Were there 40 year "winners?" Gold and silver are great buys as of December, 2015. They might have their peak before 40 years, but, generally, you would do well with gold and silver for a buy and hold. You have decent odds with the S&P as long as inflation and the US dollar continue with their erosion and decline and, generally, monetize stock prices upward. How about individual stocks? Will Apple, Samsung, Google, Pepsico, Coke and others hit the 40 year mark? Will the 40 years be well spent as an investment?

The success of a 40 year stretch on individual stocks might depend on buying near the inception of the company or near the beginning and riding it out for 40 years. At any given time, there will likely only be far less than 1 percent of the stocks traded that will have a good 40 year track record. Gold and silver can have a great 40 year track record if you pick the right time to buy.

The S&P or other market indexes have an opportunity to give a good nominal return over a 40 year period on the condition that we still have a government that is inflating the money supply, growing debt and spending. So far, there has been no sign of those things changing.

Each candlestick in the above chart represents one month. You can see that you can spend years of time dollar cost averaging where you buy shares of a fund that continues falling. Each week the shares you bought the previous week are worth less. Is this sound advice? If you have no basic sense of markets, governments and investing then this may be sound advice. Are you are plagued by undue fear of a market top and miss years of a rally? Do you fear a market collapse and miss years of a rally? If these are some of your fears and inhibitions then buy and hold dollar cost averaging each week could be your best choice.

If you dollar cost averaged and bought shares every week or every other week from your paycheck then your average price could be somewhere in the ballpark of the middle of the price range? It depends on if more weeks were spent buying at the top or if more weeks were spent buying at the bottom. A "blind" buy and hold strategy might be defined where everything is done automatically each pay period. The success of this strategy has more to do with luck than anything else.

You may need up to 4 factors or more to succeed over a 40 year stretch. First, you may have needed to buy at the right time. Next, you needed to buy the right individual stock, stock index or gold or silver. Then you need the price action, if you had weekly or bi-weekly payroll deductions, to spend a majority of the time (weeks) at the lower end of the range so that you had more low priced buys than high priced buys. Finally, you would need to retire at the "right" time when your investment is at the highs.

There are a few people who through luck or skill were able to do a 40 year buy and hold. They are the exception, not the rule. Yet, you still hear "professionals" advocating not to time the markets. Unless they figure you are as intelligent as cattle or hope you are as lucky a leprechaun then this is not sound advice. What the "professionals" want is to time the market for you. They may say they are not timing the market. Inevitable, someone is timing the market. It may come in the form of the technical indicators programmed into computer software programs. Someone programmed the technical indicators in the program to time the market (give buy and sell signal in a certain way).

If we have a currency collapse of the US dollar, going all in could be the only thing that keeps you from being completely wiped out like the Weimar Republic or Zimbabwe. With the exception of the fiat British Pound, no fiat currencies such as the US dollar has survived more than 70 years. There is risk involved with every investment choice we make. In some cases, going all in is the least risky choice in my opinion. I have been successful one hundred percent of the time that I've went all in (sometimes that process took a year or two and initial losses, but, the forecasted event occurred and was profitable by the conclusion of the trading). If you are going to need cash or make withdrawals then take that money out beforehand (in case losses precede gains before the conclusion of the trade or investment). Going all in runs against the standard advice you are given by investment advisers. Standard advice is not to time your investments. Standard advice says that you should cost average through a buy-and-hold strategy through weekly payroll deductions.

Timing is everything. I cannot stress this enough. I want to shake up people's myths and preconceptions about making their own investment choices. I think that doing nothing may be the most risky decision of all. This complacent thinking is what allows "smart money" to exploit "dumb money." Inflation will constantly erode the value of your holdings. Hyperinflation or deflationary recessions (negative GDP growth) or depressions (prolonged negative

GDP growth for years) can also wipe out the value of your holdings. I would, at least, go down fighting. Smart money is constantly in the process of thinking of new ways to take money from the uninformed. Government's help or hindrance in the process changes from time to time, but, the process continues.

If dumb money is more aware that smart money, can and most likely will, take almost all of their money through theft and/or cunning then dumb money can become informed money and make the right changes in their plans and investments.

Most people believe that things will happen down the road. How many people imagined the housing crisis? Despite the devastation of the "great recession" of 2008, how many people know what a derivative is? How many people can explain securitization? How many know the acronym CDO or CDS for Collateralized Debt Obligations or Credit Default Swaps? If you do not understand the causes and tools of the past and present then how can you expect to make future gains? The future bubbles and crisis may well come out of many of the same themes, causes and tools of the "great recession" of 2008.

There is an age and/or wealth amount that a person may shift from appreciation to preservation. A person might think that they are in preservation mode but how far does that go? What if you are down 50 percent during a recession? Does that change the picture of preservation? I imagine that many workers had a buy-and-hold preservation mentality toward their 401(k) in 2008. They held the company directed mutual fund. Something viewed as preservation or flight to quality or flight to safety is all relative. Every investment will fail or already has failed. Even gold has sizable retracements or years of decline.

You can preserve your wealth. It takes timing. Many financial advisors tell you not to time the markets. They tell you to buy-and-hold. How many of these of advisors told you to exit stocks in 2000 or 2008? How many financial advisors told you to sell your house in and buy gold? The housing bubble, most likely, took five years to recover your losses if you are all in long stocks such as a 401(k) mutual fund from your employee plan. Perhaps you needed to retire and had to use your retirement money even if that retirement money was half of what it was. In this sad case, you lost 15 years if it took you 30 years to accumulate assuming the approximate 50 percent drop that we saw. A retired person using that money may never get that lost money back. On one hand, if you are close to retirement then be very careful about any all in approach as a balanced approach may be better if you need some money immediately for retirement (hopefully, at least one of your balanced investments do not fall in value). On the other hand, all the balanced investments may fail and going all in on an investment or two might have been better. So, of course, the stakes are high. There is no autopilot for investing. Cash has the danger of inflation.

Some might say to take the "balanced" approach and balance a basket of investments with a varied percentage of your overall portfolio. The investments that make money are supposed to be sold and reinvested in the losing investments.

The hope is that the winners will pay for the losers and everything will balance out and no timing is ever needed.

Balancing and rebalancing several different asset classes such as stocks, bonds, money markets accounts, etc. is supposed to preserve your wealth. What happens when several asset classes fall at once? In 2009 stocks indexes and commodities fell. Bonds alone was left to balance the falling classes. There is a huge impending bond bubble that is forming. What if bonds are the bubble this time and bonds take the stock market down and commodities fall with them. There may be no long side winners. What's the point of balancing and rebalancing?

Stock indexes and commodities will not go to zero. The commodity will always have value. A market index will never go to zero because there should always be a market for the 30 - 3,100 companies (30—Dow Jones, 500—S&P, 3,100—Nasdaq) in the index. An index such as an ETF (Electronic Traded Fund) that track just a few individuals companies (especially in a sector) can go to zero or below. So going all in on an individual company is almost always the wrong call to make. Even some ETFs have some theoretical danger if they only track a few companies. Still, people go all in on the individual company. They hope it will all work out well. The individual company may be approaching the FDA for approval for the very first time. They may hope whatever science is being applied actually works. Investors may feel like they can go all in on the risky trade.

How can I help my all in approach?

Demand. This is guaranteed demand for the timeframe that you need to trade or invest in?

Replacement can this be replaced in any way for the time-frame that you need to trade or invest?

Catalyst what is the catalyst that may be causing an once-in-a-lifetime opportunity? How long can the catalyst influence the share price?

Supply how long can the supply stay at current levels?

For example, I went all in on with oil and silver in 2009. Oil—**demand** for oil was unquestionable in 2009 with over 99 percent of all vehicles using oil at that time. Demand is guaranteed. Some of the thinking behind the fallen prices might have been a perception that overall demand could fall because of the downturn in the overall economy. Unemployment and less produced and transported goods may have lower demand for oil. This negligible effect in demand wasn't really seen in the price as we rallied from around 38 dollars to around 90 dollars in less than a year. With a well-timed 2X ETF or better you could make 2X to 3X. Obviously **replacement** is small-scale even in 2016. The number of vehicles still using oil may be close to 99 percent oil based or oil-gas/electric. There are pure electric and natural gas cars, but, are still likely less than 1 percent of the total number of vehicles. The **catalyst** was fear that sent the stock markets down 50 percent or more. There is not a 50 percent destruction in the economy. It may have been more in line with up to 4 percent. We went from around 1 percent to 2 percent GDP to negative 1 percent to 2 percent negative GDP. Negative GDP is a recession. Therefore the great recession as it is claimed was begun. So obviously, a huge drop in oil was overdone. The **supply** was not disrupted short-term or long-term. This was a slam dunk 100 percent opportunity to go long oil. I knew I may never see oil prices that low again.

Silver—**demand** for silver, to me, is controversial. There is an exhausted or low supply physical market and an over-abundance, oversold, cheap paper market. On one end, there may be a government conspiracy that is orchestrated by the Rothschilds and central bankers to prop up the dollar? On the other end, silver is a free market that trades freely. You see a big block or suspicious volume from time to time, but, not the conspiracy level intervention in gold and silver. From around late 2008 to early 2011 we went from around 700 dollars to over 1900 dollars in gold and from under 9 dollar silver to almost 50 dollar silver. If the conspiracy was so strong, where was the intervention then? So, what is the demand? There is commercial and industrial demand for silver, but, until this physical market shortage is fully realized then the physical market doesn't seem to move silver. The physical market shortage wasn't realized in 2009. Though there could be a time when we have to do cash settlements not metal settlements. The paper markets are driven mostly by fear of economic collapse and government instability. We had fear in spades in 2009. While the initial knee-jerk reaction sent metals down they rallied with a fear induced panic afterwards. So, demand existed.

There is no **replacement** for gold and silver. The **catalyst** was fear. Silver has value and demand. The fear will be temporary. What made this an all in scenario was the speed and severity of the multi-year lows or the speed and severity of the fear. We lost over 50 percent in less than 3 months from around 20 dollars to a little under 9 dollars. There are **supply** issues. There would be major supply issues if futures and paper markets needed metal backing. Currently, the supply is not affecting the price. Though, that could change. In 2009, supply did not affect the price. Overall, I felt that fear was a short-term catalyst that would also drive demand. The supply picture only helps and there is no replacement for the valuable commodity silver. I gave it "an all in rating."

Individual Stocks—**demand**. Now let's compare that, to say, Apple stock and new version of the iPhone. Demand is purely discretionary. People can live without Apple cell phones. **Replacement** is all around, Samsung, HTC, Motorola, etc. As a discretionary product, opinion is the key driver of replacement. **Catalyst** is a new version of the iPhone. The impact of the catalyst depends if there are some great futures, apps or platforms then the catalyst could affect share price. There is no short-term or long-term **supply** issues.

We just used Apple stock for a failed all in approach. Demand, replacement and catalyst are not "guaranteed" in my opinion. Early feedback from word of mouth or reports can enhance or diminish demand. A diminished demand will lead to replacement and affect the catalyst of the new version launch. There are too many unknowns and variables. I believe any individual stock should not be used in an all in trade or investment. Demand and/or catalyst can always fail. Whether it's an approval, sales, safety, laws, regulation, competition, replacement, you can never be 100 percent sure of the direction of the demand due to the catalyst. Most of the time being more than 70 percent sure is rare.

The stock indexes themselves can be 100 percent Going All In certainty. Multi-year lows of the last recession were a 100 percent certainty. Unless we return to the gold standard or create other sound money through commodity or other value based backing, inflation favors the long side of any stock. The US dollar is a fiat, inflationary tool that applies nominal upwards pressure on all prices. Of course, shorting the stock indexes would be trying to go against the inflationary dollar, inflation on dollar denominated goods and services and greed filled bubbles. The deficits, debts and bubbles can always go higher than you can imagine. If you lose money going all in, you didn't do it right!

Most likely, retirement folks are on a fixed income pension, annuity or Social Security monthly payment cycle. One day, when the dollar collapses, there will be a retirement collapse where retirees could go under with hyperinflation. Unless a retiree has assets that are properly invested away from fixed income instruments then the retiree is doomed. I hope that there are some prepared retirees out there that have additional investments!

So, how do you go all in the right way? First, that takes some awareness of the potential bubble or crisis to come. Is the potential upcoming event deflationary or inflationary? If the potential upcoming event is a potential deflationary event such as a deflating bubble then we have a few options. You can choose an approach such as going at a bubble directly or a passive approach of waiting to see how the bubble deflates and seeing what the most depressed markets are afterwards. To go at a bubble directly, you could take the ultra-risky position of going long in the direction of the bubble. If your timing is fantastic then you can make money on the bubble's growth and then sell the long position and take a short position and make money on the way down. Perhaps, if you believe that you are close to a market top then you won't follow the herd down as the bubble deflates. Of course, there is no bell that rings when you hit the market top or when the bubble starts deflating. You could take the opposite position of the bubble and go short the direction of the bubble. You could sustain some short or medium term losses as you wait for the bubble to deflate. If these losses become long term losses then either your timing is off or the bubble is more sustainable than you imagined or not a bubble at all. Another option, you could go (or stay) cash and wait until the bubble has deflated and pick the most depressed markets at the peak of fear when events have moved prices to multiyear lows.

If the potential upcoming event is a potential inflationary event then long stock indexes or gold and silver or even oil might be possible considerations.

Any trade involves risk. Past performance may not be indicative of future results. There can always be a black swan event that you may never see coming. You could do everything correctly going all in and have a large open loss. You could diversify correctly and have a black swan event that may create losses in all your diversified investments. Your diversification could have missed the investment(s) that might work in the particular black swan event that might occur. I don't want to give anyone false illusion or hope. Any investment can be a loser. Since any investment can be a loser, it is better not to use margin on any investment as you could get forced out of a position that may have needed more time and/or you could lose more than your original investment regardless of whether you were right or wrong in the long run.

You will not have the tools to go all in with this book alone. Understanding technical analysis properly will take one or more books. Understanding fundamental analysis will also take one or more books. One of the best fundamental approaches deals with asking the right questions and seeing what answers you get.

My main goal is to try to stress that having cash, checking accounts, brokerage accounts, bonds, etc. can give you a false sense of security. There is no timeless investment that can preserve your wealth at all times. Even gold, silver and cash take timing to preserve and not depreciate in value or price.

What To Look For

A standard 40 position single dial padlock has 64,000 combinations. At any time, an investment might have different things that can affect it. What can affect an investment at one point in time may have no effect at another point in time. The effects can change in duration and intensity at any time. While by no means inclusive, I want to provide some basic things that a person can look at. I just want to provide a few items to use with technical and fundamental analysis books and tools. What you will find if you track items from this list is that many have convergent technical movement. Many have divergent technical movement. While some of the convergent movements are in the same sector, some convergence is not in the same sector.

Unemployment
Interest rates
Inflation
GDP growth
Price of oil, gas and other commodities
Position of prices. Multi-year highs?
Trade balance for imports/exports
Political Risk
Risk of terrorism
Risk of war
Natural Disasters
Price/Earnings on different sectors
Commitment of Traders CFTC (U.S. Commodity Futures Trading Commission)
Viewing fundamentals or technicals in a vacuum
Seasonal expectations
Time frames across yearly, monthly, daily and down to the minute
Major Indices (S&P, Dow Jones, Nasdaq, Russell)
S&P 500 PE Ratio
Shiller PE Ratio
Cyclically Adjusted Price Earnings Ratio (CAPE)
Price/Earnings 10 Ratio
S&P 500 Price to Sales Ratio
S&P 500 Price to Book Value
S&P Earnings Yield
S&P Earnings
Trailing Twelve Month earnings (TTM)

Dow Jones Transportation Index
Technology Select SPDR (XLK)
Financial Select SPDR (XLF)
Energy Select SPDR (XLE)
Health Care Select SPDR (XLV)
Consumer Staples Select SPDR (XLP)
Consumer Discretionary Select (XLY)

    The Dow Jones Industrial Average has 30 companies in its index. The S&P 500, as its name implies, has 500 companies in its index. Nasdaq has about 3,100 companies in its index. There are around 5,000 companies that trade on the indexes (which include the mentioned indexes and the Russell, etc.). There are over 18 million businesses in the United States according to *dmdatabases.com*. It is easy to let the success or failure of the 18 million businesses that surround us influence our feelings in some way to the 5 thousand companies listed in the indexes. The listed companies are often multi-national companies doing business across the world. So, events here in the US for good or ill may have limited or no impact on the direction of the share price overall. This is especially true of the 30 cherry picked companies that "star" in the Dow Jones Industrial Average. Just how "industrial" is that average? Companies that aren't stars are tossed from this average. So, the markets tend to outperform the overall economy most of the time. The flip side of this are the penny stocks or the OTC BB (Bulletin Board and Pink Sheet markets). Many companies here are scams, shell companies or just overpriced.

    While most brokers use conventional approaches, many of these brokers advocate the use of margin. One single day can wipe out a margin account in a heartbeat. On January 15, 2015 the Swiss Central Bank made a surprise announcement that they would no longer peg the Swiss Franc currency to the Euro currency any longer. A Swiss Franc Futures contract at that time (which may be the same by the time this goes to print) is 125,000 Swiss Francs that you could buy for around 3,000 to 5,000 dollars. So, if you spent 5,000 dollars on a Swiss Franc contract you would control 125,000 units or Francs. On January 15, we moved from 98 cents to 1 dollar and 22 cents and closed above 1 dollar and 14 cents for 6 consecutive trading days, so, there was no way to wait out a margin call if that was a plan.

If you were short the Swiss Franc then a move like that is around a 25 percent loss on 125,000 Francs or around a 30,000 dollar loss on your 5,000 dollar contract. It is no surprise that investors were wiped out in a heartbeat and some brokerage houses such as Alpari and Global Brokers NZ that had to cover gaps that the investors could not cover to meet their "margin calls" to the exchanges were also wiped out. Conventional tools such as a preexisting stop-loss order were useless at this point. There was a straight vertical gap up that stayed above 1 dollar and 14 cents for 6 consecutive trading days. Conventional traders shorting the Swiss Franc were instantly "gapped" into a loss of up to 600 percent in a heartbeat!

Conventional investing tells us to wait for confirmation before buying. On steep falls, waiting for a swing high that is higher than the last swing high is good advice such as the fall from 50 dollar silver to 26 dollar silver. The harder part for me is the ambiguity of what many people consider confirmation. Is confirmation getting above a 10 day moving average, a swing high that gets above the last swing high, a certain low RSI (Relative Strength Indicator—Indicating oversold conditions) reading, or any moving average, stochastic, Bollinger Bands, etc.?

I find common technical indicators to be unreliable. I believe that each individual company, commodity, indices, etc. has its own story to tell. The price and volume has all the information that you need. You can draw your own trend lines, support, resistance, etc. based on the price and volume. If there is a huge spike up or down, I would rather judge that for myself. Most technical indicators take price spikes and average them with equal weighting into a moving average. Should that price spike be included in an average? If so, should it be equally weighted with all other price information?

Every stock, bond, commodity, etc. is dynamic. For me, forcing static measures and tools on a dynamic entity is a losing proposition. Price action is shoved into Fibonacci's, moving averages, Bollinger bands, strength indicators, etc. Bollinger bands and Relative Strength Indicators can be overbought or oversold for days and weeks on end. These static measures can give you so many false signals. This problem of false signals is compounded when many of these measures and tools can be weighted in many different ways. A static tool that might work with one commodity may not work with another commodity.

Every feed or quoting system has the same basic information. Opening price, closing price, high price, low price and volume. I prefer to spend my effort dissecting this basic information relative to the individual story of the stock, bond, commodity, indices, etc. If I used common technical indicators, in most cases, I might have around the same odds as a coin flip. In the case of Bollinger bands and RSI, I would say less than a coin flip's odds. Many brokers believe that they can increase their odds if they increase the number of technical indicators that give the same signal. To me, that is much like flipping more coins and believing that I am increasing my odds.

In a more basic sense, I have a hard time with the basic premise of using mathematics or technical indicators to predict human behavior. I prefer reading investor emotions, psychology, reason and philosophy to a mathematical approximation of human behavior. Many prefer math and that is fine. They prefer not to use their own judgment on investor state of mind and reasoning. Maybe there can be a mathematical equation for everything. How many trading systems predicted the collapse of 2008? There may have been one or more? I can think of a few people who saw the collapse of 2008 coming and exited the market without the use of a trading system.

What to look for depends, of course, to what you are investing or trading in. Investing in currencies, for example, are affected by almost everything under the sun in my opinion. Most currencies are fiat currencies that have no value. They are actually government debt. Every time a government increases (they may never decrease) the supply of money, the government increases its debt. There is no off-setting increase in the supply of a commodity or other item of value earmarked and stored to "back" the fiat currency.

When most investors and traders buy or short something, they are looking to make money. When the government "invests or trades" through "open market transactions" they have entirely different goals. The government might be looking to provide artificial liquidity to equity markets, keep interest rates low or high, increase employment, modify inflation, raise or lower the price of the US dollar. The government's tools to achieve these ends involve currencies and government bonds and securities. Any investment in these markets involve the government as a major player. Any investment in these markets are affected by whatever the government might be attempting to do at the moment.

The most basic emotional-based trading strategy may be the best. Buy fear, sell greed. If you sell greed correctly then you have sold at a much better price than waiting until the tippy top and usually exiting as the "herd" stampedes in a fall off the price cliff. You may not catch the very top selling greed, but, you will usually be much better off than the fear driven panic that sets in after a steep fall that can quickly set in as everyone heads for the exits at the same time and there are much more sellers than buyers.

Another common adage is buy the rumor, sell the news. My favorite trading strategies is buy the fantasy, sell the reality. It is similar to buy the rumor, sell the news. I call it buy the fantasy, sell the reality because the fantasy can consist of rumors and news. The fantasy can become a belief that can span years. A fantasy is usually longer than a rumor. A rumor is usually a single event that is eventually proved or disproved. A fantasy can contain many rumors and have actual news infused with the rumors. Most fantasies cannot be proved until reality can finally set in. Fantasies usually involve things such as potential sales of a new product. Approval or development of a new product. Safety, functionality, efficacy, popularity of a new product. People's imagination about these things are usually much greater than what reality can deliver.

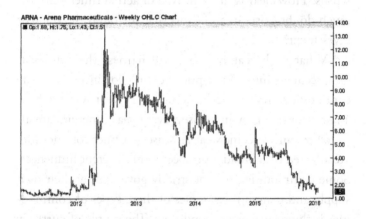

You can see the fantasy develop as the price of Arena goes from 1 dollar to 13 dollars. Fear and reality start to set in as Arena starts falling from the day of approval of its first FDA approved weight loss drug Belviq from 13 dollars to under 2 dollars. The peak of fantasy which is often the day of approval (binary event catalyst) formed the top of the price chart.

The consensus of agreement is part of the difference. Agreement and sentiment could point one direction while the direction that people are actually buying and selling point another way. The recovery in Wall Street from the Great Recession of 2008 has been widely viewed as hated by Main Street. Despite widespread pessimism, the overall market grinded higher. Most everyone is bullish gold and it has overwhelmingly bullish sentiment. This sentiment has not pushed gold prices near any multi-year highs in many years. The confidence of the consensus is a factor. Do extreme emotions such as fear and greed form the consensus? How clear is the perceived or actual timeline? How much doubt exists in all factors that surround the trade or investment?

What is the catalyst that will harness the consensus of agreement into actual price action? For instance, some commodities have specific events every year. Grains have a fairly specific growing season every year. Energies are affected by fairly specific weather seasons. Other commodities are affected by a broader perspective of different influences. Some commodities are not strictly governed by their own supply and demand. Examples of these types of commodities include currencies, bonds, etc. The supply of currency and bonds are artificially provided by the government.

Metals, such as gold and silver, cannot physically cover their paper-represented counterparts such as futures contracts in metals, ETF shares representing long or short metal positions and any derivatives or swaps. The actual metal to back the paper positions may be under 1 percent. There may be a time when futures markets have to settle in cash. Cash settlement might spike metal prices to amazing levels.

I think the main reason that metals have avoided their supply problems is because the government does not report metal supplies. Oil and natural gas, for instance, have weekly storage reports by the US Energy Information

Administration. The Department of Agriculture has weekly reports tracking prices, acres planted, weather impacts, etc. Metals investors have no weekly tracking by the government. If metal investors saw declining storage every week and could compare the current year's storage and supply with the previous year's storage and supply or a 5 year average storage and supply then we could see a rally based on the current supply picture. This is how energy and grain prices work. There is a direct correlation between supply and the consequent price that follows.

The catalyst itself must be judged as to whether it is a make or break for the stock company or will it really move the commodity or indices etc. What is a range of possibilities for share price percentage moves up or down? What is the strength of the catalyst? There are so many things to consider. There is always a danger of making new multi-year lows or highs after breaking a fresh multi-year low or high.

Now at this point a few astute readers might start to think about how these government departments might exist in a Voluntary State? The Department of Agriculture already should exist as explained in the Voluntary State chapter. The SEC, and FTC, for example, could be funded by high frequency traders and the markets that collude with them. As we learned in the Markets chapter, high frequency traders are committing a crime. The courts should be punishing the high frequency traders and the market exchanges that house the computer servers that sit on the market "floors" that help with the extra speed needed to "front-run" the trades.

A settlement for the marketplace might include payment for all the money that the market exchanges received from the high frequency traders. The computer servers would be removed from the market exchange floors. The high frequency traders would be heavily regulated where they could no longer prey on retail investors and brokerage houses. High frequency trading firms would have to be like any other investor. They would have to use technical and/or fundamental analysis and try to pick winning stocks and funds or design a computer program that might help pick winning trades. In any case, the former high frequency trading firms would not be able to do high frequency trading any longer.

For the short-run, any settlement between the courts and high frequency traders could provide short-term funding for the government regulatory agencies such as the SEC and FTC. This settlement could be payable over many years to keep the businesses intact if they want to become a legitimate firm. The long-term funding would come from the market exchanges. The market exchanges would have to pay for their own regulation. Market exchanges might naturally pass some or all of these costs to the brokerage houses. The brokerage houses might naturally pass on these costs to their clients in the form of higher trading fees and commissions.

At this point you may be wondering why the retail investor is getting a double dose of victimization. The investor was never compensated for his losses from high frequency trading and now he will have to pay higher trading fees and commissions. There will not likely be an accurate way to track and calculate who was robbed and by how much for transactions that occurred in less than a second whose digital footprints may be short-term. To compensate millions of victims for trillions of transactions would be very difficult indeed.

As far as paying more in *visible* fees and commissions, let me remind you of the costs that might be more "invisible" or require some digging. High frequency traders can steal money on every share that you trade. On thousands or millions of shares even fractions of a penny can be thousands or tens of thousands of dollars. So, an extra buck or two in fees or commissions if they prevent these losses is money well spent.

CHAPTER 10
ODDS AND ENDS

BOUNDARIES

There are certain boundaries that you cross that are very difficult to return from. Once you allow the majority to control your own income then you become a beggar for your own money. There is no magic stopping point, the majority can spend your money on anything under sun. You can become a financial slave.

Another boundary is when we sacrifice ourselves to the state. There are things worse than the coercion involved in turning people into their own financial slaves. Once you begin to sacrifice yourself there is no magic stopping point, you may sacrifice your own morality and any personal individual value. Nazi Germany was one example of when the individual was entirely sacrificed to the state and the Fuhrer. According to the Nazi value system, this total sacrifice was the only moral choice that an individual could make.

Individuals need to recognize and understand the difference between selfishness and selflessness. Individuals must draw that line between selfishness and selflessness themselves. It can be an individual line that varies from person to person. We can selfishly cooperate and work together at our jobs, sports or other endeavors. Many might mistake the selfish cooperation of employment, sports, etc. with the false belief of "cooperating" through majority rule. While we recognize the cooperative effort of theft as a crime when thieves steal our personal property; we may not recognize the cooperative theft of majority rule as a crime.

If an individual gave you money out of the blue then you might consider that kindness or charity. If the government gives you money then it is an entitlement that you deserve? Not everyone will pay enough into the "system" to cover their retirement, healthcare, disability, unemployment, welfare or other government benefits.

Some boundaries are very easy to cross in some ways. A social safety net with unemployment and welfare might be a desired reason to bring in collectivism or the state to help? Once you cross the line of collectivism, it is difficult to contain a certain level of collectivism or to go to individualism. In the A Voluntary State chapter, I showed how private charity and property rights could provide a social safety net. At worst, a larger property owner that might pay more than he takes in from property rights could merely sell his property and stop paying property fees which give him a positive cash flow balance on the property fee payments he receives.

If you fell on hard times or wanted to sell your property for any reason then you could simply sell and no longer pay property fees and be only a recipient of property fees. People that we consider citizens would be property owners in the land. They would be eligible to become a recipient of property fees. On one hand, the more people that are considered citizens eligible for receipt of property fees, the lower the average property fee payment may become if they do not become property owners. On the other hand, these added citizens may become property owners themselves and may or may not offset their added numbers with added property fee payers and payments and rising land prices (which could cause other problems such as higher costs of housing, food and other production).

There is a literal boundary when it comes to labor and natural resources. We have a literal boundary with Mexico and Canada. The Canadian/United States border is almost entirely unmanned. There is some relative economic and financial balance between Canada and the United States. The Mexican/United States border, as we know, is manned and monitored.

On one hand innovation and entrepreneurship can create jobs. On the other hand, innovation and efficiency create a lower supply of jobs for the same output. Additionally, there is only so much land and natural resources and commodities. There is a balance between the size of a country, the natural resources and commodities the country contains or can contain and the number of people needed for the defense, health and security of the country.

The Libertarian Party has traditionally been an advocate for open borders through the years. Their 2014 platform allows for open borders while giving an apparent nod to rising terrorism and security issues. They state that

> Political freedom and escape from tyranny demand that individuals not be unreasonably constrained by government in the crossing of political boundaries. Economic freedom demands the unrestricted movement of human as well as financial capital across national borders. However, we support control

> over the entry into our country of foreign
> nationals who pose a credible threat to secu-
> rity, health or property.

Market forces are an amazing thing. Free markets can accomplish incredible feats. There is an optimal balance, equilibrium, optimum utility or other name you might give to it. It is not a specific point or quantity, but, more of an area. An area where labor, innovation and natural resources are in balance or have reached an optimum utility. With the exception of the United States, if you compare the top 10 countries with the highest population densities with the 10 countries with the highest per capita income; as of 2015, you will not find the most densely populated countries to be the wealthiest countries (List of countries by GDP (nominal) per capita, *Wikipedia*, February 2016; List of countries and dependencies by population, *Wikipedia*, February 2016).

Population can play a role in the status of the economy. You could point to periods of time and industries where rising population was a good thing. You could have all kinds of innovation and entrepreneurship, but, if you have diminishing land and natural resources with increasing prices for the land and natural resources then there is a point or area where per capita income declines and standards of living can decline as land and natural resources become scarce. I would venture to estimate that there are far more businesses and industries that do better under a strong economy versus a weak economy. It should come as no surprise that the most densely populated countries struggle with starvation and a social safety net. Even under a Voluntary State, the more people that are considered citizens eligible for receipt of property fees, the lower the average property fee received may become. While it would be nice if the solution to all of our problems was a totally free unhindered market that even covered all functions of the government; there are barriers to the market that cannot be overcome without at some point diminishing utility. These barriers include land, population and natural resources.

A dividing line for the state and, perhaps, even ethics is the source of production. Production is a requirement of survival. Whether you cooperate voluntarily, steal, defraud or murder; it affects the nature of your personal ethics and morality. In large numbers, the choice regarding production has an impact on the form of the state that you have. For instance, dictatorships and Fascists choose murder. Communism and democracy choose theft. The Voluntary State chooses individual choice and the choice to cooperate voluntarily.

2008 RECESSION

What led to the fall and recovery of the 2008 Great Recession? While we could point to derivatives, subprime lending, easy credit terms, rapid bubble in housing prices, etc.; I want to draw attention to the "natural" part of the equation which is that paper wealth reached an overbought point. In a technical sense, we had returned to the overbought point of the year 2000. In 2008, we didn't have individual stocks that were as overbought. In 2008, we had overbought housing, credit and derivatives that were more overbought than, perhaps, the individual stocks were in terms of price, earnings and debt. The stock market had reached a critical technical point on a 25 year or multi-year chart. We had reached the 1,600 S&P area that we failed (crashed) on in the year 2000. If we had got to this level without overpriced housing and derivatives then maybe we would have sailed on through this level?

Many might say that lowering interest rates and Quantitative Easing "saved" the day. If saving the day is defined by rising asset prices then it raised asset prices as any rise in the money supply might do. Without added production of goods or services when more supply (money) is injected into the market or economy it takes more supply or money to buy the same good or services. Prices or stock prices might rise due to the added supply.

What would I call the *real* causes for the recovery? Supply and demand had to rebalance or come to a new equilibrium. Demand for houses had peaked. Housing affects many markets. Building, construction, retail, home furnishings, building supplies, etc. It also affects the credit and financial industries. Excess equity dried up for many people overnight. Money from second mortgages and home equity loans to invest in the stock market, buy cars and second houses and a myriad of other goods and services largely were reduced or dried up.

Before you can have any meaningful discussion on causes for the recovery, you should determine recovery from what? In 2009 there were discussions of what a stock index level might look like without the debt, extra money supply and Quantitative Easing. Let us imagine that we were at those levels. It doesn't matter, for the sake of our discussion, whether the level of the S&P was 800,700,500,900 or 1000...

What led to a *real* recovery in the absence of artificial measures of the government? Reducing the workforce to account for lower demand. Eliminating middle management jobs and bonuses for upper and lower end management, eliminating new projects, new expenses, new stores, new or unneeded operations and buildings. Streamlining the business. Eliminating or reducing parts of the business that doesn't target consumers with lower disposable incomes for the majority of people in the economy. Restructuring the business to cater to changing consumer budgets, price points and more affordable goods and services products and packages. These are *real* causes that I believe led to the 2008 recovery.

The government can't help itself and must put its hands in the mix. There are many reasons for this artificial government manipulation or intervention. Any excuse to inflate the money supply is a win for the politician. The national debt can be monetized with more money supply which erases some of the impact of the debt. Politicians can claim (steal) the victory of all the work the businessmen did. Politicians can claim it was QE that caused the recovery. Whatever president who happened to sit in the White House at the time can claim (steal) the credit from the businessmen.

It was the businessmen who reallocated, streamlined or eliminated their business that were the *real* cause of recovery after 2008. The politicians throw their artificial plan into the mix at the same time and then claim (steal) credit for the recovery that follows. All the while it is the artificial meddling that will make the next recession that much worse because of the politician's artificial intervention.

MONEY AND ECONOMY

The Voluntary State has no artificial money supply and no artificial debt. It is a clear line. This clear line regarding money supply will never be realized or understood until we remove all the falsehood regarding how an economy actually works. This message must extend beyond the Austrian or other Schools of economic thought. Beyond books and writings. It must extend beyond the business boardrooms. It must extend beyond the brokers and brokerage houses. It must move into mainstream understanding and knowledge.

Otherwise, each recession will be worse than the last as each recession will need more artificial money supply and debt to overcome the lack of production and demand and growing debt and money supply.

When we allow our national currency to be inflated there is no magic stopping point or easy point of return. When we allow a belief in liquidity of money, Quantitative Easing and other bond buying programs as a "cure all" for recessions usually brought on by government in the first place there is no magic stopping point or easy point of return. Whatever liquidity such as trillions of dollars in bond buying will come back around and make the next recession much worse. The 600 trillion in the notional value of derivatives, that we had in the year 2008, has more than doubled in size and may more than triple in size by the next recession. Note that I did not say if we have another recession. I said "by the next recession." The way that we handle the money supply and the economy guarantees recessions and even hyperinflation at some point. It is not if these events will happen, it is only the order and timing in which they occur that is in question.

Fortunately for our congressional kings, the majority of voters have no clue of what a derivative is or even the existence of a derivative. The majority of voters have no clue of the Keynesian or Monetarist economic schools of thought used to control the money supply. The majority of voters have no clue to the reasons why Keynesianism and Monetarism are failed economic policy and theory disproved long ago. Voter ignorance might be detrimental as politicians know better, but, use the money supply to their political advantage.

Economists who accept Keynesianism and Monetarism as part of their models as a "given" don't provide alternate models of how things would look with a correct money supply and without Quantitative Easing and national debt. Economists have become like news reporters who report the news. Economists rarely ask questions as even an investigative news reporter might do. Here is your Keynesian and Monetarist economic numbers. Here is our projections based on those numbers. Economists may as well be saying, here is how long the breadlines might be based on Keynesian and Monetarist economic numbers that helped create the breadlines.

Sure, economists write books, I have read innumerable quantities of these books. Some warn of recessions, inflation or asset bubbles. A couple go at Keynesianism. I have not read any that solve the problem of taxation, debt, majority rule or democracy to name a few problems. Some might state that this is not the area of the economist. Unless an economist wants to label themselves as a micro-economist then any "macro" issues should apply. Taxation, debt, majority rule and democracy are macro issues. Do economists believe that the task should be left up to the philosophers to handle? Do the philosophers believe that monetary issues should be left up to the economists to handle?

THE STATE AS AN END

Though, socialism, Marxism, fascism and other ideas were disproved long ago; we keep much or most of the machinery for those ideas intact. The machinery of collectivism is being ignited by treating the state as an end instead of a means. Treating the state as an end which has primacy over the individual further ignites the machinery of collectivism. Collective tools such as democracy, taxation, civil asset forfeiture, fascism, Marxism, etc. are all just different tools of the machine of collectivism. Once you legitimize the collective machine then the various tools follow that keep the machine running.

When do we draw the line on collectivist theory? If the machinery of collectivism is unleashed then there is no magic stopping point. You can end up at the logical conclusion of your philosophy. The Nazi State was the logical conclusion to putting the primacy of the collective over the individual. The Nazi State was the logical conclusion to subordinating the individual to the collective.

I was not born with a life-long social contract. I was not born with *social debt*. While I may feel that I owe a debt of gratitude to past generations, I will not sacrifice my individualism. I will not sacrifice my right to my own income and my right to self-rule. I may be coerced into sacrificing my income and some individualism. This sacrifice on my part is due to coercion not agreement. I view myself as a consumer of state goods and services. I only pay for what I consume. I do not pay for the consumption of others. I do not owe others a social debt.

LIFE

What you believe about the beginning and the end of human life on earth can affect how you live your life on earth. Whether you believe there is or is not or could be an afterlife. Whether you believe conditions of life exist by nature, cooperation, force, birth, bloodline, geography, family, race, culture, production, etc.; can affect your belief of whether we are born free, born to a social contract with debt and duty, born as an individual, born as a member of society.

These may seem like questions with obvious answers. They are not so obvious, I believe. For instance, should we be born to a forced and coerced social contract? Our democratic predecessors have us inherit a certain social order and social contract. The social contract can involuntarily exert immense duties and obligations on us.

THE ONE PERCENT

We have heard of the 1 percent controlling most of the wealth in this country with the top 5 percent controlling up to 40 percent or more of our national wealth. We have heard the charge of powerful corporations progressively oppressing the weak employees as freedom increases. The truth is that freedom provides increasing opportunities both good and bad. Under freedom, it depends on the participants of the "game." Corporations may erratically use manipulation and aggression to get the results that they want? Employees are voluntary participants in the job market. There are millions of businesses and jobs in the United States, but, only one government and one choice that is pure aggression (the choice of exile or the Involuntary State). There is only so much manipulation and aggression that you might willingly accept as an employee. Aggression comes into full-force when an "employee" is an involuntary or uninformed citizen (who votes in favor of an involuntary social contract in the form of our current state or government).

Artificial government manipulation (taxation, inflation, devalued currency, mandated participation in health and retirement plans, compliance with a myriad of regulations, etc.) collusion and negligence are what I might call oppression. The artificial picture is a result of the government and democracy enabling the powerful and oppressing the weak. The applicable artificial picture was best detailed in the Victim Identity section of the History and Identity chapter of this book. The government and democracy coercively make everyone pay for the Involuntary State. This oppression makes it much more difficult to become a business owner or entrepreneur as much more income and maybe all of your savings go to the Involuntary State. Without the competition of more business owners and entrepreneurs because of this artificial government manipulation; powerful corporations and businesses become wealthier and have a larger market share because of reduced participation of new business owners and entrepreneurs entering the field.

Some of the congressional kings might point out that the mere existence of wealth inequality is a call to action. We should ask "how" and "why." Was the wealth accumulation a zero sum game or the result of aggression? If no aggression was used to secure a higher share of wealth then the disparity of wealth may be valid despite any distaste of the wealth disparity. Is the wealth of the top 5 percent a zero sum game taken directly from the plate of the lower 95 percent? Wealth under a free market is not a static function, wealth is dynamic in a free market. The use of aggression can increase the risk of entrepreneurship and profitability. The best way to increase overall wealth is not wealth redistribution and aggression, the best way to increase overall wealth is risk reduction through the elimination or reduction of artificial and other barriers and obstacles.

So, generally, as the government increases, the powerful in government increasingly oppress its voluntary and involuntary citizens. Voters do not recognize this sabotage and continue to use democracy and pay exorbitant salaries and benefits to the congressional kings to continue to oppress them as the congressional kings offer them a financial pittance and point the finger of blame at everyone except themselves. Wealth redistribution which is usually the real goal of such inequality schemes (as the attention that the wealth inequality of the 1 percent garners) will reduce overall wealth by increasing risk and decreasing reward and risk-taking opportunities undertaken.

Reduction of aggression and risk is the best way to

increase wealth and decrease the inequality of wealth. Unfortunately, our current state appears to be in the business of increasing aggression, risk and wealth inequality.

CONCLUSION

At first blush, many ideas may seem incredible to believe. Creating the world in six days or the universe coming about from a single electron? Creating woman from a single rib or evolving from a primate? One man ruling a million or one man ruling himself? For me, these are some of the most relevant ideas and questions that still persist in mainstream thinking. Without any prior knowledge of any of these topics, on their face, almost every single question should appear to be untrue. For me, the only statement that, on its face, at first blush that should be true is for man to rule himself. If there was no Bible then there would be no reason for reasonable people, many of whom call themselves Christians, to believe that any heavens and earth were created in six days. Christians, to properly follow the Bible, must believe in a single universe that began with a god that created the universe in six days. For Christians to believe in a multiverse or a universe that might have arisen from a single electron would be a contradiction of a single universe that was created by a god in six days.

How much is riding on six days of creation? The existence of a god. The truth of a Bible. Heaven and hell. A beginning of time. A single universe supporting a beginning of time. How much is riding on the universe coming from a single electron? Nothing. Science moves on to another idea of how our universe started. What is at stake if woman was not created from a single rib? The truth of the Bible and whether anything in the Bible can be believed. What is at stake if we did not evolve from a primate? I would imagine that we would have to go back and reexamine the steps of evolution that led to that conclusion. Science is dynamic and we can examine everything and anything if we have the desire and ability. Faith is static and starts with preconceived assumptions and premises of the truth of a creator and an inspired text to support the existence of this creator.

What is at stake for one man to no longer rule a million? Everything that was stolen by the one man from the million. The problem is that most people do not know most of what they conceded and what was stolen. The concessions and theft may be viewed as hard fought freedom purchased from the blood of patriots. So much went in to putting the one man in power of a geographical territory. Any thoughts of freedom or self-rule may be overshadowed by thoughts of the fear of others in a state of nature. Though, freedom and self-rule will likely always be a natural feeling on some level.

One man ruling himself is overrun by fear. The one man has tried to escape fear with kings, congressional kings, presidents, dictators, Prime Ministers, tyrants, gods, a monotheistic god, popes, prophets... The one man or individual has fought for religious freedom—separation of church and state—the freedom to believe in mythology with many tax free privileges. The individual has not fought for the right to his own income. The individual has not fought for the freedom from aggression, civil forfeiture, eminent domain or the right to end his life or take certain drugs or medicines which are unapproved or illegal by the FDA that could save his life. The individual spends more time enslaving himself than freeing himself.

At first blush, we may know what is true. We may allow inference and necessity to override this first impulse of what is true when it comes to faith. Faith has two steps to allow the belief of anything. The belief of god and the belief of the Bible are the two steps that can circumnavigate anything. If god and the Bible are true then we can infer that anything that god "says" in the Bible or anything from the Bible must be true. This is a possible sequence of belief for the Christian. The Bible says the heavens and earth were created in six days. The Bible says the creation of woman came from a single rib of the first man. There is no scientific or logical basis or natural laws that support either of these two biblical assertions, so, Christians use some supernatural basis to believe in these assertions despite any supporting proof or evidence and overwhelming proof and evidence against these biblical assertions.

So many people have died in the name of faith and the fight for the afterlife. Or, at least, that has been the excuse in many cases. There is no afterlife. The lack of an afterlife makes our time here on earth of crucial importance. We cannot take anything with us after we die. We can only leave behind a gift or a curse. While we can live for our self as individuals, everything we do can be for the future generations to possibly have an improved experience on earth. We have evolved past a point where we can now understand how we can help others. We can see *ought* from *is*. We can see people as subjects not objects. It saddens me that some faiths still seek to murder in the name of a god. I must confess that I love my cats. It is hard to imagine that even animal life has no afterlife. In the Bible, animals were sacrificed to god, so, it is no surprise that animals were not given a soul and afterlife in the fictional story of the Bible.

An afterlife is not determined by who has the "right" version of fictional mythology or religious faith. We cannot rely on some god to suddenly exist and appear. We got to this point in evolution through incremental change through natural selection of a fraction of one percentage point at a time taking a couple steps forward and a step back at times.

We may gather the knowledge and ability to create immortality, but, could we manage this immortality. While we seem able to build and manage knowledge in the natural sciences such as physics, biology and technology; our ability to move forward in economics, philosophy and learning from history is impaired.

Morally, we have made great strides since the Crusades and the Dark Ages (except in fundamentalist religious faith). Politically, we have sat idle for hundreds of years. We have replaced feudal lords and kings with congressmen and presidents. We have merely provided a modern update on Old World politics. We used to burn "witches" and heretics at the stake. Now, we "only" decapitate heretics (infidels) in certain fundamentalist faith based parts of the planet. Different method, but, same result.

Faith affects our investments, economy, intellectual advancement and even our health and any possible immortality. Trade involving profit or interest was banned by the church as usury. We have culturally evolved past usury (again, except in some Islamic areas). We are now stuck misallocating resources to church buildings and lands. Faith attempts to block stem cell research. It is stem cell, multi-stem, cloning and regenerative medicine research that is more likely to give humans eternal life than a nonexistent god. A Christian belief that life or a soul is inherent at the cellular level might impede these medical advancements. The money spent for church resources could go to charitable donations. Helping actual people who need help would be better than worshipping a moral monster described in many religious texts.

Why do Christians need churches? Obviously, Christians are mandated to worship their alleged creator and maintain fellowship and church government. Implicitly, though, Christians may often need the support of fellow Christians to believe without evidence—faith. Supernatural beliefs do not lend themselves to empirical evidence or natural laws. Churches need prayers, songs, sermons, baptisms and other acts and other Christians to validate their myth and delusion. At this point, a Christian may believe that they do need these validations in order to believe. If that was the case then why do most Christians just believe in the supernatural events alleged in a single book, the Bible? Why not believe in all supernatural events? Why does one book allow a person to suspend the laws of nature, empirical evidence and logical thought and reason?

Atheists do not need a church or other building to meet once a week to believe in proven empirical laws. Atheists do not need to worship or sing songs of praise to natural selection or the Law of Gravity for instance.

Science can advance better without the limits that

religious mythology places on it. Limits that might include doubting or exploring the multiverse (or even if acceptance of the multiverse then the time and effort wasted on religious mythological explanations for god existing in a multiverse). Limits that might include working on theories of time. Any religious premise that begins with god starting time and our universe can be deeply limiting to the possible results. I am unsure just how effective compartmentalizing any conflicting religious and scientific views truly are to the best scientific results and advancements? A Christian belief that life or a soul is inherent at the cellular level might impede these medical advancements.

This is usually the point in the book where an author writing on economics or political theory offers hope that if his suggestions and recommendations are followed then we can still turn the corner for democracy and the economy. Most of the time the authors are merely making small revisions to democracy or economic policy. It can be difficult to convince people of a single topic. I have the topics of reality, faith-based morality, atheism and morality, free will and morality, science and morality, justice, anti-democracy...

Entire books have been written on each of these single topics. I have all of these topics in this single book in addition to one of the main topics of the Voluntary State. If the Voluntary State was marginalized then it could be blamed for the failures of other ideas or policies. Many things are called "market failures" that are no failure of the market. Many people try to interject envy, altruism, equality and call it a failure of the market because the market didn't produce a certain ("equal or fair") distribution of goods.

The market, at its core, is a very simple idea. A market is voluntary exchange between buyer and seller. People, institutions and society often place so many things in front of voluntary exchange. When these personal, institutional and societal ends are not reached then the market is often blamed for failures of these ends.

The Voluntary State, at its core, is also a very simple idea. For the most part, the Voluntary State is voluntary exchange between buyer and seller. The market and Voluntary State should be individual choices and exchanges. Both are likely to be viewed, by many, as having failures. Failures because the voluntary, individual choices were not socially optimal for the collective.

The social safety net of the Voluntary State may not be broad enough to satisfy everyone. It may lead some to believe that you could "tweak" individualism with collectivism to broaden the social safety net. The social safety net created through property ownership should feed people. It may not be broad enough to avoid all levels of suffering. I believe people can and will help those who are suffering through donation and aid. I do not believe that we need coercion to force us to help. Collectivist thinkers will seize on this sentiment of need and promise less suffering for the children. Children of drug addicts, broken families, orphans, etc. will be victims in any state. Collectivist thinkers may work hard to show that making people do "the right thing" (coercion) is needed in this case. Individualistic thinkers may have to be creative and create additional ways to voluntarily help these children through donation and charitable organizations, educational foundations and profit motive to help these children.

A child might become the hero of a collectivist movement. The role of hero and villain must be understood at a child's level. This simple level of understanding is not just for children. Religion, for example, has a patient, loving hero of miracles and forgiveness. His name, of course, is Jesus. Children and adults focus on Jesus and forget or ignore the history of millions murdered in the Old Testament. People might focus on the suffering of some children in the Voluntary State and forget or ignore the suffering and death of the Involuntary State.

Children know more about some aspects of science than adults did thousands of years ago. Children know of a round earth that rotates around a sun. Children can grasp the relative size of the earth and the immense animal life and might understand that stories such as Noah's Ark are fictional. These are facts that adults thousands of years ago did not have. Despite how charming the fictional hero role of Jesus might be, the facts of science will eventually show how fictional this story is on a child's level. A child may eventually understand an existence of a multiverse as easily as a round earth revolving around the sun. A child may eventually understand the relative infinite nature of time and gravity—past and present—in the scientific context of time as easily as a child understands time beginning and ending in the biblical context of time.

The harder part, I believe, will be roles of hero and villain in any Voluntary State. Children might be the victim or hero as the villain might be the "selfish" capitalist in the collectivist story. Individualist thinkers may have to inspire heroes of old and new. Heroes such as John Galt and Howard Roark. Heroes more vivid and inspiring that can define how children and adults see the world.

At first blush, we know that democracy is wrong. If we took 10 people and had 6 people tell the other 4 people what they can eat, drink or smoke; watch on television or radio; what income they could take home as a paycheck; what guns they are allowed to have; how many rounds of ammunition they are allowed to have; how many rounds of ammunition they are allowed to put into a magazine; how long or how fast their gun can fire rounds of ammunition; what toilets and allowable water flow they can have; what rainwater, if any, they are allowed to collect on their own property; having their phone, email and internet monitored; how much cash they can keep on their person or in their vehicle; how tall their grass can be; how tall their fence can be; who they must declare war against; who they must fight against; who is allowed to take money through high frequency trading; what the value of their money will be worth; the interest rates of their money, the inflation of their money; then, of course, the 4 coerced people would object and fight the 6 dictator, tyrant acting people to the bitter end.

If we took 10 people and had 6 people make 4 people terrorists (while having the 4 "terrorists" pay for the 6 people's wants and desires) and enemies of the state by declaring a National State of Emergency and allowing the ability to declare martial law (and deny trial by jury and other rights) then we can make the 4 "terrorists" pay for mandatory financial participation in socialized entitlement programs;

pay for health and retirement regardless of individual use or potential loss of use through means testing; pay for the cost of educating everyone's children. Any alternative or additional education must also be paid by the 4 "terrorists." The four must pay for special PERA retirement which is superior to their own Social Security. The four must pay for half-priced HUD homes for teachers through the Good Neighbor program (as if teachers are automatically the best neighbors). All the while, these US teachers provide about the lowest quality education in the world at the highest per capita price in the world the nine months out of the year that the teachers work. The 4 "terrorists" must pay for Federal Reserve Banks (Quasi-public), art, foreign alliances, buildings, parks, fireworks on the fourth of July or other times, recreational facilities, trails, dog parks, swimming pools, tennis courts, running tracks, skate parks, basketball courts, boat docks and air shows. We have the water, electricity, capital expenses, land (or opportunity cost that the land could be generating in revenue and property fees), wages, salaries, pensions, maintenance equipment, maintenance buildings, maintenance vehicles, maintenance workers to maintain these facilities. Under these circumstances, of course, the 4 coerced people would object and fight the 6 dictator, tyrant acting people to the bitter end.

If we took 10 people and had 6 people make 4 people help pay for the cost of their collectively owned businesses such as:

Amtrak
Commodity Credit Corporation
Conrail

Corporation for Public Broadcasting
CSS Industries
Export-Import Bank of the United States
Farm Credit System Insurance Corporation
Federal Crop Insurance Corporation
Federal Deposit Insurance Corporation
Federal Retirement Thrift Investment Board
Federal Savings and Loan Insurance Corporation
Holdings of American International Group
Legal Services Corporation
Mercury Filmworks
NeighborWorks America
North Dakota Mill and Elevator
Overseas Private Investment Corporation
Pension Benefit Guaranty Corporation
Picatinny Arsenal
Reconstruction Finance Corporation
Resolution Trust Corporation
Rural Edge
Securities Investor Protection Corporation
Stribling Productions
State Justice Institute
Tennessee Valley Authority
Toon City
United States Postal Service

Then, of course, the 4 coerced people would object and fight the 6 dictator, tyrant acting people to the bitter end. If the number of coerced people is increased from four people to four hundred million people then somehow it is okay? We now call tyranny—democracy just by increasing the number of people involved. Whether four people or four hundred million people, we are just as philosophically and morally bankrupt.

Somehow if the number of people involved increases then tyranny—democracy is legitimized somehow? One reason that many might want to legitimize democracy is that there are goods or services that we like from democracy. To get the goods or services that we want, we must pay for the goods and services of everyone involved in the democratic state. It would be much cheaper to pay out of pocket for the few things that we want versus paying for all the goods and services for the entire democratic state.

Of course, if we could choose individual goods or services then we have no need to pay for the services of political parties and other government administration. If we have no need to pay for all the goods and services of the Involuntary State then many would not pay for all these goods and services out of their own pocket if people were given (or able to make) the choice. Many people pay no taxes and get the entire set of government goods and services for free. Democratic leaders (politicians of every political party) focus on what they give not what they take and who they will take it from. They focus on photo opportunities of some struggling people. They espouse a virtue of duty and obligation not rights of the individual. For democracy, heroism is defined in duty.

We should understand the alternatives to the ideas and practices that currently exist in democracy. The tools are out there to move to a Voluntary State. There is a viable alternative to democracy. There is an alternative to collectivism.

364

There is an alternative to the selfless identity. There is an alternative to the morality and distributive justice that currently exists.

Back to hope. The hope that an author often tries to share at the end of a book. Science continues to disprove theology, there is hope in this development. Theology hid behind a flat earth and an earth in the center of the universe. Theology may continue to try to hide behind thermodynamics and a single universe. The hope is to abandon our reliance on some omniscient, omnipotent, omnibenevolent being or god. The hope is that our planet will avoid a cosmic event such as an asteroid or comet collision or other cosmic event. We can hope to have enough time to begin to figure out how to create our own afterlife of sorts. We may gather the knowledge and ability to create immortality, but, could we manage this immortality? While we seem able to build and manage knowledge in the natural sciences such as physics, biology and technology; our ability to move forward in economics, philosophy and learning from history is impaired.

We are impaired by philosophers and intellectuals who can do more harm than good. Nissim Nicholas Taleb in *The Black Swan* explains that philosophers can often extract time and energy from real problems. I would certainly agree. I will offer up my own example of this extraction occurring. Jean-Paul Sarte was awarded a Nobel Prize, helped develop existentialism, but, was a Marxist socialist. I believe that validating and perpetuating socialism as a Nobel Prize winner (whether Sarte accepted the prize or not) does more harm to the survival of the human species than any benefit that existentialism might bring.

The United States can go from a first-world nation to a third-world nation in the space of a few centuries. Politically, we have been in an overall rapid decline for centuries. The unravelling political picture is spilling into growing debt and economic distress. A third-world nation is unlikely to be making profitable cutting edge advancements in physics, medicine, regenerative medicine, cloning, time travel and space exploration to name a few. We really have a lot to do to avoid all memory of our species being wiped out. If we cannot save our species from extinction then the best that we may be able to hope for is what they refer to in football as a "Hail Mary" play where the human species might send out our knowledge, DNA and other biological material in satellites like messages in a bottle across a sea of space and time or bury our "bone (knowledge, DNA and other biological material)" like a dog buries a bone in some heat resistant container in some underground structure or hole. I hope it does not come to only an attempt to save some of the knowledge of the human species without saving a single member of the human species.

Time travel may not be fiction someday. The Voyager 1 satellite launched in 1977 travels at around 11 miles per second or around 39,000 miles per hour. The speed of light is about 186,000 miles per second and 671 million miles per hour. With propulsion and time dilation greater speeds and distances may be reached within a person's lifetime if they were travelling through space. Hopefully, a far enough distance to a habitable planet or traversable worm hole to another universe. Or, we could terraform a planet or create a traversable worm hole? We know that gravity is a common feature throughout time and space. What we know about electrons, black holes and traversable worm holes may eventually lead to time travel. By simply changing the charge of an electron (negatively charged electron) to a positively charged electron or positron can change the arrow of time and move backwards in time. Tachyons can move backwards in time with faster than light speed. Electrons or antielectrons as a wave of probability can sometimes be in two places at one time (or we have fooled ourselves with the "double slit" experiments). We should be able to figure out how to travel in time.

We might be able to change the axis of the earth and/or knock the earth out of its orbit away from the direction of the sun. Perhaps, directed explosions way outside the earth can create energy and shockwaves that could move the earth away from the sun. There are frozen planets that are well within reach that may offer support. The frozen moons of Saturn may thaw and become habitable as the sun heats up. Titan, a moon of Saturn about half the size of our planet Earth, appears to have an earthlike atmosphere and may have frozen water. Titan is 886 million miles from the sun versus the 93 million miles that the earth is from the sun. The human species can ill afford to keep all its proverbial eggs in the one basket of Earth. Perhaps, we could steer Earth within a million miles of Titan or something to help support another human colony as the sun thaws Titan. Satellites have already visited Titan, a manned expedition may be a future prospect.

We may be more "under the gun" than we can imagine. We have about a half-billion years until carbon dioxide levels kill off much of the tree and plant life. Our oxygen and food base will be diminished. If human life extends past a billion years, it may never reach about eight billion years (at least not on this planet at the earth's current location of 93 million miles from the sun) as the sun will have expanded to the point of burning up the earth as the sun would now burn helium and would become a huge red giant.

You can save the past without affecting the future. A person from the future will still exist if his parents were never born by changing the past. Matter from the future in the form of a person does not does not destroy itself if the person's parents were never born as a result of trip(s) to the past. The matter (person) exists. The fact of the person's (matter) existence does not change regardless of where the matter (person) travels in time and space. You could save a life by extending their life in their own time through cloning, brain transplants, regenerative medicine, stem or multi-stem technology and/or other measures or you could save a life by transporting a person to another place or time that has these life-extending measures.

I would venture to say that many children could be affected by visitors from the past. The conception time for children born after visitors from the past might vary or not occur at all. Varied conception times might lead to a different birth gender, hair color, eye color or genetic composition. A way around this problem might be something like the simultaneous arrival of many visitors (and/or the delivery of a simultaneous "message" throughout time) from the future spaced 30 years apart which may require over 30 million people to pull it off if the human species survives on earth for a billion years. To people living in the future this would not affect their lives. They would continue to exist regardless of what happens with people travelling back in time. Only people living in the future who wanted to be a part of time travel would be affected as people nowadays who choose to work in space exploration. If these measures could be delivered while the person is still living and conscious then their life could be extended. Of course, there are many problems not the least of which include who to save and how to handle known crimes and criminals. Which leads us to a problem that we may face with or without immortality. What is the carrying capacity of the human species?

As far as countries and nations, with the exception of some individual families, generally, birth rates increase as education decreases. Birth rates also tend to increase as religious extremism increases. Case in point—Africa and the Middle East lead the world by a large margin for birth rates in the last twenty-five years. Also, generally, as income levels increase religious faith decreases.

The Muslim threat is growing. It is fairly impossible to denounce the Koran while the Bible is supported. As long as god and Jesus are thought to be real supernatural beings then that gives validity to both the Koran and the Bible. At this point, it becomes very difficult to isolate certain aspects of violent Jihadism when god and Jesus and biblical history are left intact. While there have been denouncements and military action against ISIS, there has been, to my knowledge, no government denouncement of the Christian or Islamic faith.

So, forget a billion years, we may not make it another one or two hundred years if faith (even faith we might believe is harmless) is allowed to flourish. While the non-Muslim world may, in some places of the world, have a birth rate near its death rate, the Muslim world will likely continue its very high birth rates. These birth rates will be an added threat and add to the necessity of having to address the threat and danger of the Muslim world.

Stabilizing immortality, if it all possible, is one piece of the puzzle. Another piece of the puzzle might be understanding what causes consciousness and what causes first person experience and individuality. Still another piece of the puzzle is storing this information and experience in some ethical manner. Perhaps, we will have clones of ourselves minus our conscious brain that can be transferred to the clone? A final piece may be managing a planet that could sustain immortality. Part of maintaining a planet that could sustain immortality is having the morality and politics to achieve it. This is where this book enters the picture.

My hope is to help provide one small piece to a much larger puzzle. Some authors believe that democracy and faith will "correct" itself over time and incorporate morality and understanding over time. That is an unlikely possibility. It is also possible that unbalanced power and ideology may bring about global devastation that could undermine our progress and even our existence. This is why we must confront democracy and faith in the most serious way possible.

Some of what I have explained may seem like science

fiction fantasy. Human consciousness or self-consciousness may have only been around for a few thousand years? It took billions of years to get us to this point without a conscious mind. Unfortunately, we may have less than a billion years before human life may not be possible on this planet. As the sun expands and burns up the remaining hydrogen, the earth will start to heat up. We have less than a billion years until higher temperatures from the sun start evaporating the oceans which causes water vapor, which is a greenhouse gas, to heat up the planet even more and evaporate the oceans even faster. We may need an immense amount of time to figure out time travel and faster than light travel and other obstacles. Still, imagine a billion years with a conscious mind... If we don't wipe each other off the planet because of religion, deterministic justice, police state militarization, politics, starvation and death because of politics then we have a chance and hope.

The chief aim of this book is a political one. The chance to solve a problem in political theory. The problem of democracy. So, I want to close on the topic of political theory. Is there hope that we could come out on the right side of some or all of the topics of political theory? Selflessness, socialism, majority rule, Keynesian economics, fiat dollars, currency debasement, inflation, debt... all have to run their course and show the major flaws and defects in their operation? Do we have to face the abyss before we make significant changes to some or all of these topics? We have had just enough capitalism, ingenuity and selfishness to prolong the day of reckoning for democracy or more properly the rule of kings.

FOR FURTHER READING

I am listing all the books that influenced the creation of this book. That influence might come in the form of agreement, disagreement or conflict. While there may be other books by the same author, I am referencing the books that happened to influence this book in some way. In some cases, just the existence of the books or writings influenced this book. Case in point—all the numerous writings by unknown authors that were never canonized or considered inspired, but, existed and may have been well known at that time. Which may lead us to the question of why every religion usually considers one or two books inspired while all others are uninspired?

Berlin, Isaiah *The Roots of Romanticism*
Block, Walter *Defending The Undefendable*
Bostom, Andrew G. *Sharia Versus Freedom*
Coyne, Jerry A. *Faith vs Fact*
Darwin, Charles *The Origin Of Species*
Dawkins, Richard
    The Blind Watchmaker
    The God Delusion
    The Greatest Show On Earth
    The Magic of Reality
Dennett, Daniel C
    Breaking The Spell

Darwin's Dangerous Idea
freedom evolves
Intuition Pumps and Other Tools for Thinking
Diamond, Jared
    The Third Chimpanzee
    The World Until Yesterday
Ferry, Luc *A BRIEF HISTORY of THOUGHT a philosoph-
    ical guide to living*
Friedman, David *The Machinery of Freedom*
Friedman, Milton *Capitalism and Freedom*
Frost, S.E. *Basic Teachings Of The Great Philosophers*
Galambos, Andrew J. *Sic Itur Ad Astra*
Harris, Sam
    End of Faith
    Freewill
    Letter to a Christian Nation
    The Moral Landscape
Hayek, Friedrich A.
    Constitution of Liberty
    The Essence Of Hayek (Nishyama and Leube)
    Individualism and Economic Order
    The Sensory Order
Hitchens, Christopher *god is not Great*
Honderich, Ted
    Mind and Brain
    The Consequences of Determinism
Kaku, Michio
    Parallel Worlds
    Physics Of The Future
    Physics Of The Impossible

The Future Of The Mind

Kennedy, James Ronald and Walter Donald *The South Was Right*

Lewis, Hunter *Where Keynes Went Wrong*

Lewis, Michael *Flash Boys*

Loftus, John W.
    The Christian Delusion
    Why I Became An Atheist

Madrick, Jeff *Seven Bad Ideas*

Mauldin, John *Endgame*

Marx, Karl and Engels, Friedrich *The Communist Manifesto*

Maybury, Richard J. *The Thousand Year War in the Mideast*

Mises, Ludwig von
    Human Action
    Socialism

Morris, Gregory L. *Candlestick Charting Explained*

Nozick, Robert
    Anarchy, State and Utopia
    The Examined Life
    Philosophical Explanations

Onfray, Michael *Atheist Manifesto*

Peikoff, Leonard *The Ominous Parallels*

Pinker, Steven
    The Better Angels Of Our Nature
    The Blank Slate

Pring, Martin J.
    Technical Analysis Explained
    Technicians Guide to Day and Swing Trading

Rand, Ayn
    Anthem

Schoek, Helmut *Envy*
Scruton, Roger
    An Intelligent Person's Guide to Philosophy
    The Meaning Of Conservatism
    Modern Philosophy
Shermer, Michael
    The Believing Brain
    The Moral Arc
    The Science Of Good And Evil
    Why Darwin Matters
Shubin, Neil
    The Universe Within
    Your Inner Fish
Singer, Peter
    Practical Ethics
    The Expanding Circle
Sire, James W. *The Universe Next Door*
Stenger, Victor J.
    GOD and the Folly of Faith
    GOD and the Multiverse
    The Fallacy of Fine Tuning
Strauss, Leo and Cropsey, Joseph
    History of Political Philosophy
Tannehill, Morris and Linda *The Market For Liberty*
Unknown Authors
    Acts of Solomon
    Acts of Uziah
    Annals of King David
    Assumption of Moses
    Astronomical Book (Book of Enoch)

The Bible
Book of the Covenanat
Book of Dream Visions
Book of Enoch
Book of Gad the Seer
Book of Parables of Enoch
Book of Jasher
Book of the Jubilees
Book of Jehu
Book of Statutes
Book of Samuel the Seer
Book of the Wars of the Lord
Book of the Watchers
Chronicle of the Kings of Israel
Chronicle of the Kings of Judah
The Epic of Gilgamesh
Epistle to Corinth
Epistle from Laodicea to the Colossians
Epistle of Enoch
Epistle to the Laodiceans
Iddo Genealogies
The Koran
Life of Adam and Eve
Martyrdom of Isaiah
Nathan the Prophet
Prophecy of Abijah
Sayings of the Seers
Shemaiah the Prophet
Story of the Book of Kings
Story of Prophet Iddo

Visions of Iddo the Seer
Wallace, Steven and Debra *The End Times Hoax*
Wells, Steve *Drunk With Blood*
Wilson, Edward O.
    The Social Conquest Of Earth
    The Meaning of Human Existence
Wright, Robert *The Moral Animal*
Zacharias, Ravi *The End of Reason*

ABOUT THE AUTHOR

Sean Wallace received his bachelor of arts degree in economics from California State University, Hayward, and he has passed the Series 3 National Commodity Futures Examination. Trading and investing in futures, options, ETFs, ETNs, and stocks, he works in manufacturing and lives in Colorado with his wife and stepson.

Follow him on Twitter: sean wallace@author_Wallace